The Story of Britain

The Story of Britain

by R J UNSTEAD
illustrated by Victor Ambrus

with 16 colour plates
and 130 black and white line drawings

Adam and Charles Black

London

Other books by R. J. Unstead

Looking at History
People in History
Men and Women in History
A History of Britain
Looking at Ancient History
Living in a Castle
Living in a Crusader Land
Living in a Medieval City
Living in a Medieval Village
Castles
Monasteries
Travel by Road
Early Times

WITH W. F. HENDERSON
Homes in Australia
Transport in Australia
Pioneer Home Life in Australia

WITH WILLIAM WORTHY
Black's Children's Encyclopaedia

ISBN 0 7136 1007 7

TEXT © 1969 R. J. UNSTEAD PUBLICATIONS LTD

ILLUSTRATIONS © 1969 A. & C. BLACK LTD

FIRST PUBLISHED 1969, REPRINTED 1970, 1972

A. & C. BLACK LTD 4, 5 & 6 SOHO SQUARE LONDON W1V 6AD

COLOUR ILLUSTRATIONS PRINTED IN GREAT BRITAIN BY W. S. COWELL LTD
LONDON AND IPSWICH

PRINTED IN GREAT BRITAIN BY MORRISON AND GIBB LTD
LONDON AND EDINBURGH

CONTENTS

In the Stone Age

About five thousand years before the birth of Christ a neck of marshy land was flooded by sea, and Britain became an island.

The islanders were few in number and their lives were hard. By this time, the weather had grown wetter and less cold than in the years of the great icefields, so the land was covered by forests and the valleys were filled with dense undergrowth and swamps. Only the chalk hills and the windswept moors were open to the sky, for there the soil was too thin for woodland trees.

Here and there, on the uplands and along the forest edges, little groups of hunters tracked the wild boars, the deer and the elk. They trapped some in pits and lamed others with rocks. They followed the herds to cut off strays and to run down the young ones, killing them with flint hand-axes and sharp sticks.

When they killed, they ate, tearing the flesh with teeth and fingers, cracking the bones for the marrow and piercing the skulls to suck out the brains. Nothing was wasted, for it might be days before they ate again. The skins, the sinews and the needle-sharp bone-splinters had their uses too.

I

These people lived where they could, in caves, in cracks among the rocks and in pits piled round with stones and roofed with boughs and turf. Their lives depended upon the animals that gave them food and clothing, and if the animals moved to fresh feeding-grounds the hunter-families followed them.

But, in this bitter struggle to keep alive, man already had his possessions. There were his weapons and scrapers, his fire to keep him warm and to cook his meat and his dogs to help him in the chase. So far, in Britain, he had little else.

Away to the south and in the east, there were men with many

2

possessions. In Egypt, Mesopotamia, India and China, where there was warmth and fertile soil watered by great rivers, people were living in towns. They had houses, temples and roads ; they grew crops, worshipped gods and were ruled by kings and priests.

Beyond the fertile valleys the mountain folk and the herdsmen of the plains were on the move. From time to time they swept into the rich river-kingdoms and took them for their own. This surge of peoples in the east was like a sea whose waves flooded the empty lands. Its farthest ripples reached Britain before the island had a name.

In the Stone Age

Men from the Mediterranean lands moved up the coasts of Spain and France. There were always some who ventured a little farther than the rest, and presently a few bold fellows crossed the sea in their skin-covered boats and came to the southern and western shores of Britain. Others, from the northern plains, landed in the south-east and made their way inland along the grassy hills.

These newcomers understood the arts of weaving and pottery. They brought hoes and long-handled spades with which they could work the light soil of the hillsides, and they harvested their crops with flint sickles and ground the precious grain into flour. In addition they kept flocks and herds, and although they never lost their love of hunting, they no longer depended upon wild animals for all their food and their clothes.

Since animals had to be tended and guarded, the herdsmen-farmers made trenches and palisades to protect their flocks and also their homes. Settlements of round huts stood on the windy uplands of Salisbury Plain, the Chiltern Hills and Dartmoor, and near to the settlements great stones, called dolmens, were set up to please the spirits that caused the seed to sprout, and the lambs and the calves to be born.

Knowledge and skills were growing. Some men had special gifts and nimble fingers ; they were the weavers, potters and artists ; they chipped and polished the great flints dug out in underground galleries, they made tools and carved figures of the mother-goddess. A few were magic-men or priests. They knew how to make sacrifices to the spirits and the right way to bury the dead in hollow graves.

Beaker Folk and Celts

From about 2000 BC a new people began to arrive from eastern Europe. They were the Beaker Folk, whose name comes from the drinking vessels that they buried with their dead. They brought with them a knowledge of metals. Their bronze weapons and their bows and arrows gave them victory over the less well-armed people of the uplands. But there was room for both and the invaders mingled with the men they had conquered and married their daughters.

It was the Beaker Folk who raised the mysterious temples of Stonehenge and Avebury, those great circles of stones, some of which were dragged on rollers and floated down rivers for hundreds of miles. No one knows why these huge circles were made with so much effort. Hundreds or even thousands of men must have laboured all their lives and have left the task to be finished by their grandsons. Stonehenge may have been a temple of the sun but we know next to nothing about the religion that drove men to such toil for their gods.

Beaker Folk and Celts

After the Beaker Folk, there were no more big invasions for several centuries; but from time to time small bands of settlers came to the western coasts, drawn perhaps by stories of Irish gold and Cornish tin whose fame had spread to Crete and Greece.

Then, from about 1000 BC, came the Celts, or Gaels, a fair-haired race who had crossed Europe and had given their name to Gaul. A few entered Britain. More joined them and then whole tribes came to settle in the south and the east, driving the inhabitants into the hills and forests of the west.

The Celts brought ploughs pulled by oxen and, from about 500 BC, their kinsmen arrived with weapons and tools of iron. Celtic smiths understood the secret of smelting ore in charcoal furnaces and their craftsmen fashioned the metal into swords, into rims for shields and chariot-wheels, into fastenings for brooches and harness.

They were lively, quarrelsome, artistic people. Led by their warrior chiefs, the Celts defeated the islanders and fought among themselves in tribal wars, defending and attacking the huge earth fortresses that can still be traced on many hilltops. But they were also good farmers and business-men who used iron bars as money and set up a thriving trade in tin, lead, iron, corn and hides with the dark-faced merchants who came from the Mediterranean city-states.

One of these traders was Pytheas, a Greek from Massilia or Marseilles, who wrote a book about his voyage to the remote

6

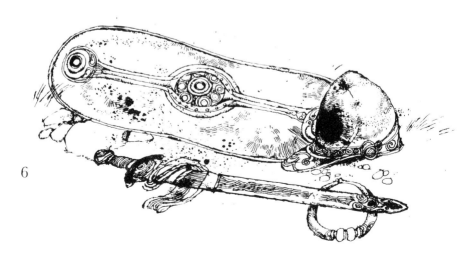

Tin Islands. In it, he described how the Celts worked their tin-mines and brought the metal in wagons at low-tide to an island, probably St Michael's Mount, Cornwall, where the sea-traders came regularly to do business.

Above all, the Celts were artists in metal and precious stones. Their brooches, hand-mirrors, drinking-cups and even their helmets and shields were wonderfully shaped and decorated with circles and curving lines, with brilliant enamels and studded gems.

Vain, handsome, furiously proud, the Celts adored finery and gaily coloured clothes. Men and women alike decked themselves with jewellery. They plaited and braided their long hair, smoothed it with combs and sometimes bleached it with chalk-wash to make themselves even fairer. The warriors took pride in their enormous moustaches and in the patterns that were painted on their bare chests before a battle.

These were the tribesmen whom the Romans fought. Their name, the Britons, came from one of the tribes called Brythons, but there were many others, the Iceni of East Anglia, the Brigantes and the Parisii in the north, the Cantii of Kent and the Belgae, a most powerful tribe who occupied nearly all the southern uplands from Sussex to Dorset. Though they were called Britons, they were not yet a nation, only a number of tribes in a wooded island where many of the earlier peoples still lived in the mountains.

7

Julius Caesar in Britain

While the Celts were raiding each other's hilltop forts and pushing into Ireland, Wales and the Scottish Highlands, a nation was growing from a handful of refugees who had built themselves a town on the banks of an Italian river. By nature and training, the Romans were conquerors. They defeated the Italian tribes, the Greeks, the mighty Carthaginians, the Spaniards and most of the peoples of the Middle East. When all the lands around the Mediterranean Sea were under their rule, the Romans pressed into Gaul, where the people were kinsfolk of the British tribes.

In the city of Rome, a pleasure-loving noble named Caius Julius Caesar bribed his way into the hearts of the common people. He gave them gifts and free circuses and they rewarded him with their cheers so that he became Consul for a year. After that, he was given command of the Roman Army in Gaul.

Although Caesar knew little about war until he was about forty, he swiftly proved himself one of the greatest generals in history. By 55 BC, he had conquered Gaul and had carried the Eagles across the Rhine to overcome the German tribes. After that, it was time, he thought, to pay a visit to the island whose shores could be seen from the coast of Gaul.

There were several reasons why the Roman general wanted to go to Britain. The tribesmen had been helping their friends in Gaul and many a defeated chief had escaped across the Channel. It seemed as if the islanders knew so little about the power of Rome that they were not at all frightened of Caesar and his legions. It was time they were taught a lesson and it would also be a fine thing to send messengers to Rome with news

of yet another triumph by the great general. Moreover, an expedition to Britain would fill the Roman citizens with pleasure and excitement.

The Tin Islands, wrapped in mist and peopled by giants and demons, had long fascinated the civilised world. It was said that there were fabulous riches in gold, tin and metals of every kind, besides unlimited crops of grain. If this were true, such riches must certainly be brought to Rome.

So, out of curiosity and military need, Caesar set sail from Gaul on an August evening in 55 BC. It was not a large force, but every man was a hardened soldier, well armed, well disciplined and absolutely confident of himself and his general. There was a force of cavalry, too, in boats broad enough to take the horses.

By morning, the Roman fleet was close to the shore of Britain. Ahead were towering cliffs where a landing was quite impossible. Caesar gave the order to sail along the coast until they came to a place where the cliffs gave way to a pebble beach. The captains were told to drive their vessels hard at the beach so that the soldiers could wade ashore.

This was done, but the men refused to jump. The shore was alive with British warriors who had followed along the cliffs and now were gathered in force upon the beach, yelling defiance and driving their war-chariots to the water's edge.

The Roman soldiers hated the sea and did not relish the thought of plunging in up to their armpits, to struggle through the waves towards a horde of painted savages. Besides, they had no knowledge of how to deal with chariots, a weapon of war that the Gauls had given up using.

At this moment, the Standard Bearer of the Tenth Brigade shouted, "Jump, lads! I mean to do my duty. Follow me!" Holding aloft the pole that carried the silver Eagle, he plunged into the surf and the soldiers, fearing the disgrace of losing their precious Standard, leapt after him.

Men from the other ships followed their example and a fierce skirmish took place in the shallow water and along the shore. Gradually, the Romans got a footing on the beach, formed their ranks and pressed the Britons back until they scattered into the woods. There was no pursuit because the ships carrying the cavalry had not arrived. So the Romans made camp and waited for the morning.

Next day, messengers came from the British chiefs. They asked for peace and said that they would send handsome gifts if the Romans would go away. In reply, Caesar upbraided the Britons for ill-treating a messenger whom he had sent before the landing ; the chiefs must send their men back to the fields while the terms of peace were being arranged.

Three days later, just as the ships carrying the cavalry were sighted, a storm blew up and once more forced them to return to Gaul. Worse than that, the fleet at anchor and the vessels that had been dragged a little way up the beach were badly damaged.

At once the Britons changed their attitude. They saw that Caesar was trapped. He could not sail back to Gaul and he had no stores to feed his men during the bad weather that lay ahead. There was no more talk of peace. The warriors looked to their arms and the chiefs sent word to their allies that they were gathering an army.

A sudden attack was made on Roman soldiers who had been sent out to collect corn. Hastily marching to their rescue, Caesar beat off the tribesmen and, as he retreated, he sent orders that every available man in camp was to set to work to repair the least-damaged ships with planks and nails from the wrecked vessels.

After one more skirmish, the Roman force embarked in the overcrowded ships and returned across the Channel to Gaul. It had been anything but a glorious expedition.

But Caesar was not the man to accept defeat. The bald,

keen-eyed general kept his men at work all through the winter, and when summer came again he had a bigger fleet and a force specially trained to meet every danger and surprise.

This time there was no fight on the beach. The British chief, Cassivellaunus, had decided that he would draw the enemy inland and destroy him in the woods. So the Roman army landed without difficulty and, as usual, set to work to build a strong base camp.

Leaving a force to guard the ships and the stores, Caesar advanced warily. His cavalry probed ahead to view the unknown countryside and to search out the tribesmen. The Britons held off. Sometimes they swooped along the enemy's flanks or darted out of ambushes, but they refused to fight a pitched battle.

The Roman legions marched on grimly until they came to the River Thames. Here the Britons held a ford in strength but, after a bitter engagement, the Romans forced their way across. Cassivellaunus rallied his warriors but the remorseless enemy pressed them back into Hertfordshire where the British stronghold was taken by storm.

The Britons lost heart. So many of the tribesmen offered to surrender that Cassivellaunus had to ask for peace. Caesar readily agreed. Already he was anxious to return to Gaul, for news had come that the whole country was about to burst into rebellion as the Gallic chiefs made a last effort to win back their freedom.

Caesar had given the Britons a taste of Rome's power. That was enough for the present. With promises of tribute and a few hostages of noble birth, he hurried away to crush the Gauls and, later, to make himself master of the Roman world. In the years of struggle and triumph that followed, he had no time to spare a thought for the remote island where he had so narrowly escaped disaster.

The Roman Conquest

Ninety years passed before the legions came back to Britain. By that time, however, Roman ideas and Roman goods were well known in the southern part of the island.

Gaul had developed into a splendid province, with wide cornfields and busy towns. Merchants crossed to Britain to sell their wares for tin and iron and slaves. Kinsmen travelled to and fro and more Belgic tribes came across to settle, bringing new ideas and heavy ploughs that could bite into the lowland clay.

The Roman Conquest

Some of the British chiefs began to live in the style that the newcomers talked about. They wore dignified robes and had gold coins made with Latin words on them ; they called themselves kings and believed that their courts were every bit as sumptuous as the Emperor's. Visitors hid their smiles and agreed that the thatched huts at Camulodunum (Colchester), capital of Cassivellaunus' grandson, Cunobelin, were as splendid as the buildings in Rome itself.

The Romans had not forgotten the name of Britain. To them, with their tidy minds and sense of order, it was not right for these half-barbaric islanders to imitate Roman ways and to boast of their freedom. When someone had time and an army to spare, Britain must be brought into the Empire. Caligula planned an invasion but he was a madman who changed his mind, so the task fell to the Emperor Claudius, a sickly, bookish man who wanted a conquest that was not too difficult.

In AD 43 an army of some 40,000 men under Aulus Plautius landed in Kent. Following Caesar's line of advance, it forced its way across the Medway and the Thames into the strongest part of the island. The Emperor himself arrived to encourage his troops by his presence and to dismay the Britons by the sight of his military elephants.

Camulodunum was captured and eleven chiefs were brought to make their surrender to the Emperor. They were told that their capital would be rebuilt in the Roman style with a temple in honour of Claudius as its centre-piece. They and their people were now subjects of Rome but, if they behaved themselves and paid their taxes, they would enjoy the blessings of trade and law.

After Claudius had gone back to his books in Rome, the legions set about conquering the whole island. It was not as easy as they had thought. The half-civilised south-east had surrendered readily, for the chiefs knew and admired the power of Rome, but inland, in the west and the north, there were tribes that cared nothing for tiled pavements and elegant robes.

14

Moreover, Caradoc or Caractacus, son of Cunobelin, was made of braver stuff than many of the chiefs.

He refused to surrender and moved into the west where he rallied the hill-tribes who lived by rough farming and robbery. Here, in Wales, Caractacus fought the legions for eight years, always losing ground but never giving up the struggle. At last the Romans brought him to bay in a hill-fort called Caer Caradoc—the fort of Caractacus. His army was destroyed but he escaped to the Brigantes, only to be betrayed into the hands of the conquerors.

Taken to Rome and paraded in chains through the streets for the amusement of a gaping crowd, Caractacus so impressed the spectators by his upright dignity that they forgot to jeer. Looking about at the lofty buildings, Caractacus cried out to his fellow-captives, " Why did the Romans rob us of our huts when they have houses like these? "

The Emperor was astonished by the prisoner's bold gaze. " Do you not know, Briton, that you are about to die? " he asked.

Caractacus looked up at him. " I did not fear death in battle against your soldiers. Why should I fear it here? Put me to death, Emperor. I shall soon be forgotten. Spare my life and it is you who will be remembered! "

" Strike off his chains," cried the Emperor. " Rome knows how to pardon a brave enemy."

Caractacus was said to have settled in Rome with his family. Another story said that he returned to Britain to his estates. If he did, he would have found that his countrymen were far from happy.

Boadicea's Rebellion

The tribes had surrendered but where, they asked, was the good life promised by the Romans? Bullying officials demanded gifts and heavy taxes to pay for the troops, the fortified towns and the long straight roads. The Britons grew sullen and their anger was fanned by their priests, the Druids, many of whom had retreated to the dense thickets of the holy island of Mona or Anglesey.

The main Roman army was on its way to Anglesey to destroy the sacred groves when, in the year AD 61, a great rebellion broke out in the east.

Enraged by tax-officials who had brutally insulted Queen Boadicea and her daughters, the Iceni tribe of East Anglia took up arms. They killed the officials and were speedily joined by a host of warriors from neighbouring tribes.

Led by their tall, handsome Queen, the Britons swept down

upon the new towns, shrieking their battle-cry, " Death to the Romans! "

The hated temple of Claudius at Camulodunum was torn down, Verulamium (St Albans) was savagely destroyed and its inhabitants massacred, the Ninth Legion was overwhelmed and the port of Londinium went up in flames.

News of these frightful happenings reached Paulinus, the Roman Governor, as he was nearing the stronghold of the Druids. Immediately he ordered his army to turn about and march south to seek out the rebels.

A vast host of Britons had gathered to destroy their enemy. So certain were they of victory that they had brought their wives and children to watch the battle from the lines of wagons piled high with plunder from the looted towns.

Paulinus took up a strong position and looked calmly across at Boadicea's great force of wildly excited tribesmen.

" Men," he cried, " today we fight for Rome and for life itself. There can be no retreat. Stand firm. Keep your ranks. Bear yourselves like soldiers of your legion. These are savages led by a woman! "

From her chariot, Boadicea also addressed her army. She reminded them that once they had been free. Now they were slaves. But they had shown that they could beat the Romans. One more victory and all was won.

" Death to the Romans! Drive them into the sea! "

The Britons answered with a great shout and charged. They hurled themselves against the Roman shields, battering with maddened courage a foe that was better armed, better led and grimly cool. The Romans held their ranks and then, as the charges grew less furious, they advanced in line, step by step, pressing the Britons back to the wagon-lines where they slaughtered them beside the plundered wealth.

In a woodland clearing, Boadicea and her daughters drank poison to escape a more horrible death. The revolt was over.

17

Agricola

On that day a young officer named Agricola fought in the army of Paulinus. Afterwards he saw service in other parts of the Empire and, seventeen years later, he came back as Governor of Britain.

Agricola had not forgotten the islanders' bravery nor the reasons why they had rebelled. He knew that they still hated the Romans but he vowed to give them peace and justice.

First he had to deal with the Druids who were still causing trouble. Then, after he had destroyed them and all their holy places, he conquered Wales and turned his attention to the Picts who lived in Caledonia or Scotland.

Although Agricola defeated the Picts, he found it impossible to carry on winter warfare in the northern forests and highlands. So he built a line of forts to keep the savage tribes in check while he took up the task of changing the rest of Britain into a civilised province.

For the Romans, civilisation meant living in a town. A town was easy to rule ; townsmen could be counted and taxed, their comings and goings were known, their work was buying and selling, hammering, writing and carrying, instead of hunting and fighting.

18

More than fifty towns were built in Britain, neat towns with straight streets crossing at right-angles, with temples, law-courts, shops, market-places and public baths. Often they were built near the site of an old settlement or at a ford or at a place where roads crossed and where it was natural for people to gather for trade or safety. In timber and brick, with thatched and tiled roofs, with pavements and stone pillars, towns went up all over Britain from York and Lincoln in the north, to Chester and Caerleon on the Welsh frontier, to Bath, Exeter, Dorchester, Winchester and London.

In the south, retired officials and former chiefs owned large corn-growing estates known as villas, where the nobility lived in centrally-heated comfort, waited upon by trained slaves.

As time went by, many Britons were proud to be citizens of Rome. They dressed in the toga, sent their sons to school and sat with their elegant wives at the theatre or the games. Humbler townsfolk followed their daily occupations and spent their wages in the market and the wine-shop just like the townspeople in Gaul or Spain or any other part of the Empire.

The Emperor Hadrian

In Roman Britain there was always the feeling of living on the very edge of the civilised world. In Wales and Cornwall and on the northern moors, the hill people still jeered at Roman law and clung to their old tribal ways. Sea-pirates from Ireland sometimes came ashore to rob and to snatch a few captives to sell to the slave-merchants.

The Picts of Caledonia were never subdued for long, and every now and then they broke through the line of forts to burn and slay and to take as much plunder as they could carry.

It was one of these raids that brought the Emperor Hadrian to Britain in AD 121. The Ninth Legion had been ordered out from York to pursue and punish the robbers. Somewhere in the wild north, the legion met disaster. Trapped perhaps in a glen, led into an ambush by a false guide or simply overwhelmed by a blizzard, the Ninth vanished with its Eagle Standard.

Hadrian landed at the port of Richborough in Kent. Escorted by the Sixth Legion from Germany, he marched up through the peaceful countryside, noting with approval its rich cornlands and prosperous towns. At York the garrison was paraded and drilled before the Emperor's unsmiling gaze and, when he was satisfied with its performance, he chose a strong company to march with him into Scotland. He would see for himself the country whose tribesmen refused to be conquered.

This Hadrian was a strange man. Brought up in Spain, educated in Rome and Athens, he had fought in wars against Rome's eastern enemies and had travelled with his uncle, the

20

Emperor Trajan, more widely than any other Roman alive. When Trajan died, Hadrian became Emperor but, after he had made his position safe in Rome by favouring the common people and killing off his enemies, he set out again on his travels.

Sometimes on horseback but usually on foot, Hadrian visited Parthia, Syria, Egypt, Spain, Gaul and Germany. By the time he reached Britain, he was quite certain that the Empire was big enough. Rome needed no more conquests but strong frontiers to keep the barbarians out. So everywhere he ordered walls, fortresses and defence lines to be built. Behind them there was to be peace, for the Emperor Hadrian was more than an able general. He loved music and painting. He wrote poetry and built libraries, theatres and temples. And he cared deeply about the people whom he ruled with justice and generosity, though they never understood him, for he seldom spoke and he would sometimes behave with horrible cruelty.

At a speed that exhausted his toughest soldiers, Hadrian surveyed the land of the Picts, walking and climbing in rough country, studying maps and measurements, as he snapped instructions to his weary officers. Then he called his Staff together and pointed to a map.

" You will build a wall," he said, " from here to here. That is the shortest distance between the seas. It measures seventy-six miles. The wall is to be ten feet thick and twenty feet high. There will be a ditch in front thirty feet wide and you will place forts, signal-posts and gates for peaceful traffic. Let it be done with speed. Your task is to put an end to these raids. In my Empire there must be peace."

The work took five years. Ten thousand soldiers dug the earth and raised the stones until Hadrian's Wall stretched from coast to coast. It was the mightiest fortification ever built in Britain. On its top it was wide enough for two soldiers to march abreast and, at one-mile intervals, there were " mile castles ", besides seventeen large forts to house the garrison troops.

The End of Roman Rule

The Wall so disheartened the Picts that, twenty years later,
a second wall, this time made of turf, was built farther north
between the Forth and the Clyde. But the new frontier could
not be held. In AD 190 some of the Roman troops were withdrawn from Britain and at once the Picts broke out, crossed the
Scottish Lowlands, forced their way over Hadrian's Wall and
went plundering far into Roman Britain.

The Emperor Severus came to drive the Picts back. He
retook Hadrian's Wall and made it stronger, besides rebuilding
the city of Eboracum, or York, which had been burnt to the
ground. But there was no second attempt to push any farther
into Scotland. The Wall was the frontier and the soldiers who
were stationed there and who retired from their service to live
nearby, were guarding the most northerly outpost of the Empire.

For another century Britain enjoyed peace, but by the year
300 small fleets of raiders from Germany were regularly attacking the coasts. They came ashore to rob and slipped away as
soon as armed forces appeared. These Saxons became such a
nuisance that the Romans had to build forts all along the coast

from Norfolk to the Isle of Wight. In command of these defences was an officer known as the Count of the Saxon Shore.

Rome's difficulties increased. Every frontier was threatened by barbarians pressing in to enjoy the riches of a vast Empire. In Rome itself there was no longer the heart and will to put right the things that were wrong. Emperors came and went. Sometimes there were rival Emperors who fought each other for power, sometimes a strong Emperor checked the barbarians for a time and tried to reform the taxes, but after he went decay set in again.

In 367 the Picts broke into Britain again and destroyed the legion at York ; the Saxon raids increased, Irish sea-pirates landed in the west and thousands of slaves snatched their freedom and joined in plundering the undefended towns.

Then there was a recovery. Law and order were restored and the legions stood on guard once more. But in 410 the Emperor sent a message to the Britons, telling them that they must defend themselves. He needed the legions to save the city of Rome.

So the Roman army sailed from Britain in the year when Alaric and his Visi-Goths sacked the capital of the world. Steadily, Roman Britain crumbled into ruins.

The Story of St Alban

In the 350 years during which the Romans ruled Britain, they brought many blessings and new ideas. To a semi-barbaric land, they gave roads, towns, education, law and improved ways of farming. Nearly all of these vanished after the Romans left, although the roads lasted longest and were later rebuilt, with many of the towns.

But one gift did not disappear. It was the Christian religion. When the Romans first came, they brought their beliefs in the old gods such as Jupiter, Mars and Diana. Then Emperors were raised to the level of gods and religions from the conquered lands gained favour—there was the goddess Isis from Egypt and Mithras, an eastern god who was popular with soldiers.

Steadily, secretly, because it was often forbidden, a new religion called Christianity made its way into Britain. Its message of hope appealed strongly to poor people and to slaves, but there were powerful persons who disliked a religion that acknowledged only one god.

Most people in the Ancient World accepted the various gods who belonged to different towns, rivers and holy places. It was their refusal to accept any other god, even the Emperor, that led the Christians into trouble. At times they were left in peace, but at others they were hunted down, tortured and put to death. Yet, no matter how they were treated, their religion spread and it took root in Britain.

In about the year 300, a young man named Alban lived in the Roman town of Verulamium. He had been born in Britain but his father was rich enough to send him to school in Rome, and later he had served his time in the army, as befitted a

24

gentleman of means and birth. Now he was living in a fine house in his home town where he was well liked for his kind deeds and for his generosity to the poor.

One day Alban arrived home to find an old man resting in his porch. He was obviously exhausted and near to collapse. Alban carried the stranger into his house, gave him food and drink and told him to rest until he felt stronger.

Presently the old man explained that his name was Amphibalus and that he was a Christian priest wanted by the Roman officials for preaching the forbidden religion. Hunted by soldiers, he had lost touch with his friends, some of whom had already been put to death. After wandering from place to place he had come to seek shelter in Alban's house.

" But why did you come to me? " cried Alban. " I am a Roman citizen, obedient to the law."

" I know that," replied the old man. " I also know that you are a good man, a helper of the needy and the poor. I beg you to help me until I am strong enough to go out and preach the Word."

By this time the old priest was too weak to be asked any more questions, so Alban put him to bed in an inner room where, unknown to the servants, he looked after him for many days.

As Amphibalus grew stronger, he and Alban often talked together. The young man asked questions about a religion that men would die for and, as the priest explained the teachings of Jesus, Alban became certain that this was indeed the true religion. He asked Amphibalus to teach him how to enter the Christian faith.

One morning, when they were praying together, a servant came running to tell Alban that he had heard that soldiers were on their way to search the house. A Christian was said to be hiding there.

Alban acted quickly. He told the old man to exchange his shabby robe for some of his own clothes, to wrap himself in a

25

warm cloak and, with a purse of money, to make his way to a place of safety. When he had received the priest's blessing, he hurried him to a side-gate and, telling him that he would delay the soldiers somehow, bid his friend farewell.

Minutes later soldiers stormed into the house and discovered a man kneeling in prayer in an inner room. Seeing that he was dressed in the robe and hood of a Christian priest, they dragged him out and took him to the Governor.

When the prisoner's hood was thrown back, everyone in the court-house saw to their astonishment that it was Alban, one of their best-known citizens. The Governor was very angry at the trick that had enabled the priest to escape but he knew that Alban was a man of good birth and reputation. For the sake of his father, an old friend, he would pardon this piece of folly. Of course, Alban must make the proper offerings to the Roman gods.

" I cannot do that," said Alban, " I am a Christian and I know that there is only one God."

His friends and even the Governor pleaded with him but he

refused to deny his religion.   In accordance with the law, he was sentenced to death.

The soldiers marched Alban out of the town to the place of execution on a hill.   So great was the crowd that it was impossible to pass over the bridge across the river, but when the soldiers thrust their prisoner down the bank to make him wade across, it was said that the waters miraculously dried up. It was said, too, that when, before his death, Alban asked for a drink, a clear spring gushed out of the ground and was known as Holywell ever afterwards.

Having heard Alban pray for those who were about to execute him, the soldier who was detailed to kill him flung down his sword, saying that he would not strike a holy man. At this, the officer in charge snatched up the weapon and killed both Alban and the soldier.

In later years, when the Christian faith was no longer persecuted, a church was built on the hill where the first British martyr died and, as the Roman town fell into ruins, the new town by the church was called St Albans.

27

How St Patrick Converted Ireland

Not long after St Alban's death, the Emperor Constantine became a Christian and his religion spread rapidly through many parts of the Empire. In Britain we know that the faith reached far into the west country and the north.

It was somewhere in western Britain, perhaps in Glamorganshire or as far north as the banks of the Clyde, that a boy named Patrick was brought up on a farm near the coast. These were troubled times, for the end of Roman rule was not far off, but the boy's parents were good Christians and his father, besides being a farmer, was a deacon of the Church.

One day, when Patrick and his friends were playing on the shore, they were surprised by a band of Irish pirates who had come ashore unnoticed. Before the lads could get away they were overpowered and thrust aboard the pirates' boat, which carried them to Northern Ireland.

Patrick was sold to an Ulster chieftain who put him to work on the land. The boy was lonely and homesick but he pluckily made the best of his hard life. He learned to speak the Irish language and found that, although the people were heathens, they were good-hearted in a rough, half-savage way. Every day, when he was alone with his master's flock, Patrick prayed to God for courage and patience, for he was certain that help would come to him.

After six years as a slave, Patrick ran away and made his way to the coast. Here he came across a ship about to sail to Britain with a number of Irish wolfhounds which always fetched a good price. The captain promised to give him a passage if he would help to mind the fierce animals. Patrick joyfully agreed for he knew, from his years on the farm, that he had a strange power to make creatures obey him. The sailors watched in astonishment when the great hounds followed him quietly on board.

The ship had not been long at sea before a storm blew up and the steersman could only run before the wind while the crew bailed hard all night long. After several days, when the wind dropped, the sailors found that they were off the coast of Gaul. Patrick was by now a favourite with the crew and they agreed to set him ashore to try to find his way home.

Months later, Patrick reached the farmstead where he was born. His parents and his brothers were overjoyed to see him for they had long believed him to be dead. He settled happily at the farm for a time but in his heart he knew that he could not stay there.

Now that he had seen something of the world, Patrick was sure that a great task was waiting for him but, as yet, he did not know where it lay. One night he dreamed that a man came to him with a message : at first he could not understand it until he heard voices saying, " Come back and walk among us as before." Then he could see the fields and woods where he had served as a slave. When he awoke he knew what he must do.

He said good-bye to his family and made his way to Gaul. At length he came to the monastery at Tours where he had been given shelter on his way home. When he explained that he wished to be trained to be a priest in order to carry the Word of God to the Irish, the prior welcomed him in. He would have to prove himself worthy to join the brotherhood of monks, and after that there would be a long training, but God would decide all things.

For seventeen years Patrick worked at this monastery and at another in Gaul, carrying out the duties and services of a monk, studying the Bible and preparing himself for the task that he hoped to undertake. At last he was made a bishop and given permission to go to Ireland.

With a small band of monks, Patrick landed on the coast that he had first seen from a pirate galley. He went to the place where he had worked as a slave, only to find that his old master was dead and his friends scattered. The people were far from friendly, but Patrick strode to the Hall of their Chief, who was at dinner with his household.

" Hear me, O Chief," cried Patrick, " I bring news that is worth telling."

Surprised to hear himself addressed in the Irish language, the Chief told the stranger to speak on. Patrick then described his adventures and dreams. He said that God had directed him to Ireland to lead its people out of their ignorance to knowledge of the true God.

When he had ended, the Chief bade Patrick to be seated with his followers. They must eat and drink, for they were his guests, and later he would hear more of this new religion.

From that day Patrick made headway. Despite the anger of the Druids, the Chief became his loyal friend and was the first to be baptised. He gave the monks a piece of land on which to build their huts and a small wooden church.

Patrick travelled to all parts of Ireland, preaching, baptising and training men to continue his work. Wherever he went, he left monks to build a church so that, when, after many years of ceaseless activity, Patrick died in the green land that he loved, Ireland was a Christian country. By this time, however, Christianity had almost disappeared in the rest of Britain.

The Angles and Saxons

After the Romans went away, there was a long period lasting for more than 150 years which is known as the Dark Ages. This is a period of history about which we know very little. It was a time of fighting and destruction, when homes, belongings and writings were burnt and people left no record of their lives.

It seems certain that, as soon as the legions sailed away, the Picts and the Welsh came swarming in to rob and kill with little fear of being driven back to their hills. Naturally the Britons defended themselves. They had weapons and many were rich, with servants and guards.

Life went on fairly well in some of the towns far from the hills, but gradually the whole system that the Romans had built fell to pieces. There was no one to take command, to fix the taxes, to organise the everyday business of town and country. Trade, law and order came to a standstill. Townspeople found that their work had gone ; some doubtless went back to the land, some tried to carry on as best they could in the dying towns and some joined the robber-bands that roved the country.

To defend their homes, men joined themselves to local leaders and soon there were petty wars, as the nobles fought for power and land.

Out of these struggles, a nobleman, Vortigern, rose to be the strongest leader of the Britons. But even he could not find enough fighting-men to keep the Picts in check. They came robbing and burning as far south as Kent and, since it was hopeless to ask the Romans for help, Vortigern thought of a

32

plan to drive the tribesmen back. He would invite the Saxons to come across the sea to fight in his army for pay ; they were splendid warriors and would be more than a match for the Picts.

The Saxons eagerly accepted the invitation and came to serve in Vortigern's army under their chiefs, Hengist and Horsa, two valiant brothers who quickly realised that this fertile land was far better than their own bleak homeland.

By the time Vortigern realised the danger, the Saxons were strong enough to defy him. It is said that Horsa was slain in a battle but Hengist took the land of Kent and made it his own kingdom.

This success brought more Saxon war-bands to the island. There was no great invasion, only a steady stream of landings, as the curved boats came up the rivers and the invaders went ashore to pillage the farms and the almost deserted towns. Wives and sturdy blue-eyed children followed the warriors, who seized farmlands and settled down under their chiefs, as ready to plough as to fight.

Although they were called Angles, Saxons and Jutes, the invaders were one race, speaking a common language and ready to band together whenever the Britons made a stand.

The islanders did not give in easily. For a hundred years they fought hard, and from time to time a leader would arise to give them hope. Arthur was one of the British chiefs whose victories over the heathens were sung and re-sung until they became a legend of a hero-king who sat with his knights at a round table in a vanished kingdom.

But if the invaders were sometimes defeated in a battle, they were never mastered or driven out. Always they regathered their forces to drive the Britons a little farther back into Devon, Cornwall, Wales and south-west Scotland.

By the year 600 the pagan Anglo-Saxons were masters of all but the hilly rain-swept fringes of Britain and the country was called England, the land of the Angles.

St Columba and St Augustine

The invaders were tribal warriors. They fought under their chiefs and settled the land, piece by piece, under their rule. So a number of separate kingdoms emerged, some of them no bigger than a modern county, as Essex, the kingdom of the East Saxons, and Sussex, kingdom of the South Saxons. Some of the other heathen realms were Kent, Northumbria, Mercia, Wessex and East Anglia.

Thor, Woden and Freya were the stark gods that the conquerors worshipped and, after death—more honourable in battle than in bed—the warriors hoped for an after-life of feasting in the halls of Valhalla.

34

But beyond these kingdoms, Christianity lived on among the Celtic people of Wales and the west. Thanks to St Patrick, it flourished in Ireland, where monks chanted their services and copied their manuscripts with loving care. So far, however, no one tried to win the Angles away from their terrible idols.

It was a quarrel over a book borrowed by one Irish monastery from another that caused Columba to make his missionary journey in AD 563. Men were killed in the quarrel and Columba, Abbot of Derry, vowed to go across the sea to win more souls for God than had been lost in the squabble.

In a tiny boat he sailed to Iona, an island off the south-west coast of Scotland, where he and twelve brother-monks built a church and a group of huts.

When he had founded the monastery, Columba made a perilous journey to the mainland and across country to the court of King Buda, ruler of the Northern Picts. Here he was able to convert the fierce tribesmen to Christianity.

As a result, Iona became the religious centre of the north at a time when the Christians in Britain were cut off from the rest of the world and knew nothing of what was happening in Gaul and Rome.

It had been an unknown Roman soldier who had first brought the Christian religion to Britain and now it was a Roman priest who vowed to restore the faith to the southern part of the island.

When St Columba was baptising the Picts, a young priest named Gregory was walking through the slave market of Rome, where captives from all over Europe were brought to be sold. He paused to look at these bewildered men and women of all races, when his attention was caught by a group of fair-haired, blue-eyed children.

" Who are these beautiful children? " he asked the slave-merchant.

" They are Angles," replied the man.

35

" Angles? " said Gregory. " They look more like angels from Heaven itself."

Gregory asked the Pope for permission to take the Gospel to a land that produced such splendid people, but the Pope had other tasks for him to do.

Years passed and Gregory became Pope. He had never forgotten that group of forlorn children in the market and he chose a prior named Augustine for the mission that he had longed to carry out.

With forty monks Augustine travelled across Gaul but, as they came nearer to Britain, they heard at every monastery where they lodged such terrifying stories of the heathen Angles that their courage failed. The monks begged Augustine to go back to the Pope to tell him that the task was impossible.

Gregory put new heart into Augustine who, in his turn, was able to persuade the monks to go forward, placing their trust in God. Besides, he had one piece of comforting news. Queen Bertha, wife of the King of Kent, was the daughter of the Count of Paris and she had been brought up as a Christian. Although she had had no success in converting her husband, she had managed to send word that a party of missionaries might succeed where she had failed. At least, she would do her best to see that they were not ill-treated.

In 597 the missionaries' boat grounded its keel in a sandy bay of Thanet. With the Cross at their head and with one of their number carrying a large picture of Jesus, the monks moved inland to the place where King Ethelbert had consented to meet them, with his Queen and nobles.

They met in the open air, the King seated under an oak-tree, for it was feared that the strangers might work magic indoors. Augustine stepped forward and spoke earnestly about the life and teachings of Jesus.

The King listened intently, but he was very cautious. " Your meaning is not clear to me," he said. " But you seem to be good men and you have travelled far to speak in this fashion. You may stay here without hurt, and speak to any who will hear you."

Queen Bertha was delighted. The King had earlier given her the half-ruined Roman church of St Martin, on the outskirts of Canterbury. Now she could invite the monks to make their homes there and to rebuild the church and to found a monastery.

The Queen's devotion to the strangers naturally aroused interest. People came to listen to them and some stayed to be baptised. At last the King himself became a Christian and then his nobles followed their ruler's example.

When this news reached Pope Gregory, he sent another party of monks to England, including a young Italian named Paulinus. Their work was to help Augustine in spreading the Gospel in Kent and, across the Thames, among the East Saxons.

Augustine, now a bishop, made a long journey to meet the Welsh Christians at a place near the River Severn. Unfortunately, his proud manner offended the Welsh, who still held Devon, parts of Somerset and Wiltshire. There was a great Celtic church at Glastonbury and others at Llandaff, St Davids and Bangor. So the bishops of the old Christianity saw no reason why they should humbly accept Augustine as their archbishop. In any case, he had come from Kent, held by the hated Angles.

However, he was a man of God, even if they disagreed about such things as the date of Easter. If he rose to greet them, they would hear him meekly. But Augustine remained seated when the Welsh bishops arrived, as if he were the teacher and they the pupils. So they said they would do none of the things he suggested nor would they have him as archbishop or help in converting the English.

The meeting was a failure and Augustine went back to continue his work in Kent, where he died and was buried in the new church of the monastery of Saints Peter and Paul at Canterbury.

Queen Ethelburga and
St Paulinus

When Queen Bertha died, the education of her little
daughter, Ethelburga, was placed in the hands of Paulinus.
The child and the tall young monk became close friends and
they were rarely separated during the troubled days that lay
ahead.

Pagan worship had not disappeared, even in Kent. Upon
the death of King Ethelbert in 616, the priests of the old religion
persuaded his son, Edwald, to throw off the Christian faith and
to return to the pagan gods. Most of the missionaries fled to
Gaul, but not Paulinus or Lawrence, the stout-hearted archbishop who had succeeded St Augustine.

Far from being frightened by the High Priest's threats,
Lawrence stormed into the King's Hall and roundly accused
young Edwald of betraying his parents' noble memory. In a
38

voice of thunder, he told how St Peter himself had appeared in a dream to warn him of the terrible things that would happen to the kingdom if he and Paulinus were harmed. The King fell on his knees in terror and begged Lawrence to take him back into God's family.

Not long afterwards, a messenger arrived in Canterbury from the distant kingdom of Northumbria. He had come, he said, to ask for the hand of Princess Ethelburga for his master, King Edwin.

Edwald, now a good Christian, replied that he would give his sister in marriage only if King Edwin promised to allow her to keep her religion and to take her tutor Paulinus with her.

The promise was given and the princess set out with a strong bodyguard for the north of England. With her travelled Paulinus and a helper named James the Deacon.

The journey from one end of England to the other was a long one and dangerous. The countryside was densely wooded, the valleys were still undrained and likely to be flooded in wet weather, and a vast area of marshes and fens stretched south from the Wash.

Homeless men and robber-bands lurked in the woods but her bodyguard and the names of two kings protected Ethelburga. King Edwin's allies and vassals sent spearmen to escort her to each vill or thane's hall at which she rested after the day's travel.

At length she came to Northumbria and was nobly welcomed by her royal lord, though he looked with some suspicion at Paulinus and his companion James.

Edwin had led a hard, adventurous life. As a child his father's kingdom had been taken and he had spent years as a landless exile until he had won back his throne by force of arms.

Older than Ethelburga, battle-scarred and wary, Edwin took little interest in the religion of his beautiful bride until he luckily escaped death from the knife of an assassin sent by the King of the West Saxons. That same night, Queen Ethelburga gave birth to a daughter.

When Paulinus reminded Edwin of God's twofold mercy, the King was still cautious. He said that his baby daughter could be baptised in her mother's faith but, as for himself, he would only consider the matter if he was given victory over the West Saxons whom he was about to punish with fire and sword.

The Northumbrians duly defeated the enemy and Edwin, a man of his word, summoned Coifi, the High Priest, and all his nobles to a meeting at which Paulinus was to explain the Christian religion. Paulinus spoke with such fiery passion that all the warrior-nobles were silent. At length, an old thane rose to his feet.

" O King," he said, " the life of a man is like the flight of a sparrow through this Hall, as we sit at meat in winter with the fire blazing. It flies in from the darkness through one door into the warmth and light and out of the other, back to the darkness.

Where it came from and where it goes we know not. Our life is as short as the flight of that sparrow. There are many things we do not know. If Paulinus can explain these things, we should follow his teaching."

Then Coifi, the High Priest, sprang to his feet. Instead of defending the old gods, as everyone expected, he attacked them for their ingratitude. He had served them all his life and they had done nothing for him. Calling for a horse and a spear, he mounted and rode furiously to the temple where he hurled his weapon at the great wooden idol. Then he called upon the people to set fire to the unholy place.

After this, Edwin and all his Court were baptised. Then Paulinus and James the Deacon went out preaching throughout Northumbria. For five years, Edwin and Ethelburga ruled happily. They travelled about their kingdom, taking Paulinus with them and encouraging the people to become Christians. At York, the old Roman capital of the north, Edwin had begun to build a splendid church of stone when disaster struck the kingdom.

In 632 the forces of the Welsh King Cadwallon and Penda of Mercia came to attack the Northumbrians. They met at Hatfield Chase where the Northumbrian army was cut to pieces. Penda had Edwin's head carried into York on the point of a spear and his pagan troops harried the land.

Ethelburga and Paulinus were forced to flee and James the Deacon went into hiding. But they escaped to the coast where a ship carried them to Kent.

King Edwald was not strong enough to take vengeance upon the terrible Penda. All he could do to comfort his sister was to give her a royal estate at Lyminge where the Queen built a small minster, a double " house ", for nuns and monks, and here she ended her days as Abbess. Her friend Paulinus stayed with her for a time until he became Bishop of Rochester. It seemed as if their work in the north had been in vain.

How Christianity Spread

But the light of Christianity had not failed. In secret places, James the Deacon preached to the faithful and taught them to sing. Then, a year after King Edwin's death, a new champion appeared. Oswald, a prince from another branch of the royal house, drove Penda out and became King of Northumbria.

Like King Edwin, Oswald had been a refugee. As a boy, he found shelter at Iona, where the monks baptised and educated him. Their kindness was fully repaid.

Having won his kingdom, Oswald sent to Iona for a priest to come and continue the work of Paulinus. The monk who came found the Northumbrians too stupid or obstinate for his liking and he returned in disgust to the island monastery. At this, his fellow-monks chose Aidan to take his place.

This humble, saintly man, working in perfect friendship with a generous king, transformed the kingdom of Northumbria. He built churches, trained boys for the priesthood and founded, on Lindisfarne, an island given him by Oswald, a monastery that was to become one of the most famous in the Western world.

Oswald, who once broke up a great silver dish and gave the pieces to the poor outside his thatched vill, did not reign long.

The heathen Penda struck again and slew him, as he slew Sigbert, the Christian King of the East Angles.

Aidan and his monks clung to Lindisfarne, living like saints in their little community and braving the perils on the mainland. They carried on their work of converting the heathen, including even the Mercian invaders.

Another leader arose in King Oswy. He rallied the hardy Northumbrians and raised an army. At long last, Penda was defeated. In 655, at the battle of Winwood, the fierce old warrior, who had been a flail to Christians for more than thirty years, was killed. With Penda dead and his own son converted, Christianity could flourish in the Midlands and north of England.

Cuthbert, who, as a shepherd-boy, saw Aidan's soul carried to Heaven and who later served as a soldier against the heathen, carried God's message to the southern Picts. Loving and gentle to others, Cuthbert was stern to himself, for he went to live as a hermit on the Farne Island, so shut off from the world that he could see only the sky above the pit where he crouched alone.

There was a great respect for hermits and only after many doubts and prayers did the monks of Lindisfarne gently pull Cuthbert out of his cell to persuade him to be their bishop.

It was in Cuthbert's time that the Abbess Hilda, friend and kinswoman of King Oswy, founded the monastery at Whitby where Caedmon the cowherd received the gift of poetic song.

As Christianity took root and spread, there was one great question to be decided. Was England to be part of the Church of Western Europe under the rule of the Pope in Rome or was it to belong to the Celtic Church of Columba and Aidan?

The Celtic saints had performed miracles of courage and faith. They had carried the Word of God into Scotland and Northumbria at a time when Britain was cut off from the rest of the world. St Augustine had not been able to make friends with the Welsh bishops, but was friendship still impossible?

How Christianity Spread

The Celtic and the Roman Churches had several differences—the Celtic bishops, for instance, did not rule a definite district for they usually roamed about, preaching and baptising—but the difference that troubled Christians most was that they held the solemn celebration of Easter on different dates.

In 663 King Oswy called a meeting, or synod, at Whitby. Abbot Wilfrid, who converted Sussex, Abbess Hilda, James the Deacon, still alive after all his adventures, bishops and clergy from all over Britain were there, including a priest from Kent who was chaplain to Ethelburga's daughter. After much discussion, they agreed to accept the Roman date for Easter.

Thus, the Church in Britain came under the authority of the Pope, although some of the clergy could not accept the change. Northern Ireland and Iona were slow to change, and in Wales they held to the old date for more than 100 years.

Five years after the Synod of Whitby, a great plague came into the land and carried off nearly all the clergy. To save the Church in Britain, the Pope chose as Archbishop of Canterbury a Greek monk from Tarsus in Asia Minor. His name was Theodore and for twenty-one years he laboured to bring order to the Church. He appointed bishops to take care of large districts in which they were to train priests for work in parishes. Theodore also founded new monasteries and encouraged the old ones to follow the Rule of St Benedict, the Italian saint whose monastery at Monte Cassino had been started in 529.

Theodore's work flowered into a golden age. English monasteries, English schools, English scholars and churchmen became famous throughout Europe. The Lindisfarne Gospel, with its wonderful illuminated capitals and covers of gold, the carved stone crosses, the new churches and the singing of the choirs in the great monasteries were the marvels of their time. The land was peaceful. There were quarrels between princes, of course, but the Welsh and the Picts were quiet and there was, as yet, no enemy from outside.

The Venerable Bede

In the north-east a wise, kindly abbot brought up a boy named Bede. They lived at the joint monasteries of Wearmouth and Jarrow, whence the good abbot made the immense journey to Rome to fetch books for his brilliant pupil.

Working in his cell at Jarrow, the gentle Bede wrote book after book. The Scriptures, of course, were the scholar's chief subject but Bede interested himself in every branch of knowledge. He wrote about saints, stars, grammar, science, history and poetry. To him came pupils from all over Europe, though he himself never left his native Northumberland.

Bede's greatest work was his *History of the Church in England*, to which we owe most of our knowledge of the country's early history. At first he felt that he knew too little about events outside his own part of the country, but his friend Nothelm enlisted the help of churchmen in many places who sent facts and letters from which Bede fashioned his masterpiece.

He was a natural story-teller and no one has ever improved upon the beauty and simplicity of such tales as how Caedmon received the gift of song, how Cuthbert served God and how the old warrior likened the life of man to the flight of a sparrow.

This great work took many years and when it was finished, Bede was an old man. There were still books that must be written. He wished to translate the Gospel of St John from Latin into Anglo-Saxon, so that ordinary people could understand when it was read to them.

Knowing that time was short, Bede wrote on and on until he became too weak to hold a pen. A scribe wrote down his master's words. Bede urged him to hurry : " Take thy pen and write quickly, for I have little time and after I am gone, I do not want my boys to read what is untrue."

The scribe went on until it was almost dark in the cell. " There is just one more sentence to write, dear master," he said.

Bede gathered his strength and spoke, " Then write quickly, my son."

Presently the monk sighed happily, " It is finished, master."

" Thou hast spoken truly," murmured the old man. " All is finished."

He died during the night, having continued to the end his work for God. This was the spirit of good men everywhere. A man had a gift ; it might be for writing or carving or building or merely for tending the sheep—whatever the gift, he used it for the glory of God.

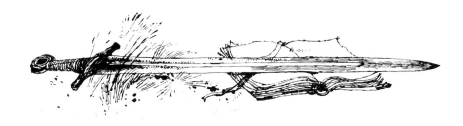

English Churchmen Abroad

Some men, like Bede, stayed at home to carry out their work. Others went abroad at this time to take into northern Europe the faith and learning that had come to England from over the sea.

The Saxon tribes of Germany were still heathens and to them went men like Wilfrid of York and Willibrod of Northumbria. The greatest of the English missionaries was St Boniface, son of a Wessex landowner, who spent his life converting the fierce tribesmen and was murdered at his task in the bleak coastland of Frisia.

Thus, when Charlemagne, the mighty ruler of Frankland, wanted to establish learning in his dominions, he naturally turned to the land that produced so many notable scholars and churchmen.

In Italy, the King of the Franks chanced to meet an Englishman journeying home from Rome with books and with the " pallium ", a special robe, for his archbishop. When Charlemagne learned that the traveller was none other than Alcuin of York, the most famous scholar of the day, he could not rest until he won consent from his king and archbishop to have him at his own court.

So, for the rest of his life, the cheerful, hard-working Alcuin acted as chief adviser to Charlemagne. He joined his travelling court and later founded the palace school at Aachen, and another famous school at Tours, where Alcuin ended his life as Abbot in 804.

Between them the English monk and the jovial, masterful emperor established abbeys and schools that lasted far longer than Charlemagne's conquests.

48

The English Kingdoms

Although the Church was now united, England was still divided into a number of kingdoms that rose and fell, according to the character and strength of their rulers.

Life was short. Only rarely did a man live as long as Penda and Charlemagne. Most men, including kings, died before they were forty and since the dead king's sons were usually boys and since there was no fixed rule about an eldest son succeeding his father, the death of the king was usually a disaster for the realm. His brothers, his wife's relatives and the great nobles usually fought and schemed for power until one came to the top and brought some kind of order to the land.

In the seventh century, the greatest kingdom was Northumbria. The influence of Iona, the work of saintly abbots and good kings brought strength and unity to the north-east. But, during the eighth century, there was a succession of short-lived kings who could not check the rise of Mercia.

This midland kingdom had only two rulers in eighty years. Aethelbald, a warrior and something of a tyrant who was told to mend his ways by the courageous Boniface, extended his rule as far as London. All the Anglo-Saxon kings south of the

49

Humber acknowledged him as their overlord until, in 757, Aethelbald was murdered by one of his own bodyguard. This led to a short period of civil war until Offa, a relative of the dead man, made himself undisputed king.

Although much of his career is wrapped in legend we know that Offa was strong enough to be called " the Great ", and to give himself the title of " King of the English ". Even the mighty Charlemagne regarded Offa as almost an equal, made a trade treaty with him, sent gifts and considered joining their two families by marriage. When a quarrel occurred, perhaps over the marriage arrangements, Charlemagne thought about invasion but, instead, he sent his friend Alcuin to patch up the friendship.

Offa was certainly powerful enough to receive ambassadors from the Pope, to mint his own coins and to crush the sub-kingdom of Kent. To defend Mercia from the Welsh, he built a huge earthwork, known as Offa's Dyke, from Cheshire to the Bristol Channel and, in this orderly kingdom, he founded many churches and monasteries, among them the Abbey at St Albans which was built in honour of the first British martyr.

When Offa's long reign came to an end in 796, the usual troubles broke out. His son reigned only five months and was followed by a distant cousin. Kent and Wessex rebelled and Mercia began to decline. It was still a kingdom to reckon with, but it was no longer supreme.

The star of Wessex was rising. This southern kingdom had been growing in strength since about 700, when one of its kings, Ine of Wessex, had the laws of his realm written down, an unusual thing to do in days when justice was based on custom known to all men.

In 802 Egbert, son of one of Offa's enemies, became King of Wessex. He defeated the Mercians and made Wessex into the strongest of the English kingdoms. By a hairsbreadth, it was to prove strong enough to save Christianity from the heathens.

The Coming of the Northmen

Out of the northern seas, from the fiords of Norway and from
the windswept islands where Boniface was killed, came a horde
of robbers more terrible than the barbarians who had once
captured Rome.

They were called Norsemen, Danes, Vikings, Northmen or,
simply, " the heathen host ", and everywhere they appeared
they struck terror by their pitiless greed and blood-lust.

In their horned helmets, carrying bright spears and two-
handed axes, the sea-pirates gloried in slaughter as they gloried
in their jewelled arm-bands and scarlet cloaks. They would
kill in a kind of frenzied joy, and what they could not carry off
in the way of loot they smashed and hurled into the flames.
Spreading terror was part of the raiders' business. People gave

them gold to go away and they came back for more in the spring, when the raiding season opened.

The first warning came in 787. A monk wrote in the *Anglo-Saxon Chronicle* :

> " In this year, the King [of Wessex] took to wife the daughter of Offa. And in his days, came three ships and the Reeve rode thither and tried to compel them to go to the royal manor, for he did not know who they were and then they slew him. These were the first ships of the Danes to come to England."

Six years after the murder of the King's Reeve, a fleet appeared off the holy island of Lindisfarne, where the Northmen went ashore to rip down the hangings of Cuthbert's church, to seize the vessels of gold and silver and to break the skulls of the helpless monks. Next year Bede's monastery at Jarrow was receiving the same treatment when a force of Northumbrians came up in time to interrupt the looting and drive off the robbers.

After this no abbey or headland or river bank was safe. Not even Charlemagne could stop the raids along his coasts. The grey sea was wide and no one knew where the Northmen would strike next. Sailing their long dragon-ships with magnificent skill, they came to unprotected shores, entered the river mouths and spread across the land on stolen horses. Villages and monasteries were sacked with merciless greed. Then, when they had thrust the bright cloth, the crosses and altar cups into the bows of their ships alongside their terrified captives, they sailed away.

Some of the Northmen went down the rivers into Russia, some along the Frankish coast and into the Mediterranean as far as Constantinople. Others crossed the sea to Scotland and the Shetlands, Orkneys and Hebrides felt their fury ; Iona itself was sacked in 802 and the robbers went on to Ireland. Here, as in Scotland and the Isle of Man, they took land and founded kingdoms with fortified towns from which they could launch fresh raids.

There were Northmen who sailed as far as Iceland and Greenland. Some, it is said, even reached America which they called Vinland, because of the wild grapes they found growing in some sheltered spot. But far easier and far more profitable was the voyage across the North Sea. They called it the Swan's Road and it led to England.

Naturally, the east coast suffered first and longest. Then, as plunder became scarce, the dragon-ships sailed through the Channel to attack the southern coasts.

No sooner had King Egbert beaten the Mercians than his own kingdom was in danger. In 835 he was fighting " a pirate host " in Cornwall and, after his death a year later, his son Ethelwulf was having to fend off the enemy all along the coast from Dorset to the Thames.

By this time the roofless abbeys and the blackened monastery walls could yield no more treasures, so the Vikings came, not in private groups of two or three ships, but in great fleets. They came to settle a land that was fairer than their own and, when they had taken farms, they showed as much skill with the plough as they had shown with sword and axe.

In the year 851 a fleet of 350 longships sailed into the mouth of the Thames. An army went ashore to storm London and Canterbury. The Mercians were defeated and Surrey was overrun. Then Ethelwulf and the West Saxons marched up from Winchester and gave the Danes the worst beating they had ever suffered.

Alfred the Great

So great was King Ethelwulf's victory that he felt able to go on a visit to Rome that lasted a year. He took with him his little son, Alfred, for he had left the kingdom in the hands of the boy's older brothers.

On their return, the travellers found that the Danes were stronger than ever, for defeat in the south had merely caused them to turn their attention to the midlands and the north.

Before he died, in 855, Ethelwulf directed that the older part of Wessex should go to his son Ethelbald and the eastern part (Kent, Sussex, Surrey and Essex) to Ethelbert. This division of the kingdom seemed to bring a curse upon the House of Wessex, for one disaster followed another.

Ethelbald died after a reign of five years. Ethelbert, who joined the kingdom together again, had just beaten off the host that captured Winchester, his capital, when he too died. Aethelred, the third of the royal brothers, became King as the Danes mounted their largest attack so far.

News reached Wessex that a " Great Army " had taken York with horrid slaughter. The whole of Northumbria, with all its store of art and learning, had fallen into the bloodstained grip of the heathens.

The King of Mercia was too terrified to fight. Aethelred led the men of Wessex up to Nottingham to offer support but the Mercians made peace. So the Wessex fyrd, or army, went glumly back to their homes. But young Alfred had seen the terrible Northmen and had noted their habit of building camps so strong that it was well-nigh impossible to dislodge them. From these fortified camps they could raid in any direction

54

they pleased and, if they met with a reverse, they had a strong-hold to fall back upon that was filled with captured stores, enough to last the winter, if need be.

In 870 the Northmen sprang at East Anglia, killed King Edmund in battle and took his entire kingdom. Then they turned towards Wessex.

The host marched to Reading in the valley of the Thames and here King Aethelred attacked their stockade. Failing to take it, he retreated into open country. The Danes followed and made a surprise attack at Ashdown when the King was still at his prayers. Alfred, however, " fighting like a wild boar ", beat the enemy off with heavy losses.

Once again, defeat did not weaken the Danes. They loved fighting and went off to spend a year ravaging the eastern part of Mercia. After that, they were ready to try another assault on Wessex.

In 871 attacks were made by land and sea. Aethelred died at Easter and Alfred, hastily elected King by the Witan, fought in nine battles that summer. His forces were exhausted but so was the enemy. The Danes withdrew into Mercia and Alfred took stock of the situation.

He was only twenty-two and, although he was by no means robust, he had been fighting since he was old enough to carry a spear. The only peace Alfred had ever known was during his childhood, when he had learnt to read at his mother's knee while his brothers scornfully played war-games. There had been a little schooling from the monks and the long-remembered visit to Rome.

But now there was no time for the things he really loved. He must fight for what was left of his battered kingdom.

As Alfred and every thane and cottager expected, the Northmen came back. Under a resolute leader, Guthrum, their main army drove deep into Dorset ; another force moved in from the west and a great fleet appeared off the south coast. Exeter was captured but Alfred was still clinging on to the fringe of the invading host when a storm wrecked the enemy fleet and strewed the shore with the bodies of thousands of Danes.

Guthrum retreated to Gloucester and the people of Wessex breathed again. Winter was coming on and the foe would quit warfare until the spring. At least, there were a few beasts left for the feasts at Christmastide.

Guthrum watched and waited. At Twelfth Night, when the season of feasting reached its height, he struck across the frozen land and took Chippenham by storm. Making this his main camp, he harried the countryside with ferocious speed.

Caught by surprise, the fighting-men of Wessex were swept aside. Their leaders were scattered or slain. The kingdom lay broken as the pagan horde swept across the land.

The Valiant King

Alfred escaped. With his family and most of his own bodyguard he fled to the Somerset marshes, where only the swamp-men knew the paths that led through shoulder-tall reeds to a patch of solid ground called Athelney. Here, Alfred built a stronghold from which he sent messengers to his friends and spies to watch the enemy.

The tale of the lonely fugitive being scolded by a cottage wife for allowing her cakes to burn was written long after Alfred's death. It may be true, but at least he was not alone. Saxons came through the Sedgemoor marsh to join him ; raiding parties went out to give the Northmen a taste of their own brew and one of these bands took the enemy by surprise and captured his Raven Banner.

Spirits rose high at Athelney. A spy came in (some said that it was Alfred himself) to tell how he had got into Guthrum's camp disguised as a harper. He had seen with his own eyes the Danes feasting day after day, using up their stores because they believed that Wessex was finished.

But Wessex was awake and ready to strike back. Alfred left Athelney and made his way, like the thousands he had summoned, to the meeting-place at Egbert's Stone, high upon the Wiltshire downs. There the men of Wessex shouted and wept to see their valiant King alive and in their midst again.

The Danes came out of camp to face the Saxons at Ethandune, fifteen miles from Chippenham. With the deep-throated roar of men who remembered their blackened farmsteads and slaughtered children, the West Saxons burst the Danish ranks and swept their hated foes into headlong flight. They did not

57

pause to celebrate the victory but drove hard after the enemy until the survivors were securely imprisoned in the Chippenham fortress.

Alfred tightened his grip. For once it was the Saxons who had food and fire but, within the stockade, the Danish stores had gone and the wounded died of hunger and cold. At last, after two weeks, Guthrum surrendered.

The time of vengeance had come. For more than a lifetime the Danes had killed and robbed without pity and now a Danish army was to meet its doom. The West Saxons looked at the prisoners and ran their thumbs along the sharpened edges of axes and spears.

But there was no massacre. Alfred gave the order not to kill but to feed his foes. In victory he showed the nobility of greatness.

Awed by such mercy, Guthrum made peace. He agreed to withdraw his army from Wessex for ever and he consented to be baptised into the Christian faith.

The Peace of Wedmore saved Wessex. Eight years later, Alfred was strong enough to occupy London and to rebuild its broken walls. He had to teach the Danes another lesson or two and, thenceforward, they were made to keep to the Danelaw, the land lying east of a line from Chester to Essex. They settled to farming and trade but Alfred could never relax.

He knew that many of the jarls, or earls, were not bound by the peace that he had made with Guthrum and there were others across the sea still hoping to find land and plunder.

To hold what he had saved, Alfred built a fleet that could tackle the enemy on the sea. The walls of London would repel an invader and, in Wessex itself, forts were built and towns made strong with earth banks and wooden palisades. To prevent the kingdom being caught defenceless again, Alfred divided the fyrd into two parts, one to tend the fields and the other, in its turn, to stand to arms.

But Alfred was not called " the Great " simply because he was a good general. At heart, he was a man of peace and, in those dire months at Athelney, he had come to realise what his people needed.

Wessex was well-nigh ruined. Trade had ceased, the farms were derelict, the churches and monasteries were roofless and empty. The people were hungry and lawless.

Almost single-handed, Alfred rebuilt the kingdom. He travelled up and down the land, praising and encouraging, building with his own hands, learning crafts and setting others to work. He fetched skilled men from abroad to teach the Saxons the arts they had forgotten, for on every side he found ignorance :

" Hardly a man in the kingdom can read his prayer-book

59

or write a letter," he said. " I would have all the boys now in England set to learning."

Schools were started and even the nobles had to go to their lessons if they wished to receive the King's favour :

" It was a strange sight," wrote a bishop, " to see eldermen and officials, ignorant from boyhood, learning to read."

Since few teachers were left alive, invitations were sent to France, Wales and Ireland for monks and scholars to come and work in Wessex. Not all of them were good men and, to Alfred's sorrow, they sometimes quarrelled. Once, two of the foreign monks actually killed their abbot. But among the newcomers was a Welsh monk named Asser, who became Alfred's greatest friend and helper.

Books had almost completely disappeared, so Alfred kept the scribes at their desks making copies of old books that had escaped the flames. Almost all were written in Latin, for there had been little or no writing in Anglo-Saxon since Bede's time. Alfred set himself to improve his own knowledge of Latin and, with Asser's help, he translated parts of the Bible and works on history, geography and science.

This wonderful man never ceased toiling for his people. He found time for building, writing and governing and was keenly interested in stars, in trade and in foreign places. He re-wrote the laws of King Ine and kept in touch with the Pope, for it was his Christian faith that gave him the strength to do so much. As one of the monks wrote :

" The King attends daily services of religion . . . he goes to church at night-time to pray secretly, unknown to anyone."

The noblest man who ever occupied an English throne died when he was barely fifty, but he left an example to his people and a message to his successors :

" I pray thee, my good son, be a father to my people," he said as he lay dying. " Comfort the poor, protect and shelter the weak and put right the things that are wrong."

The Sons of Alfred

At his death, Alfred's kingdom was not England, but Wessex, the southern part. Even so, his victory over the invader had placed Wessex far above the other kingdoms and they never rose again. There were to be no more independent kings of Mercia, Northumbria and East Anglia. It was Alfred's family that would supply the true kings of England.

Edward the Elder, Alfred's son, who reigned until 924, spent all his life fighting the Danes to extend his father's boundaries. He was a splendid soldier and his companion-in-arms was his sister, Ethelfleda, Alfred's eldest child.

At sixteen, Ethelfleda had married a war-scarred Mercian nobleman named Aethelred. This marriage linked the two kingdoms in friendship, although much of Mercia had been lost to the Danes. With a puppet-king in the enemy's power, Mercians looked on Aethelred as their leader and, for several years, his wife rode to war at his side and, when he died, she took over leadership of the army.

Known as " The Lady of the Mercians ", Alfred's daughter worked in perfect harmony with her brother when he became King of Wessex. Indeed, she brought up his son, Athelstan, a handsome boy who grew into a great general through assisting his dauntless aunt in her campaigns.

Edward the Elder and Ethelfleda developed a new way of fighting the Danes. After she had defeated the Welsh and made her border strong against attack by those tribesmen, Ethelfleda harassed the Danes along Watling Street, while her brother attacked them in the midlands. As they advanced, they built forts called burghs, so that they could not easily be dislodged from the territory that they were steadily winning.

These tactics succeeded. The Danes were still strong but they had no leader like Guthrum to unite them. Instead, they fought under a number of chiefs, called jarls or earls, whom Ethelfleda defeated one by one, while Edward pressed into East Anglia and won a great victory near Huntingdon.

Derby was taken by storm, Leicester surrendered and the Danes of York had agreed to yield to the Lady of the Mercians when she died at a fort on Watling Street in 919.

By the time Athelstan succeeded his father, the Danes had been pushed so far back that he was able to advance north of the Humber into what had been the kingdom of Northumbria. Here the Norwegians (who had settled along the coasts of Ireland and western Scotland) were in command but, in 937, Athelstan won a great victory at a place called Brunanburgh.

We do not know where Brunanburgh was but the writer of the *Anglo-Saxon Chronicle* was so moved by the victory that he turned to poetry to describe it :

> " In this year, Athelstan, Lord of the warriors,
> with his brother, Prince Edmund,
> Won undying glory with the edges of swords
> In warfare round Brunanburgh.
> With their hammered blades, the sons of Edward
> Clove the shield-wall. . . .
> There lay many a warrior
> Of the men of the North, torn by spears,
> Shot o'er his shield : likewise many a Scot,
> Sated with battle, lay lifeless.
> All through the day, the West Saxons in troops
> Pressed on in pursuit of the hostile peoples
> Fiercely, with swords sharpened on grindstones,
> They cut down the fugitives as they fled."

After this battle, Athelstan could truly claim to be King of England, for he ruled, or was overlord, from the Isle of Wight to the River Clyde in Scotland. But, as long as the Danes submitted, he left them to live their lives and to follow their own customs.

When the great Athelstan died in 941, it seemed as if the new-found strength of the kingdom might ebb away. Three kings followed each other in quick succession. They were Edmund, stabbed by an outlaw, Edred, his warrior-brother, and Edwig, who ruled badly and drove St Dunstan, then a bishop, out of the kingdom.

Fortunately, Edwig's reign was short and Edgar, who became King in 959, when he was only sixteen, ruled the kingdom so well that he was called Edgar the Peaceable.

An old story tells how Edgar, to show his mastery of the whole islands, had himself rowed in a boat on the River Dee by a crew of six " kings ". At all events, his reign was quiet enough for him to be able to follow his passion for building monasteries.

When Dunstan had fled abroad, he had stayed at a monastery in Flanders where he found monks living far more strictly than the easy-going English. This impressed him and, on his return, when he was Archbishop of Canterbury, Dunstan set to work to reform monastic life in his own country. With the enthusiastic help of King Edgar and two bishops, new Benedictine monasteries were built on land given cheerfully by the King and less willingly by the nobles. Lazy and sinful monks were turned out of the old abbeys and there was a revival of learning in the Church.

Under a good King and a great Archbishop, Anglo-Saxon England was rich and peaceful, except in the ravaged north. The King was only thirty-two and there seemed to be a long period of prosperity ahead, when Edgar died suddenly in 975. At once the kingdom fell into evil hands.

Ethelred the Unready

By his first marriage Edgar had a son named Edward, and then he married a widow, Elfrith, who bore him a second son, Ethelred. Neither boy was old enough to rule and a struggle took place between the supporters of the elder son and the powerful friends of the Queen who wanted to see her son upon the throne.

The Witan chose Edward but, in 978, when on a visit to his stepmother, at Corfe in Dorset, the young King was treacherously murdered and hastily buried without so much as a church service. Men dared not say that the Queen had planned this crime but no one was punished for it and her son Ethelred became King, as she had hoped.

At a later date the murdered boy, known as Edward the Martyr, was buried at Shaftesbury where miracles were said to have occurred at his tomb.

Thus, hoisted to the throne by murder, Ethelred's reign began badly. As he grew older, it was clear that he had none of the qualities of his great ancestors. He was not brave or skilled in arms ; owing, perhaps, to the events of his childhood, he had no trust in himself or in others. With his evil mother forever at his elbow, he presided weakly over a quarrelsome Court, where nobles betrayed each other and plotted to recover the Church lands that they had been made to give away in Edgar's time.

The name Ethelred meant " noble counsel " but it was not long before men added the bitter nickname, " Unraed ", meaning " no counsel ". Ethelred the Unraed was " Noble Counsel—No Counsel " or, in modern speech, " the Unready ".

65

But, apart from the King, the whole country was unready for the disasters that were about to fall upon it. New packs of sea-wolves came out from the Danish islands, where training-camps had been set up to teach young warriors the secrets of successful raiding.

The first of the new-style raids occurred at Southampton in 984 when most of the inhabitants were killed or captured. Thanet and Dorset were the next to suffer and, in 991, Olaf Tryggvason came to Folkestone with ninety-three ships, burnt all the countryside and the town of Sandwich, crossed into Essex, captured Ipswich and defeated the Saxon army at Maldon.

The raids grew worse when Olaf was joined by Sweyn Forkbeard, the ferocious son of the King of Denmark. They captured London in 994 and did tremendous damage. King Ethelred, instead of calling every man in the realm to arms, feebly invited the Danes to Andover where he had Olaf baptised and made him a gift of gold.

From that time on, Ethelred's only plan was to buy off the Danes. A heavy tax called the Danegeld was laid on the people. The invaders came killing and robbing ; then they were given money to stop. They took it, laughing, and went away. Soon they were back for more.

Yet what could Ethelred do? He was no soldier himself and his nobles were treacherous. They failed to protect each other's land and sometimes, when it suited them, they actually joined the robbers. In the south, the leaderless people had no heart to fight, and in the old Danelaw the inhabitants were not likely to oppose their own kinsfolk.

In his difficulty, Ethelred gave land in southern England to certain Danes on condition that they would fight for him. Among them was the jarl Pallig who was married to Gunnhilda, sister of Sweyn Forkbeard.

In 1002 the Vikings harried Devonshire and all the country

66

as far as Southampton. Pallig, who should have come to help the King's forces, did not appear and the King and the Witan were forced to find another huge sum to buy off the victors.

Ethelred was furious. In his rage, he gave secret orders that every Dane living in England was to be killed on November 13th, St Brice's Day.

The massacre took place and among the slaughtered were Pallig and Gunnhilda. When Forkbeard heard this news he swore a great oath to avenge his sister's murder.

For ten years the Danes raked the land with fire and death. Each summer they harried the countryside, and in winter they retired to the Isle of Wight or to their favourite base at Reading. Some returned to Denmark and came back in the spring with fresh recruits for the marauding host.

By 1013, when Sweyn and his eighteen-year-old son, Canute, landed with yet another army, the stricken people were sick of pillage and slaughter. To put an end to their sufferings, they offered to take Sweyn as their King. Ethelred the Unready fled to his brother-in-law in Normandy.

But Sweyn was never crowned. He died suddenly in London and young Canute, uncertain what to do, went back to Denmark to seek advice from his older brother.

Edmund Ironside

At once Ethelred returned. He was full of promises to rule well and he brought with him his son, Edmund, a young giant, full of courage and determination. While Prince Edmund put his heart into rallying his countrymen, Ethelred and Edric, his boon-companion, were busy taking revenge on those who had accepted the Dane for King.

This Edric was a Mercian earl, so renowned for his greed that he had earned the name of Edric the Grasper. With a force of his own picked ruffians, he was seizing land and riches when Canute appeared in East Anglia with a strong army.

Prince Edmund naturally expected that Edric would bring his Mercians to join the Men of Wessex. But the Grasper was jealous of the valiant prince and he marched away to offer his services to the Dane.

Edmund was forced to retreat, as all the north and the midlands surrendered. He fell back to London and here his father died. The stout-hearted Londoners, who had known many a siege, acclaimed Edmund as their King and manned the walls as Canute drew near.

The King slipped away, for his last hope lay in Alfred's country. The farmers of Wessex were still the best fighting-men in England and they flocked to Edmund's standard.

As in Alfred's day, they were equal to the best of the Danes when their own King was in the thick of the fight, swinging his war-axe and roaring the old battle-cry. They fought the enemy, drove him back, closed in and fought him again. Edmund's prowess at this time earned him the name of Edmund Ironside.

There was a battle that lasted for two days in Wiltshire,

where Edric the Grasper, serving with the Danes, tried to snatch victory by a trick. Hacking off the head of a fallen man, he held it up, crying, " See, the head of your King! Fly, Saxons, fly! "

But Edmund tore off his helmet to show his face, " I live! I live! " he shouted. " Edmund is here! " The enraged Saxons tried to reach the traitor but, although they broke the Danish ranks, Edric escaped from the field.

Canute fell back and Edmund was able to relieve London. He cleared Kent of the Danes and chased them across the Thames into Essex. His army was drawn up opposite the foe when the Grasper himself came into Edmund's camp and offered to do homage if he could serve on the Saxon side.

Edmund hesitated. The earl was a traitor but his Mercian soldiers would make victory certain. Edmund gave his hand to Edric and placed him on his army's right wing. At this, Canute decided to retreat to his ships for he knew that he was outnumbered.

Seeing his chance, Edmund gave the order to charge but, at the crucial moment, Edric played him false. He wheeled his men about and took no part in the fight, so that Canute recovered and was able to drive back the dismayed Saxons.

Once more Edmund retreated to the west and Canute followed cautiously. But, in Gloucestershire, instead of offering battle, he asked for a truce. The two leaders met on an island in the River Severn and agreed that peace was better than war between men so well matched in valour. Canute was to rule in the north and the east ; Edmund would rule in the south. When one died, the other would have all.

Within a year, Edmund Ironside was dead. No one knew how he died. Some said it was a sudden illness, but others whispered that Edric had poisoned him to win Canute's favour. If he did, it was in vain, for the Dane put him to death for his crimes.

Canute the Sea King

Swearing to rule by the laws of Alfred and Edgar, Canute was crowned King of England in the year 1016. He was a remarkable man, this Viking who had first come as a robber but had stayed to be King. Moreover, he was to rule as well as the best of those who followed Alfred.

First, Canute made sure of his throne by banishing Edmund's little sons to distant Hungary. Then he married King Ethelred's widow, Emma of Normandy, and he recruited a bodyguard of housecarls to guard him night and day. Having thus made sure that he would not be removed by rivals or by an assassin's knife,

Canute gave the people order and justice. He allowed Saxons and Danes to live according to their own customs and he refused to favour one race more than the other.

Born a heathen, Canute became a Christian and did his best to make amends for all the damage done to the church. He went on a pilgrimage to Rome and, in England, he built monasteries, including one at Bury St Edmunds in honour of the East Anglian king slain by the Danes. At Canterbury, he had a rich shrine made for the bones of St Alphege, the archbishop whom the Danes captured in 1012 and killed during a drunken feast when they hurled their meat-bones at their captive until he died.

Soon after he became King of England, Canute succeeded his brother as King of Denmark and, later, in 1028, he seized the throne of Norway, with dominion over Greenland, the Scottish Isles and the Isle of Man. Thus, he was master of three kingdoms, of the North Sea and the Baltic. This may explain the story of courtiers flattering him by saying that he commanded the ocean, whereupon he proved their folly by placing his chair at the edge of the sea and vainly ordering the waves to go back. Had Canute lived longer, England might have become part of a Scandinavian sea-empire, but he died in 1035 and was buried beside the Saxon kings at Winchester.

His younger son, Hardicanute, was fighting in Norway when his father died, so his stepbrother, Harold Harefoot, became King of England without opposition. Within two years he was dead and Hardicanute took the crown. He must have been a worthless man and a drunkard, for the chronicler wrote of him, " he never did anything worthy of a king while he reigned and he died as he stood at his drink at Lambeth ".

In 1042 the Witan chose the king of the " rightful " line, for they elected Edward, the forty-year-old son of Ethelred the Unready and Emma of Normandy.

71

Edward the Confessor

As a boy, Edward had been taken for safety to his mother's land, where he was brought up at the court of his uncle, Duke Richard. The delicate, timid lad came to think of himself as a Norman ; he had Norman tastes and Norman friends, he spoke Norman-French and he felt that he was a stranger in England.

The Normans had come from the same creeks as the sea-robbers who had attacked King Alfred's realm. Their great-grandfathers had ravaged the coasts of France, until one of them named Rollo had been given or had taken the province that came to be called Normandy.

Their Viking energy went into farming and horse-rearing, into fighting the dukes of France and, presently, into church-building. The Normans took up Christianity with enthusiasm and soon became famous for their splendid churches and for the strict lives of their monks and clergy.

It was this side of the Norman character that Edward inherited. Where most high-born knights had an appetite for battle and wealth, he had a passion for religion. It was not that he was particularly kind and good, but he loved churches, ceremonies, prayers and holy relics, such as the bones of saints and those scraps of wood and cloth that were supposed to have some marvellous power.

Despite his reputation for holiness, Edward was not popular in England. The greatest man in the kingdom was Earl Godwin of Wessex, who meant to be the power behind a weakling's throne. But, although Godwin managed to marry his daughter Edith to the King, he and his sons were cold-shouldered at court.

Edward brought some of his Norman friends and priests

with him. Others came to join them and it was not long before they were hated for the arrogant contempt with which they treated the Queen and her countrymen.

One day, the Count of Bologne, who had been visiting the King and was on his way to his ships, rode into Dover with his men and demanded food and lodging from the local house-holders. A townsman lost his temper when spoken to like a dog ; blows were struck and, in the brawl, the men of Dover killed several of the visitors.

King Edward summoned Earl Godwin, whose lands stretched from Dorset to Kent, and angrily ordered him to burn Dover as a punishment. Godwin refused, declaring that the upstarts had only got what they deserved. For this dis-obedience he and his turbulent sons were banished from the realm.

Queen Edith was sent to a nunnery and Edward, greatly pleased with himself, invited his Norman friends to help themselves to Earl Godwin's lands.

Among the visitors from Normandy was Edward's cousin, the grim young Duke William. He looked around and liked all that he saw. It was a brief visit but, before he departed, he obtained from his childless cousin a promise that he should one day have the crown of England. If William had made enquiries, he would have discovered that the promise was worthless, for the crown went to the man chosen by the Witan.

Earl Godwin was known to be a hard, ambitious man but the English were in no mood to have their own countrymen exiled for a pack of foreigners. It was not long, therefore, before the Earl deemed it safe to return from Flanders and his son, Harold, came with a fleet from Ireland. Together, their forces were too much for the timid King who agreed to restore their lands, to recall Queen Edith and to send his Norman friends away.

Godwin did not enjoy his triumph long. He died within a

few months and his titles and most of his lands fell to Harold, who became the real ruler of the kingdom.

As time went on, the King became known as Edward the Confessor. He was content to leave earthly affairs to the able young nobleman, for his own thoughts were fixed on Heaven and on the great abbey that he was building at Westminster.

Harold ruled well. Short but immensely strong, he had energy, good looks and a leader's power to make men love him. When Griffith, King of Gwynedd (North Wales), made an alliance with the treacherous Earl of Mercia, Harold crushed the rebellion with impressive skill. His fame grew, for he was as generous and fair-minded as he was brave. It was clear that he would have justice in the realm and he sternly warned his unruly brother Tostig, Earl of Northumbria, that he must mend his ways and give better government to the people in the north.

But, for all his talents, Harold was a luckless man. In 1065 he was sailing in the Channel on the King's business when a storm wrecked his ship on the coast of France. Captured by the surly Count of Ponthieu, he was handed over to Duke William of Normandy.

His rival concealed his glee and entertained the Englishmen

with lavish hospitality, but he would not let them go home.

At length, desperate to get away, Harold fell into a trap. He agreed to swear an oath that he would support Duke William's claim to the English crown. In his heart, he meant to break his word, for a man could not be held to a forced oath. But William understood his rival's thoughts. After the oath was made, a cloth was removed from the chest on which Harold had laid his hand and, to the horror of the Englishmen, it was seen that the chest was filled with holy bones. It was no ordinary oath that had been sworn and, in the future, Harold would be called oath-breaker and his men's hearts would be filled with dread.

Back in England, Harold had to deal with a rebellion in the north caused by his brother's misdeeds. Showing no favour to his own family, he sent Tostig into exile, an act of justice that was to cost him his throne and his life.

Meanwhile, King Edward was dying. Too ill to attend the opening of Westminster Abbey, he died in January 1066 and was buried in his great church. The Witan met in London and chose Harold to be King of England. The claims of Edmund Ironside's grandson, of the King of Norway and of Duke William were not even considered.

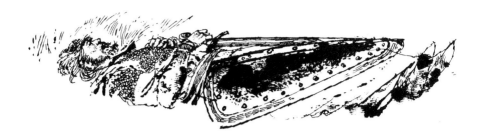

Harold, Last of the Saxons

When William of Normandy heard the news, he broke into a rage and proclaimed a crusade to win his " rights ". While an invasion fleet was being built, hundreds of knights rode in to join his army, attracted like flies to honey by the thoughts of plunder and land. The Pope himself sent his blessing and a banner, for William had made his tale good, although his claim to England was no more than an excuse for a military adventure.

Harold did not fear the Normans. Indeed, he longed for them to come all through the summer of 1066, for he had a splendid army assembled in the southern counties, far stronger than any seaborne force that William might bring. He was as good a soldier as the Duke, though more hot-headed, and he had an excellent fleet that would have given the Norman ships a rough passage in the Channel.

The summer wore on and the Normans still did not come, for the wind blew steadily from the north and kept their ships from sailing. As the corn grew ripe, the English soldiers became restive, thinking of their farms and harvest-time. Surely the Normans would not come so late to risk the autumn storms and a winter campaign?

Harold had just disbanded his army and sent the fleet to the Thames, when a call for help came from the north. Three hundred longships had sailed into the Humber and an army of Norsemen, led by Harold Hardrada, King of Norway, was ravaging the land like a pack of wolves. Earl Tostig was there with the invaders, for he had invited Harold Hardrada, the

76

giant Viking who had fought all over Europe, to come to take his brother's throne.

Hardrada defeated the Earls of Mercia and Northumbria, and made them promise to help him against Harold. Then they waited for the English King at Stamford Bridge, a wooden bridge that crossed the Derwent, seven miles from York.

With housecarls and as many fighting-men as he could gather, Harold came north at furious speed. In York, he learned that the enemy was only a short distance off, so, refusing to rest, he drove his tired men on without a pause. They came to Stamford Bridge, where the Norwegian host was camped on both banks, their armour laid aside and their ranks unformed.

Harold sent a message to Tostig. He would pardon him and restore his earldom if he came across to the English side.

"And what land will my brother give to Harold Hardrada?"

Angrily, Harold replied, " To the King of Norway, I will give six feet of English earth. No, seven feet, seeing that he is taller than other men and needs a longer grave! "

Then he gave the order to attack. The English broke through the forces on the west bank of the river but were checked by a gigantic Viking who held the bridge until he was speared from below by a soldier who had crept under the timbers. Once across the river, the English infantry cut the host to pieces and, as Harold Hardrada and Tostig lay dead on the field, they chased the remnant back to the ships.

Harold had kept his word. The most famous war-captain lay in his seven-foot grave, the pirate army was destroyed and only a few survivors were sailing ruefully back to Norway. The English buried their dead and tended the wounded, as the monks sang the Thanksgiving in York Minster.

But the wind that carried the Norwegians away brought the Normans to the coast of Sussex, where William landed his army without so much as a fishing-boat or a ploughboy to oppose him.

Like all great commanders, William made the most of his luck and turned every unexpected happening to his favour. When he stumbled on landing and heard his men groan to see him fall, he leapt up with his hands full of earth and cried, " See, I have England already in my hands! "

Then he chose a strong place to build a fort and sent his cavalry out to terrify the countryside and to bring in food for men and horses. He knew his man and could afford to wait for Harold.

Blazing hill-beacons and hard galloping carried the news to York at the other end of the kingdom. Leaving the wounded behind, Harold broke camp and marched south at headlong speed. Many of his battered foot-soldiers could not keep up and the northern earls hung back out of disloyalty, but Harold rode on. His army marched at more than thirty miles a day and, as he came, the King gathered soldiers and sent messages for all his troops to join him without delay.

By the evening of October 13th, Harold had reached Sussex. He camped his tired men on a ridge of the Downs, where a single apple-tree, bent by the wind, was a landmark. Less than half the army had arrived. Many were still trudging down from the north, some were coming from the shires and the western fyrd was still a day's march off.

Harold's brothers urged the King to wait. The Normans had had two weeks' rest ; his own men had fought a great battle, had twice marched the length of England and were utterly weary. Better to wait ; fresh troops would arrive in a day or two and the invaders would be outnumbered by two, three or five to one. Let the Norman Duke cool his heels, they said: burn all the barns and drive off the cattle, so that his men would have to fight on empty bellies.

Harold refused to listen. His people looked to him for protection and he would not burn their farms. Had he not slain the wolf of Norway? Would he not thrash this Norman

78

dog, this son of a tanner's daughter, who had played him false when a guest in his land?

With everything to gain by caution and a kingdom to lose through rashness, Harold's hot temper betrayed him.

At dawn on October 14th, the Normans advanced towards Senlac Hill where Harold offered battle. As usual, the English had dismounted, for they fought on foot, trusting to axe, spear and sword, to a shield-wall, as their fathers had done. They had taken up a strong position on the ridge, with the giant housecarls in the centre, guarding the King and the Royal Standard. On either side were the thanes and the fighting-men of the shires, but too many of the troops were ill-armed peasants hastily drawn into the army while better men were still marching to serve their King.

The battle began at nine o'clock, when the Norman archers advanced. The English, who had few bowmen, bore the hail of arrows and waited stolidly for the real fighting to begin. Then, when the foreign knights came up the slope to the shield-wall, they were met by spears, javelins and showers of stones tied to pieces of wood so that they were hurled like throwing-axes. Those who reached the shield-wall were assailed by the great

79

English axes that cut through chain-mail as if it were parchment.

A second attack was thrown back. The shield-wall was unbroken. In front lay piles of Norman dead and dying, among them Tallifer, the Duke's minstrel, who had ridden up the slope singing and twirling his sword like a juggler. By afternoon the Normans were almost spent.

Suddenly a cry went up that the Duke was slain. His men wavered and some of the English levies, forgetting their orders, rushed downhill in joyous pursuit. But William was not dead. Snatching off his helmet to show his face, he rallied his men, checked their flight and ordered a ferocious counter-attack. The English who had left their position were cut down and the Norman cavalry charged towards the weakened places in the shield-wall.

Then, as a last throw, the Duke ordered his archers, who had now replenished their stock of arrows, to fire high over the heads of his cavalry, so that the arrows fell like a deadly rain on the English. Harold himself was struck above the right eye and, from that moment, the spirit of the English army began to falter.

As dusk approached, some of the levies began to steal away and the Norman knights rode through gaps in the wall. Then the English army was broken into knots of valiant warriors who stood their ground and fought back-to-back against a mounted foe who could circle and charge at any point of weakness.

When light faded, the last of the housecarls were still grouped round their slain King and his brothers. Refusing to fly or to yield, they swung their axes in stubborn defiance to the end. Even the Normans were awed by such courage.

It was night when the Duke's servants pitched his tent among the slain. In a single day, by luck and daring, he had won a kingdom, for the men who might have led the English to avenge the battle of Senlac Hill lay dead in the darkness with their King.

William the Conqueror

The Battle of Hastings may have been a lucky victory but Duke William had the genius to take advantage of his good fortune. Leaving orders for an abbey to be built where the battle was fought, he marched along the coast and captured Dover. This gave him a strong base close to the Continent from which he moved inland to Canterbury. Then, making no attempt to capture London, he crossed the Thames at Wallingford and pitched his camp at Berkhamsted in Hertfordshire.

There, twenty-six miles from the capital and in command of the routes from the west and the north, the Conqueror waited for the English nobles to come to him. Meanwhile, with practised skill, the Norman horsemen laid waste the countryside.

On hearing news of the disaster at Hastings, the Witan had chosen Edgar the Atheling, Edmund Ironside's grandson, to succeed their fallen king. But Edgar was only a lad, and when the northern earls showed no sign of fight, there was no other leader to raise an army against the Norman invaders.

Deeming it hopeless to resist an enemy who had already

beaten Harold and the best fighting-men in England, the Witan sent the Archbishop of Canterbury and young Edgar to offer the throne to the Norman Duke.

On Christmas Day 1066, William entered the Confessor's church at Westminster. Presently, the congregation was heard to accept the new monarch with a loud shout. But the Norman soldiers on duty outside the church, mistaking this noise for the sound of revolt, set fire to the neighbouring houses and began to massacre the inhabitants.

After this violent beginning, the new reign proceeded quietly. Englishmen had known foreign kings before this, and when William declared that he was their lawful king, they accepted him, not gladly, but in the hope that he would prove to be another Canute.

At first there were few changes. William certainly rewarded the chief of his followers with the lands of those who had fought against him but he would not allow the Normans to strip the country bare. Surrounded by a hostile population, the new-comers had to obey the man who had led them to victory.

All seemed so quiet that, by March 1067, William felt able to leave the kingdom to attend to matters in Normandy. No sooner was his back turned than the Norman knights began to help themselves to what they thought were the proper fruits of conquest.

They taxed and robbed the English with such brutal greed that, by the time William returned in the autumn, the country was seething with revolt.

Rebellions broke out in several districts but there was no plan and no accepted leader, and William was able to crush the risings one after another with the ferocity of a man who meant to keep the land that he had won.

All of southern England was mastered when Harold's sons were defeated in the west. Then a more serious revolt broke out in the north, where the men of Northumbria acclaimed

82

Edgar the Atheling who was also supported by Malcolm Canmore of Scotland and by a Danish fleet that sailed into the Humber.

When he had crushed this rebellion, William laid a dire punishment upon the north. He sent his horsemen across the land until there was not a house standing nor a human being left alive. In Durham and most of Yorkshire, the cattle were slaughtered and even the ploughs and farm tools were smashed, so that if any survivors crept back to their blackened acres, they would find no means to till the soil. Those who escaped the massacre fled into Scotland where many sold themselves into slavery. For years great stretches of northern England remained an almost uninhabited waste land.

The last of the English rebels took refuge in the swamp-surrounded Isle of Ely. Here, a thegn named Hereward the Wake, so called from his skill and watchfulness, was joined by Edwin and Morcar, the northern earls, who realised, too late, their folly in not supporting Harold. Under Hereward's leadership, the fugitives defied the Normans until the relentless king built a road across the fens and took Ely by storm. As for Hereward, men said that William pardoned his heroic foe and gave him command of an army in France where he died in battle or by the hand of a jealous Norman.

It was a grim-faced king who returned to his capital after the harrying of the north and the capture of Ely. He had tried mildness but now he would rule by fear. Any act of disobedience, any move that suggested rebellion was punished with gruesome cruelty and the English were steadily removed from their lands. By the end of the reign, nine-tenths of England had passed into the hands of Norman lords.

Meanwhile, in many a town or on some nearby hillock, sullen peasants were made to pile up earth into a mound that was crowned by a wooden tower. Each castle, manned by its Norman garrison, was part of William's plan to overawe the

towns and to hold down a nation with a few thousand well-armed troops.

The man who laid his iron grip on England was born to rule. He was eight years old when his father, Duke Robert, failed to return from a crusade and the boy grew up in a turbulent land where his friends were murdered and he had to fight long and bitterly to master the treacherous nobles.

He succeeded because he was brave and cunning. His thick-set body was as strong as a bull's and his spirit as unyielding. The Normans came to know that he had a better brain and more resolute will than any of them and, if they did not love him, they feared and obeyed him like a pack of half-savage hounds.

So cruel that he once had the citizens of a rebel town flayed alive and their skins hung on the walls for mocking his descent from a tanner, William had a kindlier side to his character. He loved his wife and his troublesome sons ; his closest friend was Lanfranc, the pious prior whom he made Archbishop of Canterbury, and, as a devout Christian, he wished to bring peace and justice to the people he ruled.

The Norman barons, however, cared nothing for the

conquered English and they grumbled bitterly about the King's refusal to let them treat their vassals as they pleased. Ten years after the Conquest, William had to deal with a major revolt by his barons and, in the fighting, he was actually wounded by his own son, Robert. Yet, when the rising was crushed, the King who could be so merciless gave a pardon to his disloyal son.

In these struggles Englishmen found themselves on the Conqueror's side. He might be a hard ruler, but they knew they could look only to him for protection against the barons and their arrogant henchmen. They did not rebel again even when, for the Domesday Book enquiry, his agents measured every rood of land and counted every pig in order that their value should be known to the last penny. And at his death, the chronicler who sighed so bitterly about the Conqueror's greed, also wrote :

> " King William was a man of great wisdom and power . . . though stern beyond measure, he was kind to those good men who loved God and we must not forget the good order he kept in the land."

85

William Rufus

The Conqueror died in Normandy in 1087. At the end, unafraid of death and pain, his mind was filled with thoughts of his difficult sons and his two kingdoms:

" I have killed thousands of those fine people in England," he murmured to a priest, " and many have died of hunger or the sword. May God forgive me."

He made gifts to the Church and the poor. Then he divided his possessions. Robert should have Normandy ; Henry, the youngest son, was to have £5000 in gold (which he weighed to make sure he was not cheated), but to William Rufus, " the Red ", his second son, he gave the crown of England.

Weakly, he tried to remove his great ring so that Rufus should take it as proof of his will to Archbishop Lanfranc. Rufus tore the ring from his father's hand and left him to die, while he hurried to England to claim the throne before his brother Robert.

Robert, known as Curthose or " Short legs ", was a jovial little scoundrel, as brave as a bull-mastiff. He had no idea how to govern a kingdom and the barons much preferred the thought of him as their ruler to his tough, bad-tempered brother.

But Rufus was more than a match for the barons. He put down a rebellion and banished their leader, Bishop Odo, to Normandy.

The new king had much of his father's ability but none of the Conqueror's honesty or respect for the Church. He made no effort to appoint an Archbishop of Canterbury when Lanfranc died, but used the Archbishop's income for his own purposes and kept the monks of Canterbury on very short rations.

86

However, in 1093 Rufus fell ill and, believing himself about to die, repented of his greed. He summoned Anselm, the saintly Abbot of Bec, to his bedside and informed him that he was to be Archbishop of Canterbury. Soon afterwards, Rufus recovered from his illness and began to regret the loss of the Canterbury gold, all the more because the gentle Archbishop refused to be bullied by a blasphemous King. The quarrels between them grew so fierce that Anselm was driven into exile and while he was still abroad Rufus was mysteriously slain.

He was hunting in the New Forest when the party became split up and, according to some reports, the King was alone with a nobleman named Sir Walter Tirel. Suddenly a stag ran out and Tirel's arrow, missing the animal, struck the King who died immediately.

The mystery was never solved. If it was not an accident, it was murder, arranged perhaps by the King's brother Henry or, possibly, by believers in a strange form of witchcraft. At all events, Rufus was dead and, for all his wickedness, Englishmen remembered " the good peace he kept in the land ".

The Conqueror's third son, Henry, was one of the hunting-party, and as soon as he learned of his brother's death he galloped to Winchester to secure the royal treasury. Three days later, he was crowned in Westminster Abbey, and there was good reason for such unusual haste. Robert Curthose, the eldest brother, was expected home any day from a crusade.

When, therefore, Duke Robert arrived to claim the crown, it was already in Henry's keeping and he had taken steps to win over the English people.

Announcing that he would put an end to " the evil customs " of his brother's reign, Henry had arrested Ranulf Flambard, the hated tax-collector, and had recalled Anselm from exile. Some of the barons took up arms in support of Duke Robert, but with the English on his side, Henry had no difficulty in defeating them.

Henry I, "The Lion of Justice"

Henry I was " thick-set and strongly made, of moderate height and inclining to fatness, but his black hair falling over his brow and the soft expression of his eyes were a contrast to the fierce look of Rufus ".

In fact, he was as violent, cruel and mean as his brothers, but, because he was a far better ruler, he earned the name of " Lion of Justice ".

Englishmen looked on Henry as one of themselves since his marriage to Matilda, daughter of Queen Margaret of Scotland, a princess descended from their own great Alfred, and they willingly fought in his army when he invaded Normandy in 1106. At Tinchebrai, they took revenge for Hastings when they stood against the Norman knights and cut them down in droves. Duke Robert was captured and Henry, showing no mercy to his brother, kept him a prisoner for nearly thirty years, until his death in Cardiff Castle.

Master of England and Normandy, as he had always meant to be, Henry ruled harshly. He loved gold and he saw that it came into his treasury and not into the pockets of lesser men. His treasurer, chamberlain, chancellor, stewards and constables were made to work as hard as their master, though he paid them little and left no room for private gain. The sheriffs who collected the taxes came to the King himself and on the black and white squares of a great chequer-board placed counters that stood for gold. Thus, when few could understand written sums, the totals were plain for all to see.

So tight-fisted was the King that he knew the pay, the number of loaves, the measures of wine and the candle-ends

allowed to every royal official. No man was allowed more than two meals a day at the royal table and the King himself lived very plainly, although, by custom, a measure of wine was poured out every evening in case he should need it during the night. Since he never drank it, the servants used to drink it themselves until a night came when he asked for his wine. The trembling chamberlain confessed what had happened and, for once, the stern King relented. " Do you really receive no more than one measure? " he asked. " That is very little for the two of us. In future, you must get two measures from the butler, one for you and one for me! "

The barons stood in awe of this masterful ruler and the people had justice. " No man durst misdo another," wrote the chronicler of his reign ; " he made peace for man and beast."

But Henry I had one great anxiety. His Queen had given him only two children : a daughter, Matilda, who was sent to Germany to marry the Emperor Henry V, and a son, William, on whom all the King's hopes were fixed.

Prince William was seventeen when his father took him on a short visit to Normandy. The time came to return and the King sailed in his own ship, giving his son permission to make the voyage in a fine new vessel called the *White Ship*. After feasting ashore with his friends, the Prince came aboard in high spirits and ordered the captain to give the sailors three barrels of wine to drink his health. There was much merry-making and delay, so that it was dusk before the vessel put to sea.

Noble ladies and knights crowded the deck ; the sailors, warmed by drink, went carelessly about their tasks and the tipsy helmsman sang lustily as he steered out of the harbour. Suddenly, with a shuddering crash that threw the passengers over, the *White Ship* struck a rock and began to sink rapidly. In the darkness and confusion, the captain thrust Prince William into the only small boat and ordered the sailors to row him to safety. They had left the stricken ship when the Prince remem-

bered that his half-sister was still aboard and he seemed to hear her voice amid the screams and prayers.

" Put back! " he cried. " I must save my sister! "

The sailors obeyed but so many terrified passengers tried to crowd into the tiny boat that it capsized and the Prince was drowned.

At dawn, some fishermen picked up a man almost dead from cold but still clinging to the topmast of the *White Ship*. He was Berthold of Rouen, the sole survivor of the company that had put to sea so gaily on the previous evening.

For three days no one dared tell the King what had happened. When at last a page-boy was made to stammer out the story, Henry sat transfixed with horror. Presently, rising as if to withdraw to a private room, he fell senseless to the ground. Later, he recovered consciousness but, in his grief, he never spoke of his son or the *White Ship*. Indeed, men said that he never smiled again.

Five years later, hearing that the Emperor Henry V had

died, Henry sent word to his daughter to join him in Normandy. When Matilda arrived from the Low Countries, the King rose eagerly to greet her. She was now twenty-three, a red-haired beauty with the proud bearing of an empress and the masterful expression of the Conqueror's grand-daughter. The King's heart leapt :

" Daughter," he cried, as he embraced her, " I have lost a son but, by God's mercy, I have found him again in you! "

He laid his plans and, at Christmas, the barons and churchmen were summoned to meet the King who told them curtly that they were required to swear an oath to accept Matilda as heir to the throne of England and Normandy. The lords of the realm were horrified. It was an unheard of thing for a woman to rule England and the notion of paying homage to this red-haired girl was an insult to their manhood. But none dared voice his thoughts. They feared Henry and they swore the oath.

Next, Henry looked for a second husband for his fiery-tempered daughter and his choice fell upon Geoffrey of Anjou, called the " Handsome " and also " Plantagenet " from his habit of wearing in his helmet a sprig of broom—*planta genista* in Latin. Again, the barons were furious, for the counts of Anjou were their ancient foes, and it went sore against the grain to bow the knee to this good-looking princeling.

However, Henry cared nothing for his nobles' discontent. The succession seemed to be safe when Matilda's marriage produced two fine sons, the elder named Henry in his honour, and in 1135 the King went cheerfully across the Channel to visit them. Shortly afterwards, when he was out hunting, Henry was taken ill and died almost immediately. According to his wishes and the barons' oath, Matilda was now Queen of England.

King Stephen and the Empress Matilda

Henry I died on December 1st, 1135, but Matilda made no haste to claim her kingdom, for she and her husband Geoffrey had decided to make sure of Normandy before proceeding to England. This delay gave Stephen of Blois his chance to take the crown.

Son of the Conqueror's daughter, Adela, Stephen had been Henry I's favourite nephew. He was liked by the barons and he had spent many years in England where his marriage to a lady descended from the Saxon kings had made him popular with the common people, especially the Londoners.

Thus, although Stephen had taken the oath to support Matilda, he was given a warm welcome in the capital where, at Christmas, he was crowned by the Archbishop of Canterbury.

93

King Stephen and the Empress Matilda

In Normandy, too, the barons accepted Stephen as their Duke in preference to Geoffrey, the hated Angevin.

Charming, brave and generous, Stephen was a failure as a king. Men liked him but they did not respect his rash generosity or fear his lenient temper. He was described as " a mild man and soft and good, and did no justice ", so that the kingdom, released from Henry I's grip, quickly fell into disorder. In a short space of time, Stephen managed to quarrel with the Church and with many of the leading barons. By 1139, Matilda's opportunity had come.

Leaving her husband to conquer Normandy, the Empress crossed to England and made her headquarters in the west country where her half-brother, Earl Robert of Gloucester, was extremely powerful.

Stephen might have captured Matilda at Arundel soon after she landed, but he chivalrously let her escape, saying that he did not make war on a woman. However, both sides took up arms and civil war broke out in which the rival armies sacked towns and devastated parts of the countryside.

Some of the barons took the opportunity to build illegal castles and to enrich themselves by making private war upon their neighbours until, in some districts, the lords who should have upheld justice were living like robber-chieftains. It was said that if strangers were seen approaching a town, the inhabitants fled in terror and " men said openly that Christ and his saints slept ".

In 1141, at Lincoln, where he fought so furiously that he broke his sword and axe, Stephen was captured and taken in chains to Gloucester where Matilda had him thrown into a dungeon. As " Lady of England and Normandy ", she rode in triumph to London.

So far Matilda had shown courage and ability, but in the moment of victory her arrogance lost her the crown. She had been an Empress. She had known the grandeur and flattery of foreign courts and she saw no reason to tread warily in a small island where she had been basely betrayed. So she lost no time in putting the barons and churchmen in their places and when the leading citizens of London came to ask her to respect their laws and liberties, she flared up in anger :

" Come you here to prate of liberties to Matilda the Empress? " she stormed. " Get you back to your counting-houses and talk no more of liberties! "

But when she laid a tax on the city, the Londoners rose against her like a swarm of angry bees until, deserted by all except Earl Robert and a few friends, she was obliged to leave the capital.

Stephen's heroic Queen pursued her with an army and besieged her so closely at Winchester that she and Earl Robert decided to break out at night. In the darkness, they lost touch with each other, and although Matilda rode through the night and came safely to Gloucester, the Earl was ambushed at a ford and captured.

Without her most faithful supporter, Matilda's cause was hopeless and she had to agree to release Stephen in exchange for Robert. The war broke out again but Matilda's cause grew weaker and weaker. She sent Robert to Normandy to beg for help from her husband, but in his absence she was hotly besieged at Oxford where Stephen surrounded the castle.

It was winter and her position became desperate. Earl Robert had not obtained sufficient troops to make an attack across the snow-covered country, and inside the castle the famished garrison was exhausted. But Matilda, as fiery as ever, had no intention of surrendering. One night she had herself and three knights lowered by ropes from the castle walls. Dressed in white garments, they passed unnoticed across the snowy fields and reached the Thames. The frozen river served as a road to lead them to an abbey where they obtained horses and rode to Wallingford Castle.

King Stephen and the Empress Matilda

Here, Matilda was overjoyed to find not only Earl Robert but her nine-year-old son, Henry, who stoutly declared that he had come from Normandy to fight for his mother.

But her chance had gone. She carried on the struggle for five more years until Robert, her valiant half-brother, died. In despair, the Empress retired to Normandy, but she refused to give up her hopes :

" Never forget that one day you will be King of England," she would say to her son after he had recited his lessons.

By the age of fifteen, Prince Henry was already a dashing warrior. After two adventurous attempts to renew the war in England, he went off to fight in France and presently he married Eleanor of Aquitaine, one of the wealthiest landowners in Europe.

At twenty, with his mother's blessing and a strong force, the Prince made yet another assault on England and this time he was successful. Stephen was still a fighter but he was growing old and when his own son died, he was ready to come to terms. It was agreed that after Stephen's death, Henry should inherit the kingdom.

A year later, in 1154, Matilda's son was crowned, but the Empress was not present in the Abbey. She refused to return to the land where she had met so many disasters. Instead, she lived to a pious old age at Rouen, although she did not fail to keep an eye on her son's possessions in France nor to send him advice on how to rule the stiff-necked people of England.

Henry II, the Law-Giver

Henry inherited his mother's energy but not her arrogance, for he was marvellously humble for so great a monarch. In him there was none of the cruelty of the Norman kings, but at times he showed the almost insane temper of his family.

By a series of fortunate accidents, he was now the most powerful man in Europe for, with Aquitaine from his wife, Normandy and Anjou from his father, and now England, his realms stretched from the borders of Spain to Scotland.

The ruler of these vast possessions was built for the task. His stocky frame, bullet head and open, freckled face revealed the strength and eagerness of a young man bursting with vigour. The terrifying energy that exhausted his courtiers and servants shone from his grey eyes with such brilliance that men came to gaze on him as if, apart from kingship, he was a man above all other humans.

But Henry's gifts were more than those of an athlete and a warrior. He spoke several languages, never forgot a fact or a face, and his knowledge of law was so deep that he was sometimes called upon to settle disputes between foreign princes and

97

cases too difficult for his own judges. He was generous, too, on a kingly scale but, for himself, he cared nothing for clothes or rich living. He would ride for days in the same old tunic and cloak and eat his meals standing up while he read documents or dealt with state business.

Once, the monks of St Swithin at Winchester tearfully complained that their bishop had forbidden three of their dishes at dinner. Henry asked how many dishes they had left and when they answered, " Only ten," he replied, " In my court, I am satisfied with three. I must see that your bishop cuts your dishes to the same."

Another instance of his rough humour occurred when he was riding with his friend, the great Becket, and they saw a shivering beggar. Turning to his companion, the King asked :

" Would it not be an act of goodness to give that poor man a cloak? "

Becket agreed and Henry cried out, " Yours be the goodness then! " and flung Becket's fur-lined cloak to the beggar.

But Henry could take a joke against himself. After excommunicating a royal forester, Hugh, Bishop of Lincoln, was summoned to Woodstock Castle, and on arrival he found the King resting from the hunt in a forest glade, surrounded by his courtiers. To show his displeasure, Henry refused to look up or to greet the Bishop, whereupon Hugh, the bravest of men, shoved a nobleman aside and sat down next to the King. The silence was unbroken until Henry, who hated to be idle, called for needle and thread and began to repair a bandage on his finger. The sewing proceeded in silence. Then Hugh, leaning sideways, murmured :

" You know, Sire, you remind me of your great-grandmother of Falaise."

Henry's ancestress had been a glove-maker, daughter of a tanner, and the King, not in the least ashamed of this fact, burst out laughing :

" Do you not hear what this impudent Bishop said ? " he cried to the courtiers. " The rogue knows that my great-grandmother was a woman of the people and he has the sauce to say that my sewing reminds him of her needlecraft! "

As soon as he came to the throne, Henry made the barons pull down their illegal castles and send away the foreign mercenaries. For the task of restoring law and order, he chose honest and capable officials, among them a London merchant's son named Thomas Becket. This brilliant young man who had been trained for the Church, rose to become Lord Chancellor and, much to the disgust of the nobles, the most powerful subject in the kingdom.

The King and Becket became boon-companions. Both were tremendous workers ; both were masterful characters ; both

99

possessed a deep sense of duty and a love of justice. The only difference between them was that whereas Henry cared nothing for his appearance, Becket, newly arrived at the pinnacle of wealth, loved to parade his riches and to live in a style far more magnificent than his royal master.

For several years, the King and his Chancellor worked together in perfect friendship and when Theobald, the old Archbishop of Canterbury, died in 1161, it seemed a clever move for Henry to ask the monks to elect Becket in his place. The highest positions in the realm—the chancellorship and the head of the Church—would be in the hands of his most trusted servant.

But Henry had made a mistake. Declaring that he could not serve two masters, Becket resigned the post of Chancellor, gave up his magnificent way of life and devoted himself to the service of God and the Church. To Henry's disgust, he found that he was opposed at every turn by an Archbishop more rigorous and determined than any since Anselm.

The fatal clash came over the question of Church courts. Since William the Conqueror's time, the Church had possessed the right to try its own wrongdoers in special Church courts where punishment was much lighter than in the ordinary courts. Besides priests and deacons, a huge class of persons could claim to belong to the clergy and the King's judges knew that murderers and thieves were escaping punishment because they lived on Church property or were able to mumble a few words of Latin.

To put an end to this scandal, Henry proposed that after a " clerk " had been found guilty in a Church court, he should be handed over to a lay court for punishment. In this and in various other matters, Becket refused to budge an inch until the quarrel grew so bitter that he felt obliged to flee abroad.

Becket and the King

Six years passed until Henry, feeling uneasy at the Pope's displeasure, made peace and Becket returned to Canterbury.

The Archbishop was as obstinate as ever. From his pulpit in the cathedral, he denounced those who had obeyed the King during his absence and he excommunicated several bishops.

The news of this defiance was carried to King Henry in Normandy. Storming up and down in a towering passion, he raged at Becket's treachery and upbraided the cowering nobles:

" What fools and cowards have I nourished in my house that not one will avenge me on this upstart clerk?"

Stung by this taunt, four knights left the hall and took ship to England. At Canterbury, they ordered the Archbishop to keep his word to the King. Becket icily refused and went into the cathedral where the monks were singing vespers. Timidly, they tried to bolt the doors.

" No," said Becket. " I will not have God's house turned into a fortress."

He was moving towards the choir steps when the now armoured knights clattered into the dark cathedral, crying:

" Where is the traitor?"

A clear voice answered them.

" Lo! I am here, no traitor but a priest of God."

Becket and the King

The assassins rushed forward and thrusting the Archbishop's cross-bearer aside, tried to drag him outside. When he resisted, they lost patience and killed him where he stood on the stone floor of the most holy church in England.

Rightly or wrongly, the blame for the murder was laid on Henry. He walked in penance through the streets and allowed the monks to scourge him at the martyr's tomb ; he made gifts and endowed religious houses and he had to give up his plan to reduce the power of the Church.

But if he was defeated here, Henry's desire for justice was unabated and he travelled ceaselessly in order to bring firm government to his vast dominions. In the north, the Scots were cleared from the counties they had taken in Stephen's reign.

In Ireland, once the most godly country in western Europe, there was perpetual warfare between the chieftains. One of these, Dermot of Leinster, rashly invited some of the Norman knights of South Wales to come to help him. Richard of Clare, called Strongbow, restored Dermot to his throne but when he died, Strongbow seized the kingdom. A number of other Norman knights followed suit and set themselves up as rulers in districts that they conquered with their swords.

In 1171 Henry II crossed to Ireland to assert his authority over the knights and their Irish subjects. All accepted him as their lord, but although he set up a government at Dublin, he did not stay long enough to make sure that the nobles ruled the Irish justly.

But Britain was only a part of Henry's domains. To keep any kind of control over the violent nobles of Normandy, Maine, Anjou, Brittany and Aquitaine, he had to travel up and down his territories, dealing out justice and fending off his enemies. The chief of these was the King of France who, at this time, ruled no more than a small area round Paris and looked with envy upon the vast Angevin possessions.

In his almost superhuman task, Henry received little support from his family.   Queen Eleanor, a beautiful, tempestuous woman, took herself back to the sunny land of Aquitaine where her court was renowned for the gallantry of its knights and troubadours.   Here, she sided with her sons as they grew rebellious against a father who gave them titles but no real power.

In 1178 there was a great rebellion when the eldest son, known as " the young King Henry " because he had already been crowned, Richard, the second son, and Geoffrey of Brittany, the third, formed an alliance with King Louis VII of France.   The Scots and some of the English barons joined the rebels but Henry II was victorious everywhere.

For a few more years he ruled in peace, but although he pardoned his sons, they were soon plotting against him and quarrelling among themselves.   " The young King Henry " died and so did Geoffrey, but Richard, now Duke of Aquitaine, refused to share any of his promised possessions with John, the youngest brother and his father's favourite.

In 1189 Richard again joined forces with King Louis' clever successor, Philip Augustus.   Making a sudden attack, they caught Henry unawares and without an army.   So many of his castles in Anjou and Touraine were taken that Henry, ill and low-spirited, agreed to accept a humiliating peace.   Lying on his bed in his castle at Chinon, he was told that his favourite son John had joined the rebels :

" Is it true that John, my very heart, whom I have loved before all my sons and for whom I have suffered all my ills has deserted me ? " he cried in anguish.

When he discovered that John had indeed played him false, he sank back and turned to the wall, crying :

" Now, let all things go, for I care no longer for myself or anything else in the world.   Shame, shame upon a conquered king."

Thus, in bitter despair, the great King died and his son became Richard I of England.

Coeur de Lion

Two years before Henry's death, the whole of Christendom had been shocked by the news that Saladin, the Muslim leader, had captured Jerusalem. All that remained of the Crusader kingdoms, won by the sword in 1099, was a strip of coast and a few seaports.

The Pope called for a great crusade and the leading monarchs of Europe, the Emperor Frederick Barbarossa, Philip Augustus of France and Henry II, took vows to put aside their rivalries in order to regain the Holy City. But Henry was growing old and his hands were full, so the role of Crusader King fell to his son Richard who was to win the title of *Coeur de Lion*—the Lion Heart.

Richard was now thirty-three, a blond giant who was already renowned as the most chivalrous and skilful knight in Europe. He had inherited some of his mother's love of poetry and music but he loved fighting above all else. Like a gifted sportsman, he was often gallant and generous to his opponents, but, in other respects, he was as cruel and greedy as his brothers.

The four months that Richard I lived in England after his

104

coronation were spent in a frantic endeavour to raise money for the Crusade. He said that he would sell the kingdom itself if he could find a buyer but, failing to do so, he raised large sums by selling offices of state and granting charters to towns. For 10,000 marks, he released William the Lion from the duty of paying homage. Then, leaving England in the care of his mother Eleanor and the Chancellor William Longchamp, Richard departed for the Holy Land with a well-equipped army. Unfortunately, he did not take his brother John with him.

In the company of Philip Augustus, the English King made a leisurely journey through France and took ship to the East, pausing on the way to conquer Cyprus, and to marry Princess Berengaria of Navarre. Meanwhile Philip Augustus had reached Palestine where a huge army of Crusaders was besieging the seaport of Acre with little prospect of success.

Richard's arrival brought zest and an expert knowledge of siege-craft to the scene, and although he fell ill, he directed operations so forcefully that the town was captured. The triumph was marred by the massacre of Saracen prisoners, in revenge, it was said, for a similar deed by Saladin.

The Crusaders were already at loggerheads. Disease had killed thousands of the troops ; the French and English knights were constantly bickering and Philip Augustus, irritated by Richard's fame as a soldier, took himself back to France, promising not to interfere with a fellow-Crusader's territories. Another enemy was made when some of Richard's soldiers tore down the flag of Austria from the walls of Acre and trampled it underfoot. Vowing to have his revenge one day, Leopold of Austria also quitted the Crusade.

Richard stayed on. He routed Saladin's army at Arsouf, captured Jaffa and pressed on towards Jerusalem. But a European army was ill-equipped to march, let alone to fight, in a land where the heat and lack of water were tortures to men in armour. Each night, the Crusaders knelt and stretched out their arms towards Jerusalem, crying :

" Help us! Holy Sepulchre, help us! "

But they never reached the Holy City, for Richard was forced to order his dwindling army to retreat. He made a treaty with Saladin that saved the pilgrims' route and the remnant of the Crusader kingdoms for another fifty years. Then, in 1192, having heard alarming news about the league between his brother John and Philip Augustus, he set out for home.

Since it would be dangerous to go through France, Richard decided to sail up the Adriatic to Venice. His ship was wrecked and he was making his way overland, disguised as a merchant, when he was recognised near Vienna. He was arrested and taken before his old enemy, Duke Leopold of Austria, who gleefully handed him over to the Emperor.

During his captivity in Germany, Richard wrote songs and set them to music. For a time, no one knew where he was imprisoned and there may well be truth in the romantic story of Blondel the minstrel, trudging from castle to castle, seeking his master by singing Aquitaine songs until an answering voice from a barred window told him where the royal prisoner lay.

After hard bargaining, during which John and Philip Augustus did their best to prevent Richard's release, the English people raised an enormous ransom for the hero-King whom they had hardly set eyes on. In March, 1194, Richard was free and on his way to London when Philip sent an urgent message to John :

" Look to yourself for the Great Devil himself is unchained! "

John fled but soon afterwards Richard pardoned his brother, saying contemptuously, " You are but a child." But he had no mind to forgive Philip Augustus. Within a few months, he had raised an army and had crossed the Channel to try to recover his lost possessions. He never returned.

Great soldier as he was, Richard found it difficult to pin down a wily enemy. He won victories and built his famous fortress, Saucy Castle, to guard the border of Normandy, but the cost of the Crusade and the ransom had exhausted England, so that he was constantly short of the men and supplies which he needed for final success.

In 1199 Richard was at Chalus, besieging a vassal who refused to hand over some treasure found on his land. The castle was weakly held and Richard, unarmoured, was watching his men make short work of its defences when a crossbowman on the wall took careful aim and fired a bolt that struck him in the chest. The castle was stormed and the soldier who had shot him was taken before the dying King:

"What have I done to thee that thou shouldst slay me?" asked Richard.

"Thou hast killed my father and two of my brothers," replied the bowman. "I shall die gladly knowing that I have slain thee."

The King ordered the man to be set free and shortly afterwards, urging his barons to accept John as his successor, he died. To their shame, his soldiers seized the crossbowman and, ignoring Richard's last order, put him to a horrible death.

King John

John was not the nearest to the throne by birth, for his elder brother, Geoffrey, had left a son named Prince Arthur of Brittany. However, Arthur was only a boy and old Queen Eleanor and the barons gave their support to John.

The new King had always been the problem-child of his family. At his birth, his father called him John Lackland because the royal possessions had already been promised to the three older sons and it was Henry II's efforts to provide a share for " Lackland " that had led to the family quarrels.

Cherished by a doting father and despised by his brothers, John grew into a talented youth whose good looks were spoiled by an expression of wolfish cunning. He made a fool of himself when he was sent to Ireland to complete its conquest, and later he broke his father's heart and betrayed his brother. Yet there were times when he could show the volcanic energy and warlike skill of Richard, and he had far more understanding of the way to rule a kingdom than his famous brother. He was a failure because no one could love him. He was utterly faithless and earned the hatred of everyone except his foreign mercenaries.

At first John did well. He visited his dominions in France and overawed the barons who had been prepared to support Prince Arthur. When Arthur obtained help from Philip Augustus and laid siege to Queen Eleanor in one of her castles, John raced to his mother's rescue with such astounding speed that he took the beseigers by surprise, routed them and captured Arthur himself.

No one knew exactly what happened to the young Prince. Some said that he was blinded and hidden away but it seems

109

more likely that he was murdered at Rouen, probably by John himself in a fit of drunken rage.

The crime did great harm to John. As the French mounted fresh attacks on Normandy, his allies and the Norman barons deserted him. Paralysed, it seemed, by a strange idleness, he did little to save the Duchy, only muttering as news came in that yet another castle had fallen :

" Let be, let be. One day I shall win it all again."

The truth was that his forces were so honeycombed with treachery that he could trust no one. Normandy was lost and John went back to England where his energy returned like a flood. He toured the country ceaselessly, seldom staying more than a day in one place, but wherever he went he sat in the law-courts, forced his officials to work as never before, ordered good coins to be minted, granted charters to growing towns, built a navy and, sometimes, was generous to the poor.

Although his chief aim was to enrich himself, John provided firm government until his disastrous quarrel with the Church. He ordered the Canterbury monks to choose one of his friends as their Archbishop but, on the Pope's advice, they elected Stephen Langton, an English cardinal living abroad. John angrily drove out the monks and seized their property :

" As for Langton," he cried, " I will hang him by the neck if he so much as sets foot in my kingdom ! "

The Pope's answer was to punish the people of England. The churches were closed, and presently John himself was excommunicated ; but, to the horror of most men, he gleefully rifled the Church treasures, and with the proceeds hired an army to attack William the Lion of Scotland.

He defeated the Scots, the Welsh and the Irish chieftains, and appeared to be triumphant everywhere. Then the Pope directed that this godless King must be removed from his throne by the Church's champion, Philip Augustus.

The French King was collecting an invasion force when John

turned the tables on his enemy. Inviting Stephen Langton to England, he made his peace with the Church by kneeling humbly before the Archbishop and by actually surrendering England to the Pope.

Exulting at his own cleverness, John now ordered his barons to join him in a great attack on France. When they refused, he sailed with a hired army but, on the continent, his allies collapsed and he came home to face a rebellion.

The King's greed and cruelty, his mocking insults and his habit of giving the chief posts of honour to foreign ruffians had destroyed the barons' loyalty. In 1215 they rode to London and drew up a charter of their rights which, they insisted, the King must accept.

John, having paid off his mercenaries, was at Windsor with only a small bodyguard. When he heard of the barons' demands, he burst out :

" They might as well ask for my crown! "

On June 15th he was forced to meet his opponents in a field called Runnymeade where, under a silk awning, he sullenly put his seal to the Great Charter, promising to rule according to the laws and customs of the realm.

John had no intention of keeping his word and when he had obtained a letter from the Pope freeing him from the Charter, he hired an army and cried balefully :

" Now, by God's teeth, I will make my barons howl for mercy. Before this year is out, there will be so little left in the land that men will pay a shilling for a halfpenny loaf! "

He struck like a hurricane, sweeping across the country to capture his enemies' castles and to ravage their estates. In the wake of his army trundled a line of wagons creaking with the weight of the barons' treasures. In despair, the barons invited Louis of France, Philip's son, to come with arms to be their king. In 1216 a French army landed and all that summer there was civil war in England.

In October, after a series of masterly manoeuvres, John was in Lincolnshire, harrying the land where the corn was still uncut. He doubled back to Lynn, near the Wash and then, although unwell, he set out for the north again, ordering his baggage train to take a short cut across the river-estuary at low tide. This was a well-known route but one of the leading wagons stuck and the others, halted, became bogged down. The sea came racing in before they could be freed and John, watching in agony from the Lincolnshire side, saw his entire baggage train swept away.

To a man who loved jewels and gold as much as John, this was a terrible blow but to a king waging war with hired foreigners, it was disaster. Numb with despair, he rode to Sleaford where, said the monks afterwards, he made himself ill by overeating ; but he was already sick and broken in spirit. Carried by litter to Newark Castle, John died there on October 19th, 1216, and a few days later at Gloucester his nine-year-old son was proclaimed Henry III. As the royal regalia had been lost, the boy was crowned with a plain gold circlet provided by his mother.

Henry III and the Barons

The crowning of young Henry did not bring peace immediately. Louis and his supporters were supreme in the south, except at Dover where Hubert de Burgh was heroically holding out in the castle ; but those who had hated John had no quarrel with his little son and many began to change sides.

When William Marshall, an aged baron and the most honourable man in England, routed Louis' troops at Lincoln, and the dauntless Hubert de Burgh took to the sea to defeat a French fleet off Sandwich, Louis gave up the struggle and retired to his own country.

For the next two years, the country was ruled by William Marshall, and after his death by Hubert de Burgh, the justiciar or chief minister. Hubert took on the task of destroying or taking for the King the numerous castles that had been built during the civil war. More troublesome were John's foreign friends such as Peter des Roches and Falkes de Bréauté, an engaging rascal who had amassed a fortune. In 1224 Hubert captured Bedford Castle, Falkes' chief stronghold, and put an end, for the time being, to the power of the foreign adventurers.

Meanwhile Henry III was growing up and, when at the age of twenty this learned youth became King, it was evident that he had inherited none of his father's wickedness—nor any of his ability to rule.

Henry III's reign was a glorious period for religion and the arts. Beautiful churches and cathedrals were built, colleges were founded and the poor friars arrived in England to win widespread love and support ; but the pious, generous King was also an extravagant weakling who ruled badly.

Hubert de Burgh was dismissed and treated like a criminal in return for his great services, while Peter des Roches came back from exile to win such influence over the King that he and his friends obtained most of the chief positions in the realm.

The barons, who now regarded themselves as Englishmen, protested so hotly against these foreigners that Henry agreed to dismiss des Roches and his hangers-on. Unfortunately, the King did not learn his lesson. After his marriage to Eleanor of Provence, he rewarded droves of her needy relations.

In addition, he annoyed his own people by allowing the Pope to impose heavy taxes and to fill many places in the English Church with French and Italian priests.

Henry, who acted as his own chancellor and treasurer, decided to invade France to recover his father's lost possessions, but the attempt was a failure. Just as expensive was his foolish plan to have his second son made King of Sicily. By this time, the King was bankrupt and his nobles were ready to revolt.

The barons found a leader in Simon de Montfort, Earl of Leicester who, oddly enough, was himself a foreigner, married to the King's sister. However, Simon's good qualities had won wide respect and he was one of the members of the council or parliament that met at Oxford to discuss the King's mismanagement. Henry reluctantly agreed to mend his ways, but hating the idea of taking orders from a council, he soon obtained the Pope's permission to break his word.

At this, the barons took up arms and in the Barons' War that followed, Simon de Montfort became their acknowledged leader, while the King's eldest son, " the Lord Edward ", commanded his father's forces.

After some royalist successes, the two sides met in strength at Lewes where Prince Edward dashed so vigorously at the Londoners that he drove them headlong from the field. In his absence, de Montfort won the battle and captured King Henry so that when Edward returned, he could do no more than give himself up as a hostage.

De Montfort's victory prompted him to summon the Parliament of 1265. This was no more than a gathering of his own supporters. Few of the nobles attended, but besides the clergy and the two knights from each shire, there were representatives from various towns and cities. Thus, because he called on ordinary citizens—the commons—to take a share in governing the country, Simon de Montfort is often looked upon as the founder of the House of Commons.

Yet the Earl's power slipped away as soon as he grasped it. He held the affection of the Londoners and the common people, but the nobles came to hate him as an arrogant upstart. Thus, when Prince Edward escaped from captivity, he was able to raise a large army and to overwhelm de Montfort at Evesham, where " the good Earl ", as the people called him, was killed.

With the opposition beaten and his capable son in charge of the kingdom, Henry III lived out the last seven years of his reign in peace. Indeed, Prince Edward restored order so well that he felt able to take the Cross and to sail to the east on a Crusade. By now the days of the great Crusades were over and the Prince found little chance to win renown apart from a dramatic escape from death. An assassin stabbed him with a poisoned dagger, and it is said that his devoted young wife, Princess Eleanor, saved him by sucking the poison from the wound.

The Prince had reached Sicily on his way home when he learned that his father had died and that he was Edward I of England.

Roger Bacon, the Learned Friar

During Henry III's reign, a clever youngster came up from Somerset to the university at Oxford. He was Roger Bacon, son of a well-to-do landowner, and he sat at the feet of Robert Grosseteste, a man of the most delightful character, who had risen from a peasant's upbringing to become one of the greatest scholars of the age.

After Grosseteste had left Oxford to become Bishop of Lincoln, Bacon continued his studies in Paris where he was able to make experiments and to talk with scholars from many countries—Arab mathematicians, Jewish physicians, Italian astronomers and doctors.

But although Bacon had a brilliant mind, his sharp tongue and his interest in strange forms of learning brought him into trouble. He believed that in the search for knowledge he need not follow the well-worn paths of logic and scripture but that he should study the marvels of the world about him—sunlight, stars rainbows, plants, chemicals and gases.

When his outspoken opinions made him unpopular in Paris, Bacon returned to Oxford where he joined the Order of St Francis. The Franciscans were well known for their interest in learning and Bacon may have entered the Order partly as a protection against his enemies. At all events, students crowded to listen to the brilliant friar who had so many novel ideas that they called him " the Marvellous Doctor ". He despised the

116

way in which most scholars decided all kinds of difficult problems by merely talking about them, for he preferred to discover facts by observation and experiment :

" There are two ways of gaining knowledge," he said. " Argument and experience. Argument gives no proof nor does it remove doubt, unless the truth is discovered by way of experience."

So he made calculations, heated substances and weighed them ; he invented a magnifying-glass, a telescope to study the stars, and, it was rumoured, gunpowder. Strange bubblings and explosions were heard at night from " Friar Bacon's Tower" where he lived, and people began to wonder if he was dabbling in the black arts. Was he perhaps the servant of the Devil?

When Bacon refused to give up these experiments, he was exiled to Paris and deprived of all his books and instruments. Luckily a Franciscan, who had formerly listened to his lectures with admiration, became Pope Clement IV and sent a message to the unhappy scholar asking him to write a book about his opinions. Bacon was overjoyed and immediately began to set down his beliefs and discoveries in science, anatomy, medicine and music. It was an immense task but at last the book was finished.

" It is done," he wrote to the Pope. " I have written what I believe to be the truth and I have called it my Great Work."

Unfortunately, the Pope died before he could study the masterpiece and it was not long before Bacon was again accused of practising witchcraft. In 1277 he was arrested and thrown into prison.

Fourteen years passed and it was not until he was almost eighty that the broken old man was allowed to return to Oxford to die.

" They have treated me like a criminal," he said, " but all my life I have only been a seeker after knowledge while they stood in the way of the light."

Edward I, "The Hammer of the Scots"

The son of Henry III was as upright and unbending as a lance. At thirty-three, when he became King, Edward was one of the tallest and most handsome men in the land and his talents matched his splendid appearance. Moreover, he had seen his father's faults and he had learned what a King must do to hold his power and to keep the respect of his people.

His first task was to subdue the Welsh. During the Barons' Wars Llewelyn ap Griffith, a supporter of de Montfort, had made himself so powerful that he was recognised as Prince of Wales and overlord of all the lesser chieftains. However, Llewelyn's own feudal lord was the King of England and, in accordance with custom, he was summoned to Westminster to take the oath of loyalty to the new King.

Llewelyn refused to go, making excuses that did not hide his intention to set himself up as an independent ruler. Edward was patient but, at last, feeling that one disobedient vassal would encourage others, he invaded Wales in 1277, striking with three armies at the south, the centre and the north. Llewelyn, a brave

and resourceful leader, was blockaded in the rocky wastes of Snowdon until hunger and cold forced him to surrender.

Edward treated the Welsh prince mildly. He made him do homage in London so that all men should know that he had acknowledged his overlord. Llewelyn had to give back the territories gained during Henry III's reign, but he was allowed to keep his title of Prince and to return to North Wales.

It was not long before the harsh behaviour of Edward's officials caused the Welsh to take up arms. Llewelyn and his brother David were the natural leaders of the revolt in the north and they were supported by risings throughout the whole of Wales.

When Edward again led his army towards Snowdon, Llewelyn had no intention of being trapped a second time. He broke through the English lines and was on his way to join the rebels in the south when he was slain in a chance encounter with some enemy troops.

David held out in the mountains for another year, but after he was captured and executed at Shrewsbury, Edward decided to put an end to the troubles with the Welsh. Dividing the principality into five shires, he set up English government and laws and surrounded Snowdon, the refuge of the rebels, with a

119

ring of massive fortresses. In one of these, Caernarvon Castle, his son Edward was born and presented, it is said, to the Welsh chieftains as " a prince born in Wales, unable to speak a word of English ".

Later, when the boy was seventeen, the King conferred on him the title of Prince of Wales and whether or not this gesture pleased the Welsh, they remained quiet for another century.

Edward I was a masterly soldier but his true greatness was as a ruler. He gave his people a series of laws that improved justice by abolishing many of the barons' private courts, and by rooting out dishonest sheriffs and judges. He encouraged the wool trade with Flanders and kept the barons in a state, not of fear, but of respect and obedience.

It is curious that Edward was honoured for an act that nowadays would be regarded as inhumanly cruel. The Jews, ill-treated and despised for centuries, were able to exist only by lending money, an occupation forbidden to Christians. Most kings, being perpetually short of money, protected the Jews when it suited them to do so and afterwards taxed them cruelly and confiscated their wealth. Edward, feeling that it would be sinful to borrow money from the Jews, expelled all of them from the country in 1290.

Had Edward's reign ended in 1295, the year of the Model Parliament, it would have been a period of unbroken success, but the last twelve years of his life were spent in a costly struggle with the Scots that led to centuries of bitterness between the two peoples.

In 1286, when Alexander III was killed and his grand-daughter, the Maid of Norway, died on the voyage to her kingdom, the royal line of Scotland came to an end and no fewer than thirteen nobles put in claims to the throne. The most notable were John Balliol and Robert Bruce, both descended from William the Lion's brother and both having estates in England for which they paid homage to Edward I.

120

The English King was invited to judge the various claims to the throne, and although this seemed to be a sensible way of avoiding civil war, the Scots were startled when he insisted that they should first do homage to him. However, they consented, and after a careful hearing Edward awarded the throne to John Balliol.

From the beginning, Balliol appeared to be no more than a puppet and the Scottish nobles felt that they had been tricked over the act of homage. Thus, when Edward summoned them to serve him in a quarrel with France, they not only refused but made an alliance with the French.

At this, Edward led an army into Scotland, defeated the Scots at Dunbar, removed Balliol from the throne and carried the coronation stone from Scone to Westminster to show that he intended to rule the country himself. Having, as he thought, settled the matter, he gave his attention to affairs in France and to a squabble with some of the English nobles who did not want to fight for him on the continent.

Meanwhile, although most of the Scottish nobles had made their peace with Edward, the Lowlanders were becoming fiercely indignant at the arrogance of the English garrison troops. One day a Scottish gentleman named William Wallace was roughly handled by a company of English soldiers. He defended himself and, in the scuffle, killed one of the attackers. Wallace went into hiding but, learning that his home had been sacked and his young wife murdered, he swore never to sheath his sword until he had taken vengeance on his country's oppressors.

Joined by a few fellow-outlaws and then by increasing numbers of small landowners and peasants, Wallace built up a force that became strong enough to harry the English troops, to capture several castles and to win a major victory at Stirling Bridge.

Edward I, who had been fighting in Flanders, hurried home and routed the Scots at Falkirk. Wallace escaped from the field, but some time afterwards he was betrayed by the sheriff of Dumbarton and carried to London to be executed. The four quarters of his brave body were sent to Scotland to be shown in the chief towns as a warning, but instead, they kindled a passionate spirit for independence.

During these stirring events, Robert Bruce, the twenty-five-year-old grandson of the claimant, had been living at the English court where he had served Edward I and had fought in his army. Roused perhaps by Wallace's example, he made his way to Scotland where he met Red Comyn, one of the Scottish leaders, in a church at Dumfries. Suspecting that Comyn was playing a double game, Bruce angrily upbraided him and, in the quarrel, drew a dagger and killed him.

Aghast at his crime, Bruce fled to the hills but presently, setting himself up as a new champion, he revived his family claim to the throne and had himself crowned at Scone.

With few supporters and no money or influence, Bruce seemed to be courting disaster. His wife and his daughter were arrested, his friends were executed and an English army scattered his meagre force so that he became a fugitive living perilously in the mountains with a handful of followers.

For a time Bruce seemed to be no more than a nuisance to the occupying forces, but as his following grew, he was able to make serious raids on the enemy and he had the advantage of being always able to retreat into the inaccessible moors and forests of the Highlands. As one success followed another, his force grew into a sizeable army and Edward I felt that it was time that he himself dealt with this rebel leader.

The King was now almost seventy and his huge frame was worn out after a lifetime of ceaseless activity, but, determined as ever, he set out to conquer Scotland for the third time. In 1307, too weak to ride but carried in a litter at the head of his army, the old warrior was nearing the Border when he died.

Edward II

Confident that he understood his son's character, the dying King made Prince Edward swear to continue the war until Robert Bruce was defeated, but the handsome, feckless Prince was already tired of army life. He scurried back to London where he dismissed his father's most trusted ministers and recalled from exile his former playfellow, a conceited young Gascon named Piers Gaveston.

Edward II speedily aroused the barons' dislike by pouring gifts and honours into the hands of Gaveston. Moreover, he and his favourite took a delight in mocking the nobles of the court, openly referring to them by such nicknames as " the Hog ", " the Black Dog of Arden " and " the Cuckoo ".

At length, the enraged nobles formed a committee called the Lords Ordainers who took over the government and banished Gaveston from the realm. When Edward recalled his crony and sent him for safety to Scarborough Castle, the Earl of Warwick,

" the Black Dog ", brought up an army and forced Gaveston to surrender. Having captured the detested Gascon, the nobles were in no mind to let him escape—" If you let the fox go, you have to hunt him again," so Gaveston's head was struck off.

For the moment, Edward was powerless to revenge his friend's murder, especially as affairs in Scotland were now in a critical state.

Robert Bruce had taken full advantage of the quarrels between King and barons in England. He united his country-men and raised an army to ravage the English counties of the north. Then he began a systematic attack on Edward I's castles in the Lowlands. Perth, Roxburgh, Edinburgh and Linlithgow were captured, and by 1314 only Stirling was holding out. Its governor was so hard pressed that he agreed to surrender if help had not arrived by June 24th.

If Stirling fell, English rule in Scotland would be ended and even Edward II felt that he must bestir himself. A great army was hurriedly raised and it arrived within sight of Stirling only one day before the promised date of surrender.

At Bannockburn the English found that Bruce was waiting to fight in a place of his own choosing. The position was fearsomely strong, but there was no time for the English to manoeuvre and, in any case, their army seemed to be over-whelmingly powerful.

But Edward II's presence meant that there was no real general in command and his discontented nobles seemed to have forgotten any of the lessons in warfare that they should have learned under the old King.

On the evening before the battle there was a dramatic incident when Sir Henry Bohun, eager to destroy the Scottish King in single combat, dashed from a company of English horsemen who were examining the Scottish position. Bruce, mounted on a pony, was inspecting his troops when he looked up to see an adversary thundering towards him with levelled

lance. At the last instant, Bruce wheeled his pony aside and, rising in his stirrups, crashed his axe down upon the knight's head. The steel helmet split in two and Bohun fell lifeless from the saddle.

" I have broken my good axe," was all that Bruce said as he returned to his cheering countrymen.

On the morrow, the English archers were sent so far ahead of the cavalry that the Scottish horsemen were able to destroy them from the flank. After this stupid misuse of the archers, Edward's mail-clad knights made a massed charge at the enemy. But the squares of Scottish spearmen stood firm, thrusting away at the chargers to bring down horses and riders, so that the English, with little enough room to move in, were hampered by the plunging masses of maddened horses and fallen men. Even so, weight of numbers might have told but for the unexpected arrival of a new army advancing with banners, a little to the rear of the Scottish position. In reality, these were no more than camp-followers who, in their excitement, dashed forward with wild shouts of " Slay! Slay! "

Panic spread through the English ranks and, as Bruce ordered an advance, they broke in a headlong rout and perished by the thousand as they floundered in the marshy ground and stumbled into the pits that Bruce had dug to protect his flank. Edward II was among the few who fled fast enough to escape from the scene of the greatest English defeat since Hastings.

Stirling Castle surrendered and English rule of Scotland came to an end, leaving Bruce free to govern his own country-men, and to ravage the north of England year in and year out.

The defeat at Bannockburn had been stained by the King's cowardice and Edward II was now a man despised by all, including his wife Isabella of France, the most beautiful Queen in Europe. He could not defend his people in the north, and two years of famine and disastrous rains caused widespread

126

suffering and discontent. Yet, in their opposition to the King, the Lords Ordainers had no thought for the common people but only for their own advantage.

From this welter of greed and treachery, Edward suddenly struck out with unexpected energy. Aided by his new favourites the Dispensers, father and son, he defeated and executed his chief opponent, Henry of Lancaster, overthrew the Ordainers and took the government into his own hands.

The Dispensers were capable men but their arrogance and greed had already brought hatred upon themselves and their master when a fresh calamity overwhelmed the King.

Queen Isabella and her fourteen-year-old son, Prince Edward, made a visit to Paris where Isabella fell in love with Roger Mortimer, an exiled nobleman who loathed the Dispensers. In 1326 Isabella and Mortimer landed in Suffolk, declaring that they had come to rid the country of the King's unpopular favourites. Edward II, having lost the respect of all classes, found himself deserted. He fled to Wales but was tracked down and captured. Forced to give up his crown to his son, the wretched man was treated with savage contempt and, after being dragged from one prison to another, he was finally murdered by his enemies in Berkeley Castle.

For three years Isabella and Mortimer ruled in the name of young Edward III until, in 1330, when he had almost grown to manhood, Edward's eyes were opened to his mother's disgraceful position and to the greedy insolence of her partner. One night, supported by a party of soldiers who entered Nottingham Castle by a secret passage, Edward seized Mortimer and, ignoring the Queen's cry of, " Fair son, have pity on the gentle Mortimer," sent the favourite to be hanged at Tyburn like a common thief. Then he ordered his mother to a country manor where she was made to spend the rest of her life in retirement.

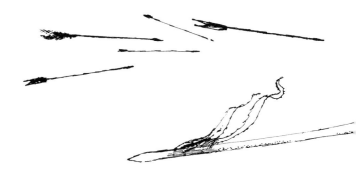

Edward III

Edward III appeared to be the perfect monarch. Tall, vigorous and handsome, he was a born soldier and a chivalrous knight whose courtesy to the greatest and humblest of his subjects seemed to spring from a noble nature set far above the common rank. Yet Edward cared little for the good of his people. For him they existed in order to provide him with the money and men for the dearest object in life, the winning of glory on the field of battle.

At first Edward tried to recover Scotland, where Bruce had died, leaving his crown to his small son, David. The English King succeeded in putting John Balliol's son on the throne and he defeated the Scots at Halidon Hill, but although young David had to flee to France, the Scots refused to be conquered. They

128

managed to hold out until Edward was drawn into a war that seemed to offer far more attractive opportunities for an accomplished knight.

The French had been helping the Scots by attacking Gascony, the English King's possession in south-west France ; in retaliation, Edward supported the people of Flanders who were at loggerheads with their overlord, the King of France. Edward also remembered that he could claim the French crown through his mother, Queen Isabella, sister of Charles IV who had recently died.

Taking the title " King of France ", therefore, Edward prepared for war with the enthusiastic support of his people who expected unlimited opportunities for glory, trade and loot.

The war opened in 1340 when, at Sluys off the coast of Flanders, the English won a notable sea-battle that gave them command of the Channel for many years. After a siege or two,

129

with some fighting in Brittany and Gascony and the usual burning and looting, both sides agreed to a truce in order to build up
fresh reserves of money and supplies.

In 1346 Edward's commander in Gascony was hard pressed,
so the King invaded Normandy as a diversion. Accompanied
by his sixteen-year-old son, the Prince of Wales (later called the
Black Prince), he captured Caen and advanced into France.
He had sacked several towns when he became aware that his
army was being tracked by an enormous host of Frenchmen
led by Philip VI.

Putting on speed, Edward marched north in the hope of
joining his Flemish allies but, having forced his way across the
Somme, he was brought to bay near the village of Crecy.
There, with his general's eye, he chose a sloping piece of ground
that was ideal for the kind of battle that he intended to fight.

The English army consisted of men-at-arms who dismounted
and sent their horses to the rear, and archers armed with the
longbow. This weapon had been developed in Wales and used
during the Scottish wars until, in the hands of practised
bowmen, it was now the deadliest weapon in existence.

On August 26th the French attacked. Their Genoese cross-
bowmen wilted under a hail of arrows and were ridden down by
the impatient French knights who charged uphill and perished
in thousands through their own recklessness and the unerring
skill of the English archers.

For a time the Prince of Wales on the right was hard pressed
when the French came to grips with their enemy. He was
knocked over but Sir Richard Fitz-Simon, covering the boy
with a standard, straddled his body and roared " Edward!
Edward! St George to Edward! " so valiantly that the mace-
swinging Bishop of Durham crashed to the rescue. To the
satisfaction of the King, watching coolly from a windmill, the
lad regained his foothold and in the end the battle was won.

The destruction of the French army opened the road to

Calais where Edward was angered by having to waste a year in starving the seaport into surrender. In the besiegers' town that grew up outside the walls, the King's court was enlivened by the arrival of Queen Philippa and many ladies from England, together with merchants and shopkeepers.

When the port finally surrendered, Edward was in no mood to treat the common townsfolk with the chivalry that he would have shown to noblemen. He had lost hundreds of soldiers from camp-sickness and the siege had cost him time and money. It was enough to spare most of the gaunt survivors and he ordered the leading burghers to be hanged like criminals as a warning to other towns that might refuse to yield.

It was at this point that Queen Philippa won the astonished admiration of Europe by pleading on her knees for the lives of six men whose claim to mercy was not noble birth but courage. To Edward's credit, he sighed, "Ah lady, for the love I bear you, I cannot refuse. Take them and do with them as you please."

In the following year a ship docked at Weymouth carrying, in the bodies of the black rats in its hold, a disease known as the Black Death which raged across England for two years. How many people died cannot be calculated. Probably a third of the population perished, not only in the densely packed towns but in the monasteries, hamlets and villages.

The effect of this disaster was worst in the country districts, for although trade and manufactures were increasing, wealth was still chiefly in land and in the food that it produced. In places there were not enough men left alive to plough the fields or to gather the harvest; wages went up steeply despite the efforts of Parliament to peg them down, and a bitter enmity arose between the peasants and their lords.

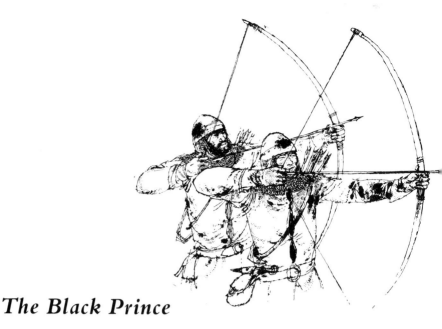

The Black Prince

In 1355 the French war began again when the Black Prince landed an army at Bordeaux, the wine-city of English-held France. Joined by the Gascon knights, he made a three months' tour pillaging and devastating the lovely countryside as far south as the Mediterranean coast.

Next year the Prince ventured into the heart of France with no more than 12,000 men. Expecting that his father and Lancaster would strike from north and west to join him, he harried the land at his leisure and then, receiving no news of his father, turned south again with his plunder-laden wagons. He did not know until it was almost too late that a huge French army was bearing down on his small force.

Near Poitiers the Prince was caught and hemmed in. So hopeless was his position that he offered to hand over all his prisoners and loot and to give a solemn promise not to fight again for seven years.

John, the French King who had succeeded his father Philip IV, refused to accept these terms, for he and his nobles welcomed the opportunity to wipe out the memory of Crecy.

The battle of Poitiers took place on a slope where the English archers had the cover of a long hedge and vineyards. Remembering Crecy, the French advanced on foot but, by the time

132

they had trudged half a mile uphill in stifling heat and in heavy armour, much of their vigour was spent. Yard-long arrows sped pitilessly into their crowded ranks and, after the Dauphin's division was beaten and the Duke of Orleans' army had quitted the field without striking a blow, the Prince boldly advanced upon King John's division, while his Gascon cavalry made a surprise flank attack.

Although King John and his little son Philip fought with splendid courage, the boy following his father and crying, " Guard on the right, father! Guard on the left! ", both were taken prisoner.

Edward III now advanced to Paris across a countryside terribly devastated by war. Both sides were exhausted and, in 1360, they agreed to stop fighting. Edward gave up his claim to the French throne in return for wide possessions including Aquitaine, Gascony and Calais. King John was released but, finding that his vast ransom could not be raised, he honourably returned to captivity and died in London in 1364.

Meanwhile, Prince Edward—the Black Prince—and his wife Joan, the Fair Maid of Kent, had gone to live in Aquitaine where, at Bordeaux, they set up a most brilliant court. Bored by this glittering but peaceful existence, the Prince led an army into Spain to assist Pedro the Cruel, the King of Castile, who had recently been driven from his throne.

By a brilliant victory at Najara, Prince Edward put the tyrant back on his throne, only to find that Pedro had no intention of paying his ally or giving him any assistance. Heavily in debt, his army riddled by a disease which he himself caught, Edward returned to Aquitaine where some of his subjects were in a state of rebellion.

Under its new King, Charles V, France was recovering. Bertrand du Guesclin, a soldier of genius, realised that the English could be beaten by new tactics. In place of the vast, unwieldy armies, small forces of professional soldiers took the

133

field against the English, nibbling away at their territories and avoiding pitched battles in order to garrison towns that were ready to throw off the foreign yoke.

One of these towns was Limoges and, although Prince Edward was so ill that he could not ride a horse, he vowed to punish the townsfolk. He captured Limoges and ordered all the inhabitants to be put to the sword. The massacre went on until, seeing a small group of knights defending themselves with the utmost bravery, Edward relented and ordered the killing to stop.

Soon afterwards, the Prince returned to England in hope of recovering but, although he lingered sufficiently long to show that he would have made a far better ruler than his father, his illness grew worse and he died in 1376 at Berkhamsted Castle. During his absence, all the English possessions in France were lost, apart from a few coast towns. By the end of the Black Prince's life, Crecy and Poitiers had been fully avenged.

At home, as abroad, the early glories of Edward III's reign had faded. The defeats in France, the King's decline into a feeble old age, the Prince's illness and his quarrels with his brother, John of Gaunt, made a dismal contrast to the days of brilliant achievement.

There was nothing to show for all the blood and gold that had been spent and, as the King lost control of affairs and the nobles jostled each other in a spiteful struggle for power, the common people looked on the government and the Church with glowering discontent.

The poet Chaucer had criticised the clergy who were lazy and dishonest, but in a poem of the time called *Piers Plowman*, William Langland expressed a savage contempt for churchmen who ignored the sufferings of the poor. In this bitter atmosphere John Wycliffe and his wandering preachers, the Lollards, found eager listeners when they attacked the wickedness of the clergy and the nobles.

Richard II and the Peasants

In 1377, when Edward III died, the Black Prince's son, Richard II, was only eleven years old, and a council of nobles was appointed to rule the country until he came of age. Early in the reign, in order to pay for the French War, the government levied a poll-tax, i.e. a tax on every poll or head in the realm ; this tax fell heaviest upon the poor, who were already in a dangerous mood.

Despite Parliament's order, wages had gone up, and in many ways the peasants were better off than before the Black Death, but they were not entirely free. Some of them still had to pay fines when a parent died or a daughter married ; some were still forced to grind their corn in the lord's mill and to bake their bread in the lord's oven and to pay for the privilege. All of them hated the name of " serf " and the threat of bondage.

On the village greens, they listened to Lollards preaching about the sinfulness of great riches, and in the taverns they chuckled over the popular rhymes that mocked the nobles. They passed on secret messages from their brothers in distant counties and they muttered the famous rhyme of John Ball " the mad priest of Kent " :

> " When Adam delved and Eve span
> Who was then the gentleman? "

The spark that set light to this smouldering discontent was the murder of a tax-collector in Kent by Wat Tyler, a brawny ex-soldier, who quickly found himself at the head of an army of angry Kentishmen.

Having freed John Ball from jail, the peasants marched on

135

Richard II and the Peasants

London to lay their troubles before the young King and to rid him of the evil counsellors who, they declared, were the cause of the country's misfortunes. All along the route, villagers and townsfolk left their work to join the ranks, often pausing to take a quick revenge on a harsh steward or a luckless lawyer. Messengers sped ahead to carry the tidings of revolt to the men of Essex, Hertfordshire, Surrey and Norfolk.

The peasants were " seekers of truth and justice, not thieves or robbers ", cried Wat Tyler but, once inside the gates of London, he was unable to control the riff-raff that tagged alongside his followers. Savoy Palace, the princely home of John of Gaunt, went up in flames ; merchants' houses were broken into, swords were drawn and a lawless mob began to loot and kill with frantic greed. While the nobles were para-lysed with fear, a party of bold peasants forced a way into the Tower and murdered the Archbishop of Canterbury and the Lord Treasurer.

Meanwhile, the young King, showing more courage than his ministers, faced the rebels and promised to grant them their freedom if they would go quietly home. Thirty clerks sat up all night writing out pardons, and many of the peasants were already trudging back to their villages when Wat Tyler and his army met the King at Smithfield, outside the city walls.

During the parley some of the King's party shouted abuse at Tyler who leaned forward to speak to Richard ; whereupon

William Walworth, the Lord Mayor, either from anger or from fear for the young King's safety, drew his dagger and stabbed Tyler.

" They have slain our captain! " roared the peasants, but the nerve of the boy King prevented a massacre. Riding forward, he cried :

" I am your captain and your King! Follow me! "

At this, the peasants lowered their weapons and presently made off home, cheerfully trusting in the renewed promises of pardon and freedom.

But once the danger was over, the nobles took a swift revenge for the fright they had suffered. With their soldiers, they hunted down the ringleaders and hanged them in market squares and at abbey gates, while the four quarters of John Ball's body were carted from town to town. As their leaders perished and the charters of freedom were torn to shreds, the peasants collapsed into cowering submission. What hope of freedom was there when the King himself, recently so brave and gracious, was touring Kent and Essex with 40,000 soldiers?

" Villeins you were," he told them, " and villeins you are. In bondage you shall abide and not your old bondage but a worse! "

Yet the revolt was not in vain. When the savage punishment was over, there were not many lords who dared to tighten the old screws of feudalism. Times were changing, and although

137

the peasants were never set free officially, they gained their freedom little by little. In time, most of them became landless labourers who worked for wages, poor and often wretched, but no longer serfs.

Richard II's moment of glory at Smithfield was his last. He had courage and ability, but as he grew up, he still showed the peevish temper and the extravagance of a spoilt child. Hating to be curbed by nobles or Parliament, he surrounded himself with elegant favourites and tried to rule like some grandiose monarch, until an opposition party led by his uncle, Thomas of Gloucester, brought him to his knees. A committee of nobles called the Lords Appellant took over the government and got rid of the King's friends by execution or banishment.

Richard, however, was no weakling. He bided his time and, a year later, he walked into the Council and asked his uncle how old he was :

" Your Highness is in your twenty-fourth year," replied Gloucester.

" Then I am old enough to manage my own affairs," said Richard coolly. " I thank you for your services, my lords, but I need them no longer."

For eight years, Richard governed well. He made peace with France, restored order in Ireland and treated everyone, including the Lollards, with tolerance and common sense. His wife, Anne of Bohemia, seemed to have a good influence on him, but when she died in 1394, Richard married Isabella, the daughter of the King of France with whom he made a peace treaty.

From this moment, Richard's character changed. Possibly his head was turned by the splendour of the French court ; at all events, he suddenly struck like a vengeful tyrant at the nobles who had humiliated him eight years before.

Overawing Parliament by a force of archers drawn up in the Palace Yard at Westminster, Richard had his uncle murdered, his old opponents executed or banished and their estates confiscated, while he himself was granted taxes *for life* and a committee of his own friends to take the place of Parliament. Soon afterwards, he found an excuse to banish his own cousin Henry Bolingbroke, John of Gaunt's son.

In a delirium of triumph, Richard plunged into an orgy of tyranny and extravagance that made men wonder if he had become insane. In 1399, when his uncle, John of Gaunt, died, he seized his estates, the property of the exiled Bolingbroke, and with the money thus gained, he fitted out an expedition and sailed to Ireland.

In Richard's absence, Bolingbroke landed in Yorkshire, saying that he had merely come to claim his father's lands. His arrival was a signal to rebellion by all the King's opponents, who by this time included most of the nobles, the clergy, the merchants and every landowner who feared for his family estates. Without striking a blow, Henry Bolingbroke found himself presented with a kingdom, for when Richard landed from Ireland, his army deserted him and he fled in disguise to North Wales where he was captured and taken to London.

Stunned by his misfortune, this strange man, so talented and so foolish, signed away his realm, declaring himself unfit to rule. Parliament then awarded the crown to his cousin Bolingbroke who thus became King Henry IV.

But there could be no safety with Richard alive, for he still had friends and he might again recover his brilliant abilities. Hustled from the Tower at night, he was imprisoned in Pontefract Castle until 1400, when a rebellion in his favour sealed his fate. His end was mysterious, but although it was given out that he had starved himself to death, he was almost certainly murdered, for despite rumours that he was alive and at liberty, he was never seen again.

Henry IV

A plain, sturdy man and far more resolute than his elegant cousin, Henry IV had sufficient character to win respect ; but as a usurper he had to tread warily to avoid offending the men who had set him on the throne. Thus, his whole reign was so beset with difficulties that he died worn out before he was fifty.

Having put down the rebellion of Richard's friends, Henry decided to subdue the Scots before they could assist France whose King was naturally enraged at the overthrow and murder of his son-in-law. But although he was a good soldier, Henry was unable to bring the Scots to battle. This failure was a blow to the King's reputation, all the more painful when the Earl of Northumberland and his son, Henry Percy, called Harry Hotspur, defeated the Scots and captured many of their leaders.

Meanwhile, in Wales, Henry was faced by a national rebellion. Owen Glendower, an educated, chivalrous gentleman, appealed to the King for justice against his English neighbour, Lord Grey of Ruthin, who had seized part of his estate. Henry, unwilling to offend one of his nobles so early in his reign, sent

140

Glendower packing and thereby roused a hornet's nest.

In 1400 Glendower sacked Ruthin and laid waste the countryside right up to the walls of Shrewsbury, but when Henry advanced with an army, the Welshmen retired to their mountains in scornful defiance. So many affairs required Henry's attention that he could do no more than leave his fourteen-year-old son, Prince Henry, to guard the border, and Owen soon became more troublesome than ever.

Henry's second attempt to crush the rebellion was no more successful. Hunger, heavy rain and incessant attacks by the agile Welsh troops forced the English army to retreat, and Owen Glendower, having captured Lord Grey, went rampaging into South Wales. There, at Bryn Glas, he defeated the English and made Sir Edmund Mortimer his prisoner.

Apart from a few castles, Glendower was now master of Wales and he lived in the style of an independent monarch, writing as an equal to the Kings of France and Scotland and making his plans for a Welsh parliament and university.

Meanwhile the Percies, having quarrelled with Henry over the ransoms of their Scottish prisoners, decided to throw in their lot with Owen Glendower. By this time the prisoner Mortimer was Glendower's friend and son-in-law.

Henry IV realised that this alliance, assisted by the French, could destroy him and he swiftly marched to Shrewsbury to tackle Hotspur before he could join forces with Glendower and Mortimer. In a hard-fought battle, Henry and his son were victorious over the rebels ; Hotspur was slain and his aged father surrendered later at York.

Glendower continued to defy the English King for several years but Prince Henry slowly ground him down and weakened his forces until the Welsh leader was reduced to wandering about the country, a defiant fugitive who refused to accept defeat or the pardon that was offered him by the Prince when he succeeded his father.

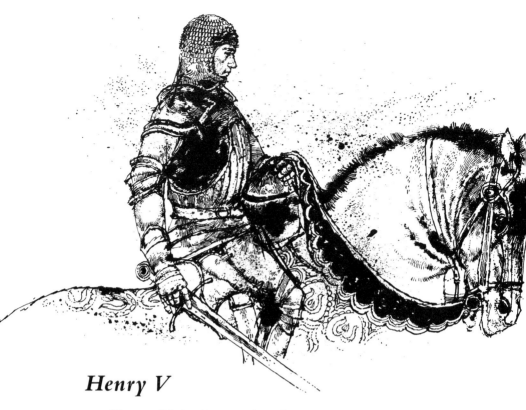

Henry V

Henry V had served a long apprenticeship to war and, during his father's illness, he had practically ruled the country. So, despite stories of wild adventures in his youth, he came to the throne well-prepared for the role that he meant to play.

One of the best-loved Kings in history, Henry looked more like a priest than a warrior, with his grave expression and clear, unwavering gaze. He was noble-minded and truly pious, although in the fashion of his age, he could bear to watch a Lollard being burnt alive and could allow civilians to die of starvation between the walls of a beleaguered town and the lines of his besieging army.

From Henry V's point of view, there seemed every reason to re-open the war with France. The nobles loved fighting and the French had long been assisting the Welsh and the Scots ; furthermore, the King of France was half-mad and his country was torn by bloodthirsty quarrels between the nobles. Lastly,

142

for the sake of his conscience, Henry convinced himself that he had a claim to the French crown, although he had not a vestige of right to it.

In the summer of 1415 a well-equipped army of archers and men-at-arms landed in Normandy and laid seige to Harfleur. The fortress held out stoutly, and by the time it fell, autumn had set in and the usual camp-fever had reduced Henry's army to half its strength.

Not wishing to return home with so little in the way of success, the King decided to send the sick and wounded back by sea, while he marched to Calais with no more than 6,000 men. It was a rash venture, for the countryside had been stripped bare of provisions and the hungry soldiers had to trudge for seventeen days through continuous rain, existing as best they could on berries and nuts. The bridges over the Somme were down and during the days spent in finding a ford, the French were able to place a huge army astride the road to Calais.

There was no means of escape and Henry accepted battle at Agincourt. His famished men felt certain that they were doomed, but so great was their discipline and devotion to the King that each one resolved to die on the morrow giving as good an account of himself as possible. Henry V, however, had neither doubts nor fear. His air of confidence, his magnificent appearance in a surcoat resplendent with the leopards of England and the lilies of France and, above all, his ringing words filled his men with a fervour of courage that only death would subdue.

Henry drew up his little army, only four deep, behind a row of sharpened stakes and presently advanced a short distance to provoke the French to attack across a newly sown wheat field which lay between two woods. Their front was narrow and as they pounded up the funnel-shaped gap, their ranks became so close packed that they scarcely had room to swing their weapons. Soon the heavily armoured foot soldiers could only flounder

through churned-up mud and piles of corpses towards the English lines where the lightly clad archers, mostly stationed on either side of the men-at-arms and often skipping through the woods, shot them down with ease and then dropped their bows and came on with axes and swords. The second French attack advanced into disaster for, the more they pressed forward, the more impossible was it for them to fight at all.

In an absurdly short time the battle was over. Thousands of French knights perished and it was said that half the nobility of France died or were captured, whereas the English lost only a handful, so that even the King, still wearing the helmet and jewelled crown that had been dented in the fight, marvelled at the extent of his victory.

Agincourt brought no immediate gain, apart from the ransoms of so many distinguished captives, and the next three years were spent in hard campaigning, mostly devoted to sieges, that led to the conquest of Normandy and the capture of Rouen after a siege even more ghastly than the starving of Calais.

The road to Paris lay open and the French asked for peace. It was arranged that Henry should marry Catherine, the French King's daughter, should rule France during that poor monarch's lifetime and afterwards he and his heirs should succeed to the throne of France.

Henry married the Princess, and after a visit to England they were back in France in 1422 when an attack of dysentery, the scourge of army camps, ended the King's life at the height of his fame and popularity. He was only thirty-three and he had begun to show far greater gifts than merely those of a successful soldier. Even a Frenchman said that he was " valiant in arms, sage, great in justice who without respect of persons, did right for small and great ".

James I of Scotland

Throughout the Hundred Years' War the Scots often assisted their French allies by making raids upon the north of England. In the year when Crecy was fought, Robert Bruce's son, David II, marched across the border but he was defeated and taken prisoner at Neville's Cross.

David was ransomed and when he died childless in 1371, the crown passed to Robert the Steward (or Stewart), son of Walter who had married Marjorie Bruce, daughter of the great King. During the reigns of Robert II and of his son Robert III, a lame and timid King, Scotland was an unhappy land torn by quarrels between its treacherous nobles and ravaged by the raids of the Highland clans upon the Lowlands and by perpetual war along the English border.

So black was the situation in 1406 that Robert III, in despair after the murder of his elder son, decided to send his other boy, James, to be brought up safely in France. Alas for his hopes, the ship with the Prince on board was captured by English pirates who handed over their captive to Henry IV.

This piece of fortune gave the English King too good a hold over the ancient enemy to let the young prisoner go home, even though his father had died and he was now James I of Scotland. For eighteen years, James lived in honourable captivity until

146

Henry V permitted him to return to his native land with his beautiful English bride, Joan Beaufort.

James was a fine athlete, a musician and a poet who had had ample time during his captivity to consider how to govern his unruly kingdom. He speedily called a parliament and made it clear to the barons that he had come to put an end to their lawless ways. Private wars were forbidden, several nobles were executed for their past crimes and the Highland chiefs were kept in strict control.

For twelve years James ruled sternly and well, but many of his nobles longed for the days when they had been able to rob and plot to their hearts' content and some had not forgotten the punishment dealt out to them and their kinsmen.

In 1436 King James and the Queen went to spend Christmas in the monastery of the Black Friars at Perth where a royal party assembled for the season of festivities and tournaments. Unknown to James, the guests included several traitors who had sworn to take revenge for the King's stern measures.

In February, 1437, when the court was at dinner, the King's chamberlain left his seat and secretly removed the keys and bolts from the doors. Having laid planks across the moat to assist his fellow-traitors, he quietly returned to his place. The feasting and the dancing came to an end, the guests went to their bed-chambers and the King and Queen were about to retire to their own bower when James, feeling thirsty, sent his page to fetch some wine. In a corridor the boy ran into a band of armed men who had just entered the monastery with their leader, Sir Robert Graham, a fanatical enemy of the King. The page delayed the assassins by desperately defending himself with a dagger and the pewter wine-jug. The clatter of arms carried to the hall.

" Bolt the door! " ordered James, but the false chamberlain had removed the heavy bar and every weapon was gone.

" The vault, sire," cried Catherine Douglas, one of the Queen's ladies. " There is a vault under the floor! "

147

Snatching up a heavy pair of fire-tongs, James set furiously to work to prise up a floor-board and he was about to drop through the opening into the vault beneath when the traitors were heard approaching:

" Can you keep the door, if only for a minute? " cried the Queen who, with her women, was struggling to replace the board and to smooth its broken edges.

Catherine Douglas rushed to the door but it was hopeless for a woman to try to hold it against a band of murderous men. In despair, she thrust her bare arm through the iron loops where the bar had been. There was a push from outside but her arm held for a moment, then several men hurled their weight against the door and burst into the room, as Catherine fell unconscious to the floor.

The conspirators looked round and the Queen faced them calmly, standing quite still so that her long skirt covered the tell-tale marks on the floor.

" The King? Where is the King? " they cried, and a ruffian held a knife to the Queen's throat.

" Leave her," said Graham. " We seek the King."

At length, believing James to be in another part of the building, the conspirators clattered out and left the women alone. Presently, hearing a noise, they came back and found that James, thinking the danger past, was trying to clamber back into the room.

Two conspirators leapt down into the vault, but the King, as strong as a wrestler, had hurled them down, stunning the one and throttling the other, when, with a vengeful cry, Graham himself leapt down and buried his knife in the King's body.

The traitors fled and although the Queen and her people pursued them until all were taken and put to a horrible end, the harm to Scotland could not be undone. The new King, James II, was a boy of six and the barons were free once more to pursue their lawless ways.

148

Joan of Arc

The baby son of the victor of Agincourt was proclaimed Henry VI of England and soon afterwards, upon the death of Charles VI, he became King of France as well, according to the treaty that his father had made.

As Regent of France, it fell to the Duke of Bedford, a worthy brother of Henry V, to try to carry out the hopeless task of governing a country that had no wish to be ruled by the English.

Despite all his difficulties and the troubles made for him at home by his brother, Humphrey of Gloucester, Bedford won several victories over the French armies. By this time, they believed that the English were invincible and the listless behaviour of the Dauphin Charles did nothing to revive their spirits.

In 1428, when it seemed certain that Bedford would capture Orleans and snuff out all resistance, a miracle occurred.

A country girl named Jeanne d'Arc, or Joan of Arc, appeared at the Dauphin's court with a story that, while she was tending her father's sheep in the fields of Domrémy, heavenly voices told her that she alone could save France from the pitiless invader. Her air of absolute certainty gained her admittance, and the situation was so desperate that any ray of hope was welcome.

" The King of Heaven," she cried to the Dauphin, " bids me tell you that you shall be anointed and crowned in the Church of Rheims."

Charles, smiling wearily at the maid's simplicity, agreed to allow her to attempt the impossible.

Clad in armour, Joan rode towards Orleans at the head of a

149

company prepared to follow her in this hare-brained scheme, and her glowing faith so inspired these soldiers that they drove the English from the strongpoint that dominated the city.

The siege was raised and soon afterwards Joan won a victory in the field at Patay. Within a year, as she had promised, Charles VII was crowned in Rheims Cathedral and the spirit of his countrymen was once more alive and strong.

Joan felt that her task was over but she stayed with the army because the soldiers' faith in her was so complete that they believed that she could lead them to absolute victory. Unfortunately they allowed her to decide military problems far beyond the girl's understanding. Naturally, she made mistakes and after failing in an attack on Paris, she was captured by the Burgundians, who handed her over to their English allies.

Tried for witchcraft by a court of churchmen presided over by the Bishop of Beauvais, Joan was pronounced guilty and, to the disgrace of the English, Burgundians and French alike, she was burned to death in the market-place at Rouen. As she died, clasping a rough cross and murmuring, " Jesus," an English soldier said : " We are lost, for this maid was indeed a saint."

It was several years before Joan's example brought the victory for which she died. The war swayed to and fro, with each side winning an occasional victory, but the French, fighting doggedly with Joan's name on their lips, slowly gained ground. Bedford, outnumbered and short of supplies, fought valiantly until his death in 1435, by which time the Burgundians had changed sides and he had rashly refused a peace offer that would have left Normandy and Aquitaine in English hands.

After this, the French won back their territories inch by inch and made such good use of cannons that, when the Hundred Years War ended in 1453, the English had lost almost everything, including Aquitaine, the great province that had been theirs since Henry II's marriage three hundred years before. Only Calais was left.

Henry VI and the Wars of the Roses

Before the war ended Henry VI married Margaret of Anjou, a fiery-tempered French Princess who naturally wanted peace with her native land. In this, she was supported by King Henry whose timid, courteous nature shrank from war.

Many of the nobles enjoyed fighting and they knew that, even in a hopeless war, there was plenty of excitement and pillage. So they opposed the Queen and her supporters (the Duke of Suffolk and his nephew Somerset) jeered at their plans for peace and blamed them for the continuous defeats in France.

So bitter was the feeling that King Henry sent Suffolk to Calais for safety, but his ship was intercepted by a vessel called the *Nicolas of the Tower* whose sailors greeted the Duke with shouts of, " Welcome, traitor! " They dragged him on deck, hacked off his head and threw his body into the sea.

This murder of the King's adviser was followed by a rising of the turbulent men of Kent. Led by Jack Cade, they defeated the royal troops and entered London where they killed two ministers and fell to plundering the citizens. The Londoners indignantly set about the rebels, who retreated to their homes ; Cade himself was killed and the rebellion fizzled out, but it showed the state of disorder into which the kingdom had fallen.

By this time, two hostile parties were arming their supporters. On one side were the Lancastrians, supporters of the King, whose badge was the red rose. On the other side were the Yorkists, wearers of the white rose, followers of Richard, Duke of York. He was Henry's cousin and heir to the throne for as long as the King had no children.

The nobles on both sides found it easy to recruit their

forces from the soldiers home from France. These hardened campaigners were ready for any ugly work, whether it was on the battlefield or in some quiet village where a landowner could be terrorised into surrendering his rights to the lord whose badge they wore for pay.

In 1453 the pious King became mad and the Duke of York was made Protector of the realm, but the delight of his supporters changed to gloom when Queen Margaret, childless for nine years, gave birth to a healthy son and heir. King Henry recovered his wits as suddenly as they had flown from him, and the Queen had York dismissed from court :

" Let the Duke know that it is our purpose to make the King safe from his enemies," she cried jubilantly, and with these threatening words, the Wars of the Roses began. It was only two years since the end of the Hundred Years War.

York and his friends, including the Earl of Salisbury, his son, the Earl of Warwick, and the powerful Neville clan took up arms and marched towards London. At St Albans, they found Somerset and the King holding the city with a strong force, but young Warwick burst through some houses and out into the streets. To cries of " A Warwick ! A Warwick ! " he took the royal troops in the rear and won a resounding victory.

While Somerset's body lay on the steps of an inn, York and Warwick found the King in a cottage having an arrow wound in his neck dressed by a tanner's wife. They knelt to him and said that they had only come to save him from his foes and to escort him safely to London.

When Henry became mad for the second time, York took control of the kingdom but Queen Margaret kept up such a relentless opposition that she was able to raise an army to scatter the Duke's forces. York fled to Ireland, while the dashing Warwick steered a small boat to Calais where he had been Governor for some time. With him were his father and Edward of March, York's eldest son, to whom he was now hero and protector.

The Queen straightway declared that the Yorkists had forfeited their lives and estates, so, with nothing to lose, they kept up the struggle and it was not long before they made another attack.

Warwick and young Edward of March crossed from Calais to Kent and, after a tumultuous welcome from the Londoners, who detested the Queen, they marched into the Midlands and defeated the royal army at Northampton. King Henry was captured and York claimed the crown. Hoping to prevent

further bloodshed, Henry agreed to set aside his son's rights and to accept York as his successor.

This betrayal of her own child inflamed the Queen's bitterness. After adventurous wanderings in the Welsh mountains where a gang of robbers were said to have protected her and her little son, Queen Margaret reached Scotland and raised yet another army. The Duke of York marched north to meet this threat, and at Wakefield his troops were defeated and he himself was slain. The Earl of Salisbury was executed immediately after the battle. His head and York's, adorned by a paper crown, were set above the gate of the city of York.

Warwick advanced to avenge his father but Margaret's army beat him at the second battle of St Albans and forced him to retreat to the Cotswolds where he joined Edward of March.

Margaret, who had recaptured her half-witted husband, had the game completely in her hands if she could have controlled her wild troops. But instead of capturing London, they preferred to straggle northwards, plundering the countryside as they went.

Warwick and Edward made a dash for the capital and, at a great meeting outside St Paul's, the citizens agreed that King Henry was unfit to rule and that Edward of March, the Duke of York's son, should be King in his place.

After this bold stroke, the mighty Earl and the new monarch, Edward IV, set off to pursue the Lancastrian army, whose troops, disgusted at Henry's order forbidding plunder, were retreating in poor spirits.

In 1461 the armies met at Towton in Yorkshire where the Lancastrians were routed with the most terrible slaughter of any battle ever fought in England. Margaret and Henry fled to Scotland and Warwick proceeded to subdue the north with gruesome zest.

Edward IV

By this time the Earl of Warwick was all-powerful, for Edward IV, handsome and indolent, seemed to have no thought for anything but banquets, tournaments and pretty ladies.

In order to make peace with the French, who had been helping Queen Margaret, Warwick arranged for Edward to marry a French princess. At the last moment, however, the King announced with an insolent smile that he was already secretly married to a beautiful lady named Elizabeth Woodville, widow of a Lancastrian.

Warwick swallowed his anger and made a great parade of escorting poor King Henry, recently captured in Lancashire, to

155

the Tower. It was clear, however, that Edward IV had grown tired of being Warwick's puppet. He was about to shake off the great Earl and to destroy his power.

He promoted his wife's relatives, the Woodvilles, to positions of influence and having rid himself of Warwick's friends, he forbade his brother Clarence to marry the Earl's daughter Isabel. Clarence slipped away to Calais, married the girl and returned with his father-in-law to raise their supporters.

Taken by surprise, Edward smilingly surrendered to the Earl who now had two Kings in his power—Henry in the Tower and Edward in his camp. But Edward was too popular to be kept a prisoner for long. Warwick was obliged to set him free and thus to bring about his own downfall. Edward collected an army and so completely turned the tables that the Earl fled to France where Louis XI was already sheltering Queen Margaret and her son.

King Louis at once put forward an astonishing plan. Since Warwick and Edward IV were now enemies, he suggested that the Earl should change sides and put Henry VI back on his throne. It took patience to soothe the Queen's hatred of Warwick but, at last, the bargain was made, and in 1470 the Earl landed in Devonshire. The Queen was to follow and their supporters had already raised a rebellion to draw Edward north.

Finding that his army was riddled with treachery, Edward did not wait to fight. Instead, he fled to Flanders and Warwick the Kingmaker brought Henry VI out of the Tower and once again rode through the streets with the poor King whose sufferings had turned him into an imbecile.

But Warwick had forgotten his son-in-law, Clarence. That faithless nobleman had been quite content to see his brother overthrown if he himself should have the crown. But it was a different matter when the Lancastrian was back on the throne. He therefore made a secret promise to desert Warwick when the time was ripe.

At this, Edward IV decided to trust to luck and his own ability. He landed in Yorkshire, gathered an army and advanced to the Midlands where Warwick was confidently awaiting the arrival of Clarence. At the pre-arranged moment, Clarence threw away the red rose and led his troops to Edward's side.

Warwick still had a sizeable army, and although Queen Margaret had not arrived he attacked the Yorkists at Barnet on Easter Sunday, 1471. The battle was fought in a swirling mist and the Earl's troops were gaining the upper hand when the cry of, " Treason! Treason! " was heard. The Earl of Oxford had arrived to aid Warwick, but in the mist his men, wearing his badge " a star with rays ", were mistaken for Yorkists whose badge was the rising sun. Attacked by their own allies, they fled. Panic followed ; no commander could make himself obeyed and Warwick's army broke.

Later the mist cleared and the victorious Edward IV was surveying the field when his attention was drawn to a body stripped of its armour. It was Warwick the Kingmaker.

" There lies the last of the barons," remarked Edward.

Queen Margaret and her son landed in England on that very day but they were defeated and captured at Tewkesbury. The Prince was killed immediately and Margaret was sent to the Tower where, it was announced, King Henry died " out of displeasure and melancholy ".

Having rid himself of all his opponents in battle or by execution, Edward IV had no rival for the rest of his life. In his cool, heartless way, he mastered the nobles and kept the respect of the middle-classes and of the common people. It was typical of him that when he took an army to France to punish Louis XI, he sensibly accepted a large sum of money instead of a battle and paid no heed to the indignation of his blood-thirsty nobles.

Richard III

Edward died suddenly in 1483, leaving two small sons. The elder boy became Edward V and, since he was only thirteen, it seemed right that he and his brother should be placed in the care of their uncle, Richard of Gloucester, who, as the late King's brother, was made Protector.

Gloucester immediately dismissed the unpopular Woodvilles, a move that frightened the Queen into taking sanctuary at Westminster, though she presently was persuaded into parting with her younger son. He was sent to join his brother in the Tower where the young King had been placed " for safety ".

With both Princes out of the way, Gloucester ordered the execution or imprisonment of all who seemed likely to oppose him. Then he claimed the throne on the grounds that Edward IV's marriage was illegal and he had himself crowned Richard III just two weeks after the date fixed for his nephew's coronation.

The two Princes were never seen in public again. Rumours

of their death went about, and twenty years later Sir James Tyrrel confessed that he and two servants had been ordered to kill the boys. This story seemed to be confirmed when two small skeletons were found in the Tower in 1674.

Richard III, nicknamed " Crookback " by his enemies, was a first-rate general, brave, charming and absolutely loyal to his brother, Edward IV, who liked and trusted him. Could such a man have murdered his own nephews? It is certain that he had grown up in the treacherous, violent years of the Wars of the Roses and he knew all too well that the way to win power was to strike suddenly without scruple or pity.

At all events, he was now King with every rival dead and nothing to fear. There was, however, just one young man left alive who could claim the throne, and luckily for him he was out of Richard's reach.

This young man, the last hope of the Lancastrians, had been sent abroad for safety and was now living in Brittany. He was Henry Tudor, Earl of Richmond, and his mother was a descendant of John of Gaunt and therefore of Edward III.

To avoid Richard III's agents, Henry went to France where he found sufficient help to decide to risk his life to win a crown.

In August 1485 he landed at Milford Haven in the land of his Welsh grandfather, Owen Tudor. Numbers of Welshmen joined him and although he had only 5000 men by the time he reached Shrewsbury, he had good reason to believe that some of Richard III's so-called supporters would hold off and others, notably Lord Stanley and his brother, Sir William Stanley, would assist him.

The King met his rival at Bosworth Field in Leicestershire, and at the critical moment Stanley changed sides. Richard III was no coward and he fought with furious courage to the end. The crown that he wore in the battle was picked up from beneath a bush and placed on the head of the victor, who thus became Henry VII, first of the Tudor monarchs.

William Caxton the Printer

Even in the most violent periods of our history, men continued to write poetry, to build wonderful churches, to found schools and universities and to manage the affairs of their towns and gilds. Among these writers, scholars and industrious citizens was a sober merchant whose achievements outshone the deeds of almost all the kings and nobles. He was William Caxton.

Born in Kent when Henry VI was a child, Caxton served as a boy-apprentice to a mercer or cloth-merchant in the city of London. When he was a young man, he went to Bruges, one of the cloth cities of Flanders, and set up in business for himself. He travelled, he grew rich and he rose to be the chief English merchant in the Low Countries, and like many rich men, he was able to enjoy an expensive hobby. His greatest pride was his collection of books—rare and beautiful books, written by hand so carefully and so slowly that a man with a dozen books possessed a proud library; but Caxton wanted more than this and not merely for himself.

He heard that Master Gutenberg in Germany had invented a way of *printing* books faster than a man could write and he went to Cologne to see this marvellous invention called a printing *press*, because it pressed sheets of paper on to wooden letters that had been fitted into a frame.

Caxton and his assistant built a press of their own, and in the reign of Edward IV they came to England and set up the press in a house close to Westminster Abbey. The wool merchant devoted the rest of his life to printing stories, poems and ballads and it was his work and the work of other printers that marked the end of the Middle Ages and the beginning of a new age.

The First of the Tudors

When, on Bosworth Field, the " crown of ornament " was placed on Henry Tudor's head, the new King had seen almost nothing of the kingdom he was to rule for the rest of his life. Half of his twenty-eight years had been spent in Wales and the rest in exile. Yet this wary, clever stranger, more Welsh than English, was exactly the man whom England needed.

To begin with Henry VII was not a warrior. He would fight if he had to but, for exercise, he preferred hunting and he liked books, music and the business of the kingdom, especially its money-accounts, better than tournaments and costly ceremonies. The country wanted peace, and he sensed that if he restored the force of law and settled the Yorkist-Lancastrian feud, he might keep the crown he had won by daring and treachery.

So he fulfilled his oath to marry Elizabeth of York, the tall, blue-eyed sister of the two Princes who had disappeared in Richard III's reign. The marriage did not put an end to all

the Yorkist plots, but from now on they flourished only in those parts which lived on discord and pillage—the northern and the Welsh borders.

As long as the great lords kept private armies to terrorise their neighbours and to overcome the law-courts, there could be no settled peace. But, crippled by their losses in the recent wars, the barons were obliged to obey Henry when he ordered them to dismiss their armed retainers. A few had forgotten the need for obedience to a royal command and, early in the reign when Henry paid a visit to the Earl of Oxford, he found himself greeted by a guard of honour wearing the Oxford badge.

" These are your servants? " enquired the King.

" They are my retainers, assembled here to do you honour," replied Oxford proudly.

" I thank you for your hospitality," said Henry, " but I like not to have my laws broken in my own sight."

Shortly afterwards, Oxford was summoned to appear before a special court which fined him £15,000, a sum so immense that it convinced the barons that it was wiser to obey the law than to risk the King's displeasure.

But it took more than fines and a successful marriage to make the throne secure. For fifteen years Henry had to overcome his difficulties by skill and cunning, for there were enemies in Ireland, France and Flanders, besides rivals in the Tower and friends at home who would change sides the moment he lost his grip.

A baker's son named Lambert Simnel who claimed to be Edward Plantagenet, was crowned in Ireland but Henry routed the boy's supporters and contemptuously put young Simnel to work in the royal kitchen. Presently, the Yorkists tried again. This time they produced Perkin Warbeck, a handsome youth who gave out that he was Richard of York and had escaped from the Tower when his elder brother was murdered. From Ireland, Warbeck made his way to Flanders where Margaret of York " recognised " him as her nephew. Henry countered by threatening to stop the Flemish wool trade, so Warbeck took himself to Scotland where he found favour and a bride of noble birth.

By this time, Henry had discovered that Sir William Stanley, whose treachery had given him the victory at Bosworth, was again playing a double game. Without a moment's hesitation, he had his old friend arrested and executed. Meanwhile, a rising of discontented Cornishmen persuaded Warbeck to try his luck in the West Country but when Henry came down with an army, the rebellion fizzled out. A few of the leaders were hanged but the rest were heavily fined and Warbeck himself was treated with mercy until his own folly brought him to the Tower and death by hanging.

After this Henry's difficulties became less. Almost every rival had been killed off and he was able to concentrate upon making the throne safe for his son. Money was the key to power and he set himself to gather in wealth by every possible means. A foreigner described him as " a great miser but a man of vast ability ". He punished offenders with fines and, as his love of gold increased, he also suggested that his subjects should make " gifts " to their royal master. To his collectors he pointed out that a man who lived in style could obviously afford to make a rich gift and a man who lived plainly must have money saved away. In either case, he had to pay! When Henry invaded France with a powerful army, he accepted a vast sum from the French King and went home without fighting, much to the disgust of his own nobles who had half-ruined themselves to provide men and equipment for the campaign.

Under this wily King, the country prospered and foreign monarchs had a new respect for England's friendship. So Henry was able to marry his eldest son Arthur to Catherine of Aragon, daughter of the King of Spain, and his daughter Margaret to the Scottish King, James IV. But Henry's interest in affairs

163

outside England was not shared his by own countrymen.

Christopher Columbus's immortal voyage of 1492 and the Portuguese discovery of a sea-route to India aroused no excitement in the English captains. Their greatest exploits were to sail their ships to fish off the Iceland coast or to trade across the narrow seas with Gascony, Flanders and the Baltic ports.

There was living in Bristol, however, a citizen of Venice, Giovanni Caboto, otherwise John Cabot who, like Columbus, had been born in Genoa and had the same notion that the spicelands of the East could be reached by sailing west across the Atlantic. His ideas aroused some interest but no financial support until Henry VII paid a visit to Bristol. Cabot was

invited to explain his plans for a voyage of discovery to the King, who was already aware that his fellow monarchs of Portugal and Spain were on the threshold of riches that would make his own hoard seem like a handful of pennies. Henry offered to provide a ship in which Cabot could put his theories to the test.

In 1497 the *Mathew*, a tiny vessel with a crew of eighteen, sailed out of Bristol and headed westward into the Atlantic Ocean. Several weeks later the look-out sighted a " new-found land ", a bleak grey headland which Cabot imagined to be the northern tip of Asia. It was in fact the coast of North America, the continent whose existence neither Cabot nor Columbus ever suspected or indeed recognised. Ashore, there was no sign of

life apart from a few bone needles and primitive traps. The sea was teeming with great codfish which could be pulled inboard by the basket-load but since he had not come for fish, Cabot sailed for home to report his meagre discovery and to ask for a larger ship so that he could go on next time to Cathay itself.

King Henry rewarded the Genoese captain with a pension and in the following year Cabot set out again with a small fleet of ships provided by the King and several enterprising merchants. Once again he reached the American mainland and this time he coasted southward, looking hopefully for a channel that would lead him to the land of silks and spices. He never found it and must have returned to Bristol a puzzled and disappointed man, for no more is heard of him except that he drew his pension a year later. The merchants left no mention of him either ; perhaps they decided to cut their losses and to say nothing for fear of discouraging others.

The King did not lose all interest in ocean voyages. Never a man to waste money, he awarded £10 a year to John's son, Sebastian Cabot, " for diligent services in and about the port of Bristol ". Sebastian, a smooth-tongued fellow with a flair for extracting money from royal pockets, afterwards claimed that he had explored the coast of North America but it seems likely that he was " a teller of other men's tales ", and in the next reign he took himself off to Spain where he prospered greatly and became Pilot-Major to the King of Spain.

Henry VII died in 1509, a sad figure whose last years were darkened by illness and the deaths of his wife and eldest son. His popularity had gone and his ministers were hated for their greed. But he left a vigorous, well-run kingdom and in the Treasury there was said to be a million pounds.

Henry VIII

The new monarch, Henry VIII, was not quite eighteen. In the eyes of his delighted subjects here was the very picture of all that a king should be. A magnificent athlete, six feet two inches tall, Henry was the most handsome and talented Prince in Europe. He spoke French, Latin, Italian and Spanish ; he liked mathematics, he wrote poetry, played several instruments and composed music. At tennis, archery, jousting and riding, there was scarcely anyone to equal him, and at dancing he leapt and pirouetted faster and higher than all the courtiers. His father had kept him hard at his books, but now this great hand-some boy, blessed with all the skills and learning of the age, burst upon the scene eager to make up for lost time by enjoying himself and impressing the world with his grandeur.

The old King's money was not allowed to lie in the treasury. Young Henry spent it with fabulous extravagance in a riot of tournaments, feasting, dancing and entertainments which fol-lowed his accession to the throne. In more serious vein, he did two things to please the people. He gave orders that his father's most unpopular ministers should have their heads cut off and he

167

married Catherine of Aragon, the widow of his brother Arthur.

The Pope gave permission for the marriage and Catherine, a grey-eyed beauty whose gaiety and love of dancing won the hearts of the English, delighted her eager husband. For the moment all was happiness in England and at court. It was not long before Henry decided to win glory in a war against France and when the older members of his council advised against the adventure, he speedily found an ambitious newcomer who was only too ready to carry out his wishes.

Thomas Wolsey came from Ipswich where his father, a grazier and butcher, was in a good way of business, for young Thomas had been sent to college at Oxford and into the Church. He was clever and he rose fast in the world. From tutor to a nobleman's sons, he became chaplain and secretary to the Archbishop of Canterbury and then to the old King himself.

Thus, when Henry VIII looked round at his council, he noted among the greybeards this young priest of brilliant talents and unquenchable greed. The minister to whom he gave his friendship was speedily raised above all the others and while Henry enjoyed himself, Wolsey managed the kingdom. With enormous gusto, he took on the arrangements for the French war and raised an army to enable Henry to cut a glorious figure on the continent. The start was disappointing but in due course he managed to provide Henry with the desired victory, even if it was not a second Agincourt. The French rode away so fast that the fight was called the Battle of the Spurs! However, a few towns were captured and Henry had the satisfaction of knowing that Europe had seen an English king in action once again.

Meanwhile, a much greater victory was won at home when James IV of Scotland, taking advantage of his brother-in-law's absence, invaded England with a large army. As Regent, Queen Catherine met the threat with great spirit. She despatched the old Earl of Surrey to the border with orders to raise the men of the northern counties, and at the Battle of

168

Flodden the English longbow won its last great victory and artillery had one of its first triumphs. The Scots were utterly routed and James IV perished on the field with a dozen earls and most of his nobles. Scotland came to be governed by the widowed Queen, Margaret, whose son James V was not born until after his father's death.

The war with France was never more than a half-hearted affair, for Henry quickly realised that his crafty allies expected him to do the fighting while they reaped the gains. So he and Wolsey turned the tables by making peace and sending Henry's beautiful sister Mary to marry the old French King. He soon died, however, and was succeeded by Francis I, a King as young and masterful as Henry himself. Indeed, if Francis was less handsome, he was even richer and more warlike.

Wolsey arranged a meeting between the two rivals who, pretending nothing but gallant friendship for each other, put on a three weeks' display of such gorgeous extravagance that it was called the Field of the Cloth of Gold. Wolsey's own splendour astonished the French and added to his sovereign's glory, but all was for show and none of the chivalrous play was sincere. Henry was already plotting with the Emperor Charles, and when it came to war, the English fought the French as they had always done.

In all these affairs, Wolsey was the master-figure who zealously managed the King's business and grew ever richer on the rewards that fell into his lap. Most of the gifts were high positions in the Church which cost Henry nothing— bishoprics, deaneries and dozens of rectorships with acres of land and fat incomes. At the height of his power, Wolsey was Bishop of Tournai, Bishop of Lincoln, Archbishop of York and Lord Chancellor of England. The Pope made him a Cardinal ; he dined in state like the King and lived in a style more splendid than the greatest noblemen of Europe. He governed the kingdom, ruled the Church, built palaces, houses, a college at

Oxford and a school at Ipswich. His power was immense because it was the King's power and as long as it pleased the King to have so fine a chancellor, Wolsey was the greatest man in the land. The people could curse him for the taxes and the lords could hate him for his arrogance, but while he stood in the royal favour, none could harm him. It was already clear that their handsome Prince had grown into a masterful King as cold and ruthless as any who had ever worn the crown.

Master of his Kingdom

By his mid-thirties Henry was an anxious man. He and Catherine, married now for eighteen years, had but one child, a clever, delicate girl named Mary. Five other children had died in babyhood and Henry longed for a son to whom he could hand on the kingdom and the Tudor name. Other men had sons but why not he? Had he sinned in marrying his brother's widow and was this his punishment? The doubt which had entered his mind grew mightily when he fell in love with Anne Boleyn, a lady of the court. She was young and pretty, with dark eyes and black shining hair, and Henry was certain that she would give him the son he wanted. He would divorce Catherine and marry Anne. Wolsey must make the necessary arrangements with the Pope.

For kings and princes, these matters could often be settled without trouble, but just at this time the Pope was in a most difficult position. The city of Rome was occupied by the Emperor's troops and the Emperor Charles V was none other than Catherine's nephew. So, whereas the Pope wished to oblige Henry, he dared not offend Charles. The matter was delayed for weeks and months and, try as he might, Wolsey was unable to obtain the answer which his master desired.

At length, a cardinal came from Rome to hear the case but delay followed delay until the King could no longer contain his fury. All his life he had had his way but now it seemed as if his dearest wish was to be denied. The fault must be Wolsey's. He struck him down savagely, banishing him from the court and stripping him of most of his wealth and appointments.

Wolsey retired to York but the King's wrath followed him

and, charged with treason, he was on his way back to London when he died at Leicester, murmuring the regrets which he never felt in his days of power : " Had I but served God as diligently as I have served the King, he would not have given me over in my grey hairs."

Having broken Wolsey, Henry gave the chancellorship to Sir Thomas More and called a parliament which he knew would support his defiance of the Pope. He then put Queen Catherine aside and had Archbishop Cranmer announce his marriage to Anne Boleyn. She was crowned at Westminster with the utmost magnificence. But the people gave " ill looks " to her as she passed by in procession.

Parliament declared the marriage legal and Henry was made " Supreme Head on earth, under God, of the Church of England ". The leading men of the kingdom were required to swear an oath accepting these changes and almost all of them did so. But among the few who refused the oath was Sir Thomas More, the kindly scholar who had already resigned from his position as chancellor. No parliament, he said, could appoint the head of the Church. The Duke of Norfolk told him that if he persisted in such talk, his life was as good as lost. " Is that all, my lord ? " replied More. " Then I die today and you tomorrow." On the scaffold, he called out calmly to the spectators, " I die, the King's faithful servant, but God's first."

After More's execution, the King's mastery was unopposed. He found, in Thomas Cromwell, a minister as grasping and diligent as Wolsey and, between them, they closed the monasteries, seized their wealth and sold their lands to the highest bidders. Thus, although the King kept to most of the forms of the old religion and had no liking for the new faith of those who called themselves Protestants, there were now many persons in England who did not want to see the Pope's authority restored. If that happened, they would have to give back the Church lands they had bought.

But, in the north, where the monasteries had not been hated or despised, a rebellion broke out, known as the Pilgrimage of Grace because the rebels were accompanied by priests carrying crucifixes and sacred banners. Henry dealt with the rising in his own fashion. Having dispersed the peasants and weavers with fair promises, he pounced on their leaders and had them executed without mercy.

Henceforward, no one was safe. The jovial monarch had become a suspicious despot who made and broke men as he pleased, a tyrant with more real power than any ruler of England before or since. In his portraits he stands like an arrogant bull, his vast frame made even broader by bolstered sleeves, his small eyes and pursed mouth conveying the cruelty of his character.

He was as ruthless in his private life as in public. On the

night when he heard of poor Catherine's death, he laughed aloud and danced merrily with Anne Boleyn. But Anne failed him. She gave him a daughter, Elizabeth, but both her sons were born dead, so she was executed on a trumped-up charge of faithlessness. Soon he married Jane Seymour who died giving birth to Edward, his longed-for son, and some time later he permitted Thomas Cromwell to arrange an alliance with the German states and a royal marriage to a German princess. When the lady proved to be ugly, she was put aside and Cromwell was beheaded for *his* failure. Execution also ended the life of his fifth wife, the lovely, sinful Catherine Howard.

On every side, Henry was hated and feared. Yet Englishmen still regarded him with a kind of terrified admiration; they liked their King to have power and Henry's power was immense. He defied the Pope and two great monarchs abroad;

175

Wales was subdued, Ireland brought to temporary obedience and Scotland humbled by another disastrous defeat at Solway Moss. The shame affected the Scottish King so deeply that he died, leaving a baby daughter who was later to be called Mary Queen of Scots.

Near the end of his reign, Henry heaved his great bulk into a new suit of armour and took an army to France where he captured Boulogne and came home well pleased with himself.

The French King, bent upon revenge, assembled a great fleet to invade England and it was as well that Henry had long been a builder of ships and dockyards and had spent some of the monasteries' wealth on building castles to defend the coast. Portsmouth was threatened, some small towns were burnt and a few Frenchmen got ashore, but the English ships, watched by the King himself, headed off the enemy fleet and caused it to retire. The English were disappointed. From as far afield as Worcester and Norwich, they had come marching towards the coast. King Harry might be an old tyrant but, with all his faults, he had their loyalty and they would have fought for him. Bald, immensely stout and plagued by an ulcer in his leg that was killing him, he still inspected his ships, troops and forts and was hoisted into the saddle to go " hawking for pheasants ". His temper was vile but his brain was as keen as ever and he realised all too well the kingdom's real weakness.

The power was his and his alone. If he should die, whom could he trust to rule the land until Edward came of age? The boy was not yet ten, so Henry chose a council of ministers to carry out his desires. He picked them carefully. Men of the old religion were included and some of the new Protestant faith. There were to be no more violent changes and, during the days before his death, Henry earnestly explained to the council how they should govern the kingdom.

Then, clutching Cranmer's hand to express repentance for his sins, he died. His reign had lasted for thirty-eight years.

Edward VI and Lady Jane Grey

No sooner had Edward VI, the boy-king, been brought to London than the council began to disobey their dead master. Within a fortnight, a party of extreme Protestants had taken charge ; and their leader, Jane Seymour's brother, made himself Protector and Duke of Somerset. They attacked the Roman Catholic religion and seized the remainder of Church property with a greed that would have shocked Thomas Cromwell himself. Riots and risings broke out and there was more disorder in one year than in the whole of King Henry's reign. Somerset was overthrown and executed by John Dudley, presently Duke of Northumberland, who became master of the kingdom and of young Edward.

The country fell into chaos. With their religion attacked and the King's authority gone, the people were distracted. Hooligans broke into the churches to smash ornaments and priceless stained-glass windows ; the ruling class plundered the possessions of the ancient gilds and schools ; rents and prices rose and the value of wages fell. England was well-nigh bankrupt.

In this situation, Northumberland's policy was merely to increase his own power. This dark ruthless man dominated everyone and, by playing upon the young King's enthusiasm for the Protestant religion and allowing no one else to come near to him, he gained a powerful hold upon the boy's mind. Until he was fifteen, Edward seemed to be quite healthy but after an attack of measles, he began to show unmistakeable signs of lung disease. His illness, aggravated by the poisonous medicines of the time, rapidly became worse and he clearly had not long to live. The heir to the throne was Princess Mary, Henry's elder daughter and, after her, the Princess Elizabeth. Next in line was Henry's niece, Frances, Duchess of Suffolk, whose daughter was Lady Jane Grey.

Northumberland easily persuaded the Duchess to pass her claim to her daughter and he next arranged for Jane to marry his own son, Guilford Dudley. Jane, a clever gentle girl, was only sixteen and she had no liking for Northumberland's spoilt son, but her scheming parents, the Suffolks, set upon her so cruelly that she was forced to accept him.

All that Northumberland had to do now was to get Mary and Elizabeth out of the way. By wheedling and threatening, he persuaded the dying King to make a will leaving the kingdom to Lady Jane Grey. The Privy Council was bullied into accepting this illegal scheme, and as soon as Edward died Northumberland proclaimed his own daughter-in-law Queen of England When she heard his words, Lady Jane cried out in anguish :

" No! No! The crown is not my right. The Lady Mary is the rightful Queen! "

Her objections were ignored and with Guilford Dudley at her side, she was taken in state to the capital. She was so tiny that she was made to wear three-inch soles on her shoes to appear taller, but the people glowered silently at the luckless girl whom Northumberland had foisted upon them.

During her nine days' reign, Jane showed unexpected strength of character and it was her refusal to allow her father to leave London that hastened Northumberland's downfall and

her own. On proclaiming Jane, he had tried to seize Princess Mary but she had ridden to Framlingham Castle in Suffolk and the men of East Anglia were soon up in arms for old Harry's daughter. Since Jane would not send her father to fight, Northumberland himself marched north with an army. By the time he reached Cambridge, his men were deserting and the game was up. Taken to the Tower, he was executed without delay and he met his end most shamefully, even denying the Protestant faith for which he had committed his crimes. Jane watched him scornfully from her prison window :

"I pray God," she said, " I nor no friend of mine die so miserably." A few months later she accepted death with far more courage. Mary's advisers warned that as long as Jane was alive there would be plots and rebellion, but the Queen had no wish to execute her cousin and hoped she might become a Catholic. Jane refused and, at the age of sixteen, she was beheaded for treason on Tower Hill Green.

Mary

Mary was nearing middle-age when she came to the throne. Years of sorrow and humiliation had given her a rather severe expression but she was brave and by nature kinder than the rest of the Tudors. The people had liked her mother, Catherine of Aragon, and they admired the courageous way in which Mary had faced Northumberland. If she had acted discreetly and had brought in changes one by one, all might have been well, for many people disliked the New Prayer Book and the Protestants.

However, Mary had set her heart upon bringing England back to the Pope's authority with all speed, and the very dangers which faced her only increased her determination to carry out what she believed to be right. At first Parliament supported her. The Commons agreed that Church services should be as they were in Henry VIII's last years; Catholic bishops were released from prison and the leading Protestants were removed from office. But no effort was made to return the Church lands.

180

The Queen's fatal mistake was to marry her cousin, Philip of Spain. She could not or would not understand the English dislike of seeing their country become a small part of the great Spanish empire. The marriage was unpopular and the Spanish priests and servants who accompanied Philip to England were hooted at and assaulted in the streets. The arrival of Cardinal Pole from Rome only made things worse, but Mary and her advisers were not dismayed by opposition. For the good of their souls, the English would have to be taught obedience.

Persecution of the Protestants began with the burning of Bishop Hooper and John Rogers at Smithfield and by the end of the year some seventy persons had died. They included Bishops Latimer and Ridley, who perished at the same stake from which Latimer cried out :

" Be of good cheer and play the man, brother Ridley. We shall this day light such a candle, by God's grace, in England as I trust shall never be put out! "

Cranmer, now old and never very firm of purpose, almost gave Mary and Pole their greatest triumph, for he confessed his errors and agreed that he was the cause of all the ills the Church had suffered. However, at the end, he regained his courage and went to the stake a Protestant, thrusting first into the flames " that unworthy hand " which had signed the confession.

Altogether about 300 persons were burnt alive, not many by continental standards, but nearly all were humble folk and their persecution aroused much wider indignation than if the victims had belonged to the upper class. Mary's own life was a tragedy. Her husband left her in order to attend to affairs in Spain, the child she longed for was never born, her religion came to be hated with terrible intensity and, persuaded by Philip to declare war on France, she had to bear the blame for losing Calais, the last English possession abroad. Seriously ill and crushed by her unhappiness, she died in 1558 after a reign of only five years.

Elizabeth

Henry VIII's second daughter, Elizabeth, had been closely guarded throughout both the previous reigns and on more than one occasion it was only her courage and sharp wits that had saved her from the scaffold.

She was now twenty-five, red-haired and handsome rather than pretty, with a curved nose, arching brows and piercing green eyes. Though her father had neglected her, he had seen that she was well educated, and she possessed his love of sport and music. From him, too, she inherited the power to dazzle all comers, to dominate the court and to bear herself like a monarch. Yet she could fling back a jest to a tipsy carter in the crowd and outswear the Thames watermen. She had Henry's zest for life, his awful temper and some of his meanness but none of his heartless cruelty. During the next forty-five years, never fully trusting anyone, never revealing the secrets of her mind, she was to inspire love and obedience such as the nation had rarely given to a man and never before to a woman.

At the time of her accession, her chances of survival seemed small. The people were not yet devoted to her and there was bitter enmity between Catholics and Protestants. If she seemed to favour one side more than the other, she was likely to invite a rebellion or a foreign invasion and she had not the soldiers or the ships to deal with either.

King Philip of Spain was naturally interested in adding his dead wife's kingdom to his empire and he offered to marry Elizabeth. She had no intention of accepting him, but was careful not to offend him by a blank refusal.

At this time, however, France was more dangerous than Spain. The French King, Henry II, had recently captured

Calais and was thirsting for further success. He already had
a powerful hold on Scotland where Mary Queen of Scots'
mother, a French princess, was ruling the country with the aid
of French troops. Henry II had married his son to Mary
Queen of Scots who, in Catholic eyes, was the rightful Queen
of England. It would suit the French King very well to unite
both kingdoms and to keep them under his own control.

In this dangerous situation, Elizabeth played her cards
cleverly. At home, she managed to settle the religious question
in a way that did not please either the Protestants or the

Catholics very much but did not drive them to rebellion. She said that people could pray as they pleased, so long as they did not upset the state, and she would have no more persecution. In the first eleven years of her reign, not one person was burnt for religion or executed for treason. As for Philip, she knew that he would not let his great enemy, the French King, put Mary Queen of Scots on the English throne, so she kept on friendly terms with him and let him go on hoping that she would marry him one day.

In Scotland she was lucky. John Knox, a fiery Protestant, returned from exile and within a year his preaching had filled the Lowland Scots with such hatred of the Roman Catholic religion that, with sly help from Elizabeth, they drove out the French soldiers and freed Scotland from French influence.

Henry II's fleet carrying fresh troops to Edinburgh was destroyed by a gale and he himself died from an injury received in a tournament. His son became King Francis II, and Mary Queen of Scots was now Queen of France and, she claimed, Queen of England too. For the moment, Elizabeth's danger was worse than ever.

However, the young King died suddenly and Mary found herself no longer welcome at the French court. She therefore returned to Scotland, a country she had not seen since babyhood.

Mary was nineteen, a gay and beautiful girl whose misfortune was to have no wise counsellors to guide her. At first she tried hard to win the hearts of the people and to come to friendly terms with Knox, but it was not long before she made the disastrous mistake of marrying her cousin, Lord Darnley. This not only aroused the envy of other Scottish nobles but Darnley soon proved himself to be an arrogant waster. His own wife despised him and gave him no part in ruling the kingdom so, in a jealous rage, he burst into the Queen's room with a gang of ruffians, who dragged out her Italian secretary, David Rizzio, and murdered him. Not long afterwards Darnley himself was found dead in the garden of a house just outside Edinburgh. Whether Mary had any part in the plot is not known ; at all events, the Earl of Bothwell, a handsome daredevil, was charged with the crime and acquitted, thanks to the presence of his own troopers in the capital.

Three months later, Mary married Bothwell. Blinded by love, she seemed to have no idea that people regarded him as a murderer or that her own conduct had filled them with angry disgust. The Scots drove her from the throne in favour of her infant son James and imprisoned her in a castle on an island in Loch Leven.

One evening, her page-boy, Willie Douglas, stole the governor's keys, unlocked Mary's room and led her to the water's edge where they scrambled into a small boat and rowed across the loch to a group of waiting friends. In Glasgow, Mary raised an army but her troops were defeated by the Scottish Regent and she galloped away to avoid capture. Unable to find a ship to take her to France, she made for England to demand help from Elizabeth.

The English Queen, embarrassed by the fugitive's arrival, followed her usual custom of not giving a definite answer to a difficult problem. If she helped Mary to regain her throne, the Protestants would be up in arms. If she handed her back to her captors, Catholics everywhere would be furious and, if she let her go abroad, Mary would certainly try to obtain armed help from Spain or France. To avoid trouble, it was best to do nothing at all. So Elizabeth refused to see her cousin and kept her, half-guest, half-prisoner, in various northern castles for the next nineteen years.

Mary, whose beauty and health faded as the years of captivity went by, never lost her courage or the devotion of her friends to whom she wrote incessant letters appealing for help. Plans of escape and plots to recover her throne filled her days and nights, but there were spies watching her and informers paid to pass every scrap of information, including the letters which she believed to be secret, to Elizabeth's agents.

Meanwhile, at the English court, Elizabeth held the stage like a great actress. Surrounded by a brilliant company of nobles, ambassadors, poets, musicians and adventurers, she played whatever part suited her mood—imperious monarch, scholarly Queen, huntress, love-sick maiden or boisterous hoyden. She adored the flattery of handsome young men, but never lost her head like Mary and never trusted the real business of the kingdom to these splendid gallants, not even to her favourite, the Earl of Leicester. Serious matters were discussed with Mr Secretary Cecil, her faithful, tireless minister, though her tantrums and refusal to make up her mind often filled him and the Council with despair. In fact, she understood far better than her ministers the value of deceit and delay. She fended off her enemies by guile because England was not yet strong enough to defy them in war.

There was one matter in which the Queen exasperated everyone. Her ministers and Parliament wanted her to marry and provide England with a son and heir of the Protestant faith. This, they thought, would put an end to Catholic plots. But although the suitors came and went—princes and dukes from France, Spain, Sweden, Germany, Scotland and England—Elizabeth never gave one of them a definite answer. She loved the elaborate wooing but she knew that almost any husband would bring disaster to the country. If he was an English or a Scottish lord, he would arouse the jealousy of the nobility ; if he was French, Spain would declare war ; a Catholic would infuriate the Protestants and a Protestant husband would provoke the Catholics to rebellion, so she continued to play the marriage game until she was an old woman. In her heart she probably never intended to marry anyone, unless it could have been Leicester, and she was too cool-headed to marry for love.

Sea Captains

Meanwhile, in England's ports and seafaring towns, there was much talk of the riches which Portuguese and Spanish captains were bringing back from distant lands and Englishmen began to awake to a sense of what they were missing. In Edward VI's reign, old Sebastian Cabot was bribed to come home from Spain to advise on ocean voyages and it was Northumberland who sent out the first important expedition since the discovery of Newfoundland. Because the Portuguese and the Spaniards had divided the New World between themselves, and the way to India was also barred by the Portuguese, Sebastian advised a voyage to the north-east, in the belief that there was a sea-route round northern Europe which could lead to India, Cathay and the Spice Islands.

Three ships commanded by Sir Hugh Willoughby set out from Greenwich but in the icy seas off Lapland, Willoughby and two of the ships were lost. Richard Chancellor brought the third vessel into a bay of northern Russia, known then as Muscovy, and, finding no way to the sunlit East, he resolutely made a one-thousand-mile journey by sledge to Moscow where he attended the court of the Great Tsar, Ivan the Terrible. A treaty was made and, although Chancellor perished on his next voyage, the Muscovy Company was set up to promote trade in furs, hides, tallow and cloth with a country which was almost totally unknown to the rest of Europe.

This modest success did not appeal greatly to those who dreamed of gold and spices. William Hawkins, a merchant ship-builder of Plymouth, made several voyages to the coasts of West Africa where he annoyed the Portuguese by trading

187

with the natives for gold-dust and ivory. Nearer home, English ships cruised about the Channel in order to rob Spanish vessels on their way to the Netherlands and when King Philip protested indignantly to Elizabeth, she replied that she simply did not know that her subjects were behaving so badly. She was well aware, however, that William Hawkins had built himself a private fleet from the profits of piracy and more lawful trade and that he would loyally use it in the Queen's service.

William's son, John Hawkins, extended the family business when he sailed to West Africa to buy or capture negroes in order to sell them to the planters in Spanish America. Philip forbade trade of any kind by foreigners in those waters but, by a mixture of charm and threats, Hawkins induced the planters to do business with him. No one thought there was anything wrong in selling slaves and the Spanish settlers could not grow sugar or work the silver mines without slave labour.

Twice, Hawkins came home with a good profit and, for his third voyage, the Queen contributed one of her own ships to his little fleet. Once again, he traded successfully along the Spanish Main and was about to return when a gale damaged his ships so severely that he was forced to enter the Spanish port of San Juan in the Gulf of Mexico. Taken unawares, the Spaniards raised no objections and work had begun on the damaged vessels when a Spanish fleet was sighted approaching the port. Hawkins had seized the harbour fort and it would have been possible for him to keep the fleet out but Spain and England were officially at peace and he would get no thanks from his Queen for committing an open act of war. So he decided to allow the Spanish ships to come in and it was agreed that neither side should molest the other.

Two days later, the Spaniards made a sudden attack, killing all the English sailors ashore and opening fire on Hawkins' fleet and boarding some of his ships. In a furious hand-to-hand battle, the boarders were driven off and, having ordered his

189

cousin, Francis Drake, to take the little *Judith* outside, Hawkins set about his attackers so vigorously that he sank two galleons and silenced the rest. Meanwhile, the Spanish shore-batteries had reduced his flag-ship, the Queen's own vessel, to a wreck, so he transferred most of the gold and silver into the *Minion* and fought his way out of the harbour to join the *Judith* at anchor for the night.

Next morning, for some reason never explained, Drake had vanished, leaving his commander in the lurch with a leaky ship containing two hundred men and very few provisions. A hundred men volunteered to be put ashore in the hope of surviving until a rescue ship could reach them from England. In fact, some were killed by Indians and the rest captured by the Spaniards. Years later Hawkins managed to obtain the release of a few survivors.

Meanwhile, the *Minion* made a nightmare voyage to England and there were only fifteen starving men left alive when Devon was sighted. Drake had already arrived and the news of the Spaniards' treachery rang through England. From that day, there was undeclared war between English and Spanish seamen no matter where they chanced to meet.

While the Queen insisted upon keeping the methodical Hawkins at home to build the royal fleet, Drake made several voyages to the New World where, in revenge for San Juan, he plundered the Spanish settlements and attacked King Philip's ships without warning. During one of his shore expeditions on the Isthmus of Panama, a runaway slave showed him a giant tree with steps cut in its side. Ascending to a platform in the upper branches, Drake caught the first glimpse of the Pacific Ocean, which no Englishman had ever seen before :

" Almighty God," he murmured, " grant me life and leave to sail but once an English ship on that great sea."

His prayer was granted when the " Master Thief ", as the Spaniards called Drake, sailed the *Golden Hind* into the Pacific

and then, having robbed the Spaniards along the South American coast and claimed " New Albion " (California) for the Queen, continued westward to the East Indies, the Cape of Good Hope and back to Plymouth Sound. This voyage round the world was important, not so much for the gold and spices aboard Drake's little ship or because he was knighted by the Queen on his own deck, but because he had inspired generations of Englishmen to set out in search of knowledge and adventure.

For the moment, the magnet that drew men to the New World was the treasure which the Spaniards wrung from the conquered peoples of Central America. In the sea-towns of Devonshire, ship after ship was fitted out, manned and victualled for the pirate trade of the Caribbean where they joined up with the other freebooters, mostly French and Dutch, to hunt down the Spanish ships and to attack King Philip's treasure-houses ashore.

Sea Captains

Besides Drake, there were many others who were urged on by greed for gold and by the excitement of finding out more about a world which had recently become so much wider than anyone had ever imagined. They took risks and accepted their failures. Sir Richard Grenville, one of the most rugged of gentlemen-adventurers, had a scheme to explore the southern seas and the unknown continent that was supposed to lie there. This came to nothing, but then Sir Humphrey Gilbert and Sir Walter Raleigh proposed to start colonies in North America where Englishmen could build new homes and still remain loyal subjects of the Queen. In Newfoundland and Virginia, their schemes failed and Gilbert, on his way home in the tiny *Squirrel*, was lost in mid-Atlantic. Friends aboard an accompanying vessel caught a last glimpse of him as the storm-driven ships came momentarily close together ; he was on deck " with a book in his hand, crying out to us . . . ' We are as near to Heaven by sea as by land! ' "

Martin Frobisher, a rougher sea-dog than the courtiers, explored the coasts of Greenland and Canada in hope of finding a sea-passage to the East and he aroused great excitement by bringing home some black stones believed to contain gold. The Cathay Company was formed to make fortunes for those who invested in ships and smelting-furnaces, but when the stones proved to be worthless poor Frobisher had difficulty in finding support for any other ventures. John Davis carried on the Arctic explorations and, in the next reign, on yet another voyage in search of the North-West Passage, Henry Hudson was set adrift by a mutinous crew and left to perish in those icy seas. The Passage did exist but it was never to become the longed-for channel to the riches of the East.

War with Spain

While Drake was sailing round the world, war with Spain was becoming ever more certain. Elizabeth still tried to avoid an open conflict but Philip, exasperated by the impudence of her pirate-seamen, at last found himself in a better position to carry out his life's ambition to restore the Catholic religion in England and the Netherlands. France was no longer a danger to him and he had seized Portugal with all its wealth and shipping.

His Dutch subjects in the Netherlands had put up a most obstinate resistance but he intended to subdue them by the ferocity of the Duke of Parma's army. Near to collapse, the Dutch sent urgent appeals for more help to come out from England and Elizabeth was prevailed upon to send a small army under the command of Leicester, whose officers included his own nephew, Sir Philip Sidney.

This gifted young poet, beloved by everyone who met him, had been denied the chances of adventure by the Queen's fondness for him. She would keep her favourites at Court, giving them minor errands to carry out rather than allow them to risk their handsome necks on active service. However, once in the Netherlands, Sidney threw himself into the struggle with far more vigour than his uncle, and he had distinguished himself alongside the Dutch in several actions when the allies advanced to threaten the Spanish-held town of Zutphen. Parma

193

despatched supplies to his garrison and an English company was sent to intercept the food-convoy. Sidney joined the ambush-party at dawn ; the supply-wagons were heard approaching when the mist lifted to reveal, not the usual light guard, but a heavy escort of musketeers and cavalry. Outnumbered by six to one, the English charged the convoy. Sidney's horse was killed and he had remounted and was back in the fight when a musket-ball, fired at close-range, smashed his thigh. In agony, he was taken back to Leicester's camp where men ran to assist him, one of them bringing water, and

he was about to put his lips to the bottle when a soldier, horribly wounded in the same engagement, was carried by. Sidney saw the dying man's eyes light up with longing and he pushed the bottle towards him.

" Drink, thy necessity is yet greater than mine," he said.

Sidney died later of his wound and the action at Zutphen was notable only because the English felt that it was there that they lost the noblest of all their young men. After this, the war went badly and the Dutch were harder pressed than ever. They got relief only when Philip finally lost patience with England.

War with Spain

The event that made Philip decide to overthrow Elizabeth was the execution of Mary Queen of Scots. Efforts to release her had been going on for years ; plots and a rising of northern Catholics had been punished with a severity that would have made Henry VIII blink ; the Duke of Norfolk and others were beheaded and for the first time in the reign, Catholics of all classes began to suffer persecution. One day, an empty beer-barrel left the castle in which Mary was a prisoner and in the bung was a letter in which she apparently gave her consent to a plot to invade England and kill Elizabeth. The brewer's dray-man, in the pay of both sides, handed the letter to the government's agent. It was enough. For years William Cecil, now Lord Burghley, had been begging the Queen to put an end to this constant danger and now, sharply supported by Parliament, he demanded that she should sign Mary's death warrant. Elizabeth yielded and two days later, in Fotheringay Castle, Mary met her death with brave dignity. She left her claim to the English throne, not to her son James, but to Philip of Spain.

At once Philip began to plan the invasion. It was a long and costly business, for warships and troop carriers had to be built and other vessels were bought in various foreign harbours and taken to Spain to be fitted out. Stores, gunpowder, shot and armour had to be amassed in huge quantities, besides the crucifixes and holy banners which the priests would carry ashore. This great fleet, or Armada, would deal with any English warships in the Channel, but its prime purpose was to carry 20,000 men and stores to the Duke of Parma. Most of the front-line invasion army would be drawn from the Low Countries and it was Parma's task to bring his tough experienced troops to the coast and to construct the flat-bottomed barges that would carry them and their horses across the narrow sea to England.

Philip's immense preparations could not be kept secret and in England there was great activity in the shipyards and on the greens where men practised their weapons and drill. In a daring bid to delay the invasion, Drake sailed his fleet past the guns of Cadiz harbour to capture and destroy thirty-seven Spanish warships besides vast quantities of equipment. Philip ruefully made his losses good and in the summer of 1588 the great Armada set sail.

On July 19th the Cornish coast was sighted and the Spanish admiral, the Duke of Medina Sidonia, ordered the fleet to take up close formation, with his most powerful warships leading the way to protect the mass of troopships and store vessels. On either side and at the rear came more fighting ships to ward off attacks. Of the 130 vessels, about 50 were warships. The fleet moved very slowly under reduced canvas, for the wind was light and it was difficult to make the cumbersome troopships keep their positions.

The English had stationed Lord Seymour in the Downs to keep a watch out for Parma's barges but their main fleet lay at Plymouth under the command of Lord Howard, with Drake, Hawkins and Frobisher each commanding a squadron. Upon news of the Armada's arrival, they had some difficulty in getting to sea but by skilful use of the south-west wind, they sailed across the front of the Spaniards and worked up wind until they had the advantage and could begin to attack.

For a week, a confused battle took place in the Channel as the Armada held its course at a snail's pace and the English attacked along its edges. Three or four great galleons were disabled and many others were damaged, but the Spaniards' gunnery was better than Drake had expected and the English, getting desperately short of ammunition, had not succeeded in breaking the formation or causing havoc among the troopships when Medina Sidonia anchored off Calais. Word was sent ashore to Parma to ask what he proposed to do. In truth, he could do very little, for his troops and barges were still some miles further up the coast and the Armada's pilots were

197

unwilling to venture into those shallow waters. The wind began to rise and the Spaniards, with no sizeable port in which they could shelter, found themselves in a precarious position.

In England, where Grenville and Raleigh commanded the West Country levies and the Queen put on armour and went down to Tilbury to address her army, there was every intention of giving the Spaniards a hot reception if they got ashore. Meanwhile Howard, lying at anchor a mile to windward of the enemy, had sent to Dover for fireships. When these failed to arrive, eight large merchantmen serving with the fleet were hurriedly got ready and at midnight, on a strong east-going tide, they were sent blazing into the crowded anchorage. In panic, most of the Spanish captains ordered the anchor cables to be cut and their ships drifted off into the darkness, colliding with one another as they tried to get out to sea. At dawn, the great fleet was scattered along the coast and the English were sailing into the attack.

All day they pounded the enemy and tried to drive him on to the sandbanks while the Spaniards fought desperately to edge out into the North Sea. Thousands of their men were killed or drowned and their ships were horribly damaged but only one was boarded and a few others were grounded or sunk. A gale came up and the battered Armada could only flee northwards pursued by the English more for show than anything, for they had long since run out of ammunition. Only fifty-three ships, fewer than half of the great Armada, ever came back to Spain where Medina Sidonia, who had done far better than most of his captains, was reviled by everyone except King Philip. " I sent you out to war with men, not with the elements," he said. Philip had no intention of giving up after one failure and, with infinite patience, he began to prepare another fleet.

The English, astonished by the completeness of the enemy's overthrow, celebrated the victory with processions, bonfires and merrymaking. Their leaders, especially Hawkins and Drake, were well aware that the destruction of a single fleet had not removed all the danger. Drake wished to attack the rest of King Philip's navy, while Hawkins vainly put forward his own plan of intercepting the treasure ships before they reached Spain.

The sequel to the Armada's defeat was less glorious. Drake's attack on Corunna failed and the Spaniards' use of fast well-armed ships for the Atlantic crossing, in place of the old slow-moving galleons, enabled them to evade the English sea-robbers. The Queen, always tight-fisted over her Navy, became less inclined to spend money on ships than on land operations in France, Ireland and the Netherlands.

Old Grenville, roaring defiance to the end, died of wounds in the last fight of the *Revenge*. Frobisher was killed in an attack on a Spanish stronghold and Drake and Hawkins both died at sea during their last raid in the West Indies. The expedition was mismanaged from the start. The Spaniards knew that their old foes were coming and the two commanders, never at ease with each other since San Juan, could seldom agree. Hawkins, worn out after a lifetime of service to the Queen, could only think of her as he lay dying : " Assure Her Majesty of my love and loyalty," he murmured, and he left her £2000 of his own money to make amends for failing to win the Spaniards' treasure.

Drake also knew that he would never be given another fleet if he returned empty-handed but there was nothing to be had at San Juan, at Nombre de Dios or on the Isthmus of Panama and he was still muttering, " We must have gold," when the greatest of Elizabeth's sea-captains died at Porto Bello.

There was, however, one last triumph in the year of Drake's death, just eight years after the Armada. Philip had amassed another great fleet at Cadiz when Howard, Raleigh and Essex sailed in, captured the town and destroyed the shipping. The Queen grumbled that they brought home too little booty but she was growing old and crotchety, and Philip himself was dying. Their long struggle was at its end.

199

The Glory of her Reign

With the sense of peril gone, some of the sparkle went out of Elizabeth's reign. As danger receded, people had time to think about the difficulties at home and to voice complaints.

The new wealth which came from better methods of farming, from mining, cloth-making, manufacturing and sea-trading, was ill-divided. It flowed mostly into the pockets of the rich.

A feature of the reign was unemployment, something never known before in a country where for centuries every man's work, usually on the land, had been as necessary as the rain and the sunshine. But the population was growing; some men lost their strips of land or sold them cheap and drifted away to the towns; vagabonds swarmed the countryside and made the roads unsafe for travellers; London teemed with rogues and cutpurses and although Elizabeth's Poor Law made it the duty of every parish to look after its poor, there was still a host of men without work. In the capital, they became a rabble, living as best they could in shacks and hovels, surviving only by odd jobs, begging and crime.

As some went down, others rose in the world. Yeomen, farmers and merchants joined the ranks of the gentry who were now becoming more important than the nobles, and as the gentry realised their power, they wanted a greater share in the government. They regarded the old Queen with awe not far removed from worship but in the House of Commons they began to question her right to decide all things with her own ministers. From time to time, they dared to draw her attention to some pressing matter or even to hold up her " supplies " or taxes and she treated them with disdain or anger or gracious courtesy, according to her mood. They loved her and she knew it and took advantage of them but they were growing restive and the day would come when, instead of beseeching the monarch's will, they would demand their rights.

In the Commons, as in the towns and some country districts, the Puritans were growing in numbers and influence. Their strict way of life, their hatred of the Roman Catholics and disgust at Elizabeth's religious settlement appealed to some of the gentry and to many of the merchants and tradespeople who as aldermen and councillors ruled the towns. For her part, she detested them and did all she could to reduce their influence.

Thus, as she grew old, Elizabeth's triumphs and achievements were clouded by difficulties. Yet nothing could dim the glory of her reign. Englishmen had found a new pride and confidence in themselves. They rejoiced in their sailors, their growing trade, their new houses and all the signs of mounting prosperity in a bustling, adventurous age. New ideas and knowledge came flooding into the country, though Elizabeth's people, eager, quarrelsome and reckless, saw nothing to envy in what they knew of foreign places. To them, their capital with its splendid waterfront, their little towns fiercely claiming the right to a market and a mayor, their lovely countryside and, above all, their own freedom to say what they liked or to die saying it, seemed beyond compare. They were a young people with a matchless Queen and a score of heroes who could write poetry, storm a fortress or plant a colony beyond the seas.

But the greatest genius of the Elizabethan age was neither a courtier nor a man of action. He was the son of a Warwickshire corn merchant and glove-maker.

John Shakespeare, one-time alderman, town bailiff and man of business, fell into debt and disgrace and there were those who hinted that his son Will would speedily go the same way. The boy had no liking for steady employment but was forever idling his time on the green or at the inn, playing the fool to other idlers by imitating the strolling players who from time to time visited the town. When he was older and had hardly a penny to his name, he married a farmer's daughter, but odd jobs and a bit of poaching were not enough to keep a family on, so Anne and her babies went back to her father's farm and Will Shakespeare left Stratford-on-Avon to seek his fortune in London.

The capital was full of country lads who had come on the same errand and Shakespeare found life as hard as the rest. His ambition to be an actor was lowly enough, at a time when actors were looked upon as hardly better than vagabonds. However, he managed to attract the attention of James Burbage, owner of one of London's two theatres, who allowed him to make himself useful and presently to take some small acting parts. It was ill-paid work and there was little enough money to send home to Stratford until the company discovered that Will had more ability for writing than for acting. Mostly, they had to rely on stories and legends into which they inserted popular happenings and pieces of tomfoolery to amuse the crowd, but now they had found a man with a gift not merely for polishing up the old tales but for writing new plays with a host of characters who held the audiences spellbound. Nothing like these plays had ever been seen before and Shakespeare's

company began to thrive so mightily that he and his friend, Richard Burbage, decided to build a new theatre at Bankside.

Courtiers, merchants, shopkeepers and apprentice-boys flocked across the river to the *Globe* where, seated in the galleries or standing in the open pit, they cheered and wept at the first performances of Shakespeare's plays. The ne'er-do-well from Stratford made a comfortable little fortune, enough to buy a fine house in his home town and to pay off his father's debts. During the next reign, he himself retired there to his garden with its mulberry tree, and when he died he was buried in the chancel of his parish church.

The great Queen fell ill in March 1603 but would neither go to bed nor take medicine. She was tired and lonely, for her old friends and enemies were dead and she was saddened by the rebellion of her last favourite, the foolish, handsome Essex whom she had sent to the executioner's block. Only when her own end was very near would she name her successor: "I will that a king succeed me, and who but my kinsman the King of Scots?"

It was March 24th, 1603, and Sir Robert Carey set out to ride full speed to Edinburgh with the news that Elizabeth was dead and James VI of Scotland was King of England.

James of Scotland and England

James, the only child of Mary Queen of Scots and Darnley, was a delicate boy who could not stand without help until he was seven. In later life, he always leaned on the arm of an attendant, and when riding he had to be strapped to the saddle, though he was a keen and reckless huntsman. As a boy he was uncommonly clever at his lessons, and his guardians made sure that he had the best and sternest tutors who did not hesitate to birch him if his answers were less than perfect.

This timid, lonely child was merely a puppet in the hands of his violent nobles, but when he grew up he managed to subdue them by trickery and by playing one off against another. He survived all his difficulties and ruled Scotland a good deal better than most of his ancestors and he took care to do nothing to offend his cousin Elizabeth. He was determined not to lose his chance of inheriting England's wealth and even when his mother was sentenced to death, he secretly assured Elizabeth that his threats of invasion meant nothing at all. Sixteen years later, when Carey brought the joyful news, he lost little time in setting out for London. His patience had been rewarded. Without the loss of a single life, he had reached the throne which all the power of Spain and France had failed to win.

The English accepted their new monarch quietly, though his appearance and manners did nothing to arouse their enthusiasm. His clothes were shabby, he seldom washed and, apart from being lame, he spoke in the oddest fashion, spluttering and lolling out his tongue as though it were too big for his mouth. Moreover, although his conversation was often full of good sense and humour, he gave the impression that he thought himself so

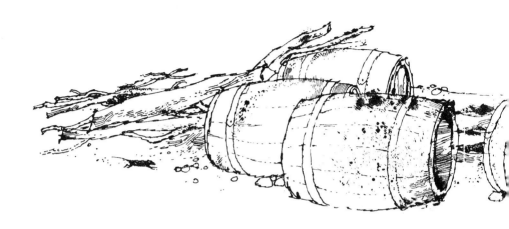

clever that everyone else was a fool. And, having come into a
fortune, he lavished enormous gifts upon the rowdy favourites
who accompanied him and he made it clear that he much
preferred Scotsmen to English courtiers.

There were nevertheless a good many who welcomed his
coming. Both the Puritans and Catholics hoped that James
would be kind to their religion but he soon disappointed them.
At Hampton Court, he treated a gathering of Puritan clergymen
with great rudeness and ended by losing his temper and shouting
that if they did not obey the rules of the Church of England, he
would harry them out of the kingdom. As for the Catholics, he
showed them much more politeness at first but, finding that this
alarmed Parliament, he allowed them to be persecuted by heavy
fines and the banishment of their priests.

In desperation, a handful of Catholic hot-heads made a plot
to kill the King and the leading men of the country when they
assembled for the opening of Parliament. The conspirators,
Robert Catesby, Thomas Percy and others, obtained the services
of Guy Fawkes, a Yorkshireman serving in Flanders with the
206

Spanish army, who was brought over to act as their explosives expert. A start was made by digging a tunnel from a cellar next to Parliament House but this was abandoned when Fawkes discovered that they could hire a large storeroom right underneath the House of Lords. Into this room he managed to take thirty-six barrels of gunpowder which he covered over with coals, firewood and bars of iron.

Leaving Fawkes as sentinel, the rest of the conspirators dispersed in order to collect arms and horses but among those in the secret was a man who did not wish to kill his kinsman Lord Monteagle. He therefore sent him a note, advising him not to attend the opening of Parliament but " to retire into the country . . . for . . . they shall receive a terrible blow ".

The letter was passed to the council and on November 4th, 1605, the Lord Chamberlain made a tour of inspection. When he looked into the lumber-room and enquired who owned the fuel, Fawkes coolly replied that it belonged to his master, a gentleman named Percy. This name excited suspicion but when, late at night, a party of soldiers arrived, Fawkes was

207

still at his post, doubtless hoping that courage and bluff would see him through. Arrested and taken before the King he did not deny his intention but, turning fiercely to the Scottish courtiers, declared that one of his objects was " to blow the Scots back to Scotland! " Under torture, he refused to give the names of any of the plotters until he learned that they had died at bay in a Staffordshire country-house. Then, so maimed that he could not walk to the gallows, he went bravely to his death.

The Gunpowder Plot ruined the Catholic cause in England, but instead of taking advantage of the situation, James I speedily fell out with Parliament. In conversation and in a book which he wrote, he put forward the notion of Divine Right, declaring that since a king was appointed by God, he could make or break his subjects " like men at chess ". They must always obey and their so-called rights and privileges were merely gifts from the King.

This kind of talk might have been all very well coming from Henry VIII but it would not do for Englishmen who, having beaten the Spaniards and overcome so many dangers, were in no mood to surrender their rights to a threadbare Scot. Their one check on the King was the ancient right to vote him the customs duties but when, instead of meekly doing so, they insisted on talking about their grievances, James dismissed them and ruled for ten years without Parliament.

By raising money in various ways, James could just manage as long as he did not have to pay for a war, and his policy, therefore, was to make friends with both the Catholics and Protestants abroad. He married his beautiful daughter Elizabeth to the leading Protestant Prince (or Elector) of Germany and he also made peace with Spain.

The First Colonies

The peace displeased those who looked on war with the Spaniards as a religious duty and a nice source of plunder. The most vigorous enemy of Spain was Sir Walter Raleigh, one of Elizabeth's favourites who had founded the colony of Virginia in her honour, had organised various expeditions against the Spaniards and had made a voyage to Central America where he believed he had only narrowly missed discovering El Dorado, the fabulous land of gold. However, early in the reign, Raleigh was arrested on a charge of treason and sent to the Tower where he spent the next thirteen years writing a history of the world and petitioning the King for his release. In return for freedom, he promised to bring him the gold of El Dorado.

While he was in prison, one of Raleigh's many schemes did get under way. His original colony in Virginia had failed, but in 1607 another party of settlers was sent out to America where they built a settlement named James Town. As in the past, it was not long before they were in dire straits. Many of the settlers were down-at-heel gentlemen, servants and petty tradesmen who had come out in hopes of an easy life, not to work hard felling trees and ploughing the soil. Bad leadership, perpetual quarrelling and semi-starvation almost destroyed them in the first year. One man saved the colony.

Even in an age of adventure, Captain John Smith's career was remarkable. A farmer's son, orphaned in boyhood, he had run away from his guardian, had fought the Spaniards in the Netherlands, had served as gunner on a French pirate-ship and had joined the Imperial Army to fight against the Turks in

209

Hungary. Thanks to his cunning and bravery, he rose to the rank of captain but, left for dead on a battlefield, he was taken prisoner and forced to work as a slave in Turkey and afterwards in southern Russia. Thence he escaped across the steppes to Poland and reached England penniless but still thirsting for fresh adventures. Having joined the colonists, Smith quickly sized up the ne'er-do-wells and made no secret of his contempt for their indolence while they, for their part, detested him and did their utmost to have him hanged.

Only when the colony was on the verge of starvation did the grumblers accept Smith as leader and he at once introduced discipline and regular work into the settlement. Unfortunately, on an expedition up-country, he was captured by the Red Indians and taken before the Great Chief whom he impressed by his courage and god-like wisdom. But the Chief, rightly believing that white men were his mortal enemies, nevertheless ordered him to be put to death. His life was saved by the little Princess Pocahontas who flung herself between the brave captain and the warriors who were about to dash his brains out.

Having contrived to return to the settlement where only thirty-eight men were still alive, Smith again restored its fortunes until, with fresh shiploads of settlers arriving every year, the colony began to prosper. Farms were established, tobacco (despite King James's opposition) became a profitable crop and, in increasing numbers, Englishmen came out to make their homes in North America.

The most celebrated of all the expeditions to Virginia never arrived there. In 1620, a party of Puritans, known as Separatists, who had already tried to settle in Holland, left England in a ship called the *Mayflower* in order to found a settlement in Virginia where they might worship God in their own fashion. One hundred and two " Pilgrims ", as they called themselves, were crowded below decks in the little ship and they had to endure the horrors of an Atlantic voyage during the autumn

gales. After ten weeks at sea the battered *Mayflower* dropped
anchor near Cape Cod, and the pilgrims found that they had
been driven hundreds of miles to the north of Virginia. Naming
the land New England, they decided to go ashore rather than
endure life at sea any longer. A settlement called New Plymouth
was started and, under their leaders, William Bradford, John
Carver and a stout little captain named Miles Standish, the
colonists settled down to face their first winter. When spring
came, barely half the company was still alive, for hunger, intense
cold and attacks by Indians had carried off all but the strongest.

Unlike John Smith's party, the " Pilgrim Fathers " were
ready to work and to live in harmony. By intense labour,

these steadfast men and women managed to support themselves and to raise crops so that at the end of the summer, when the harvest was in, they held a feast of thankfulness for God's mercies and this is still kept as a holiday called Thanksgiving Day in America. After this, the colony grew steadily, as the Indians were pushed back and new towns and villages were built.

Two years before the *Mayflower* sailed, Raleigh himself was dead. Shortage of money had prompted James to let him out of the Tower in order to fetch the gold from El Dorado. On no account must he molest the Spaniards. This was really an impossible condition for, even if the gold existed, it was absurd to believe that the Spaniards would tamely allow a party of Englishmen to carry it away. James probably hoped that if the expedition succeeded, he could pretend he knew nothing about it.

Overjoyed at his release, Raleigh collected a fleet of fourteen ships and set out for Guiana where the Spaniards, warned of his coming, were already on the alert. By the time the mouth of the Orinoco River was reached, Raleigh's health, ruined by long imprisonment, had broken down and he was too ill to accompany the exploring party which proceeded up-river in boats and pinnaces. He remained aboard ship and was still in his cabin when an exhausted survivor returned with a tale of disaster. Having gone ashore, the Englishmen had attacked a Spanish fort guarding the route inland and had been repulsed with heavy losses, including Raleigh's own son. The expedition was a complete failure and there was nothing left but to return home.

Raleigh made no attempt to escape punishment. The Spaniards were demanding his head and after King James had considered handing him over to them for trial, he decided instead that the death sentence passed years before should be carried out.

Ill, and disappointed in all his grand hopes, Raleigh met his end with cheerful courage, remarking to the bystanders at the scaffold, " I have a long journey to make and I must bid the company farewell," and then, running his thumb along the axe's edge, added, " Here is a sure cure for all diseases! "

But if Raleigh's death was meant to please the Spaniards, the royal marriage plan only led to worse ill-feeling than ever. Prince Charles and his friend Villiers, the Duke of Buckingham, made a secret trip to woo the Spanish Princess in her own country, but the foolish pair behaved with such conceited arrogance that the Spaniards declared they would rather throw their Princess down a well than see her married to such a fellow. So, having made themselves the laughing-stock of Europe, the silly young men came home without the lady.

James's hopes for the Protestant alliance failed just as dismally. His daughter and her husband became King and Queen of Bohemia but the Catholics drove them out within a year and Elizabeth, known as the " Winter Queen " from the shortness of her reign, went to live in exile in Holland where, penniless but gay, she held court to her admirers and raised a large family, including a headstrong lad named Rupert.

James died in 1625, leaving the kingdom much weaker than when he had come to England 22 years previously. Not all his difficulties were his own fault. Many of them went back to Elizabeth's time—the shortage of money, Parliament's demands to have a bigger say in the government, the rising influence of the Puritans and the widespread feeling that the Church of England was too much like the Church of Rome. But whereas Elizabeth had been able to manage her people and parliaments, James lacked her dignity and tact. He had no charm and he never knew when to yield gracefully. Worse still, he was never successful at anything. War with Spain had started again, the fleet and the army were hopelessly weak and Parliament trusted neither the King nor his ministers.

Charles I

The son to whom James left these difficulties was a much more attractive man than his father. Charles I looked like a king. Handsome, with a noble air of dignity, he was also kind and generous, a good husband and lover of beautiful pictures and artistic treasures. Regarding himself as a man of honour, he honestly believed that he conducted himself like a Christian gentleman, and he never understood that beneath his good qualities he had faults that were to bring him to ruin.

Charles had been brought up to believe in the Divine Right of Kings. Since God had made him a king, he was above the laws which common mortals had to obey and this allowed him to break promises and to deceive even his own friends. He lacked the power to make sharp decisions and had a genius for taking bad advice. Worst of all, his love of double-dealing made it impossible for anyone to trust him.

The reign opened badly. Buckingham, whom Charles adored, speedily arranged for him to marry Henrietta Maria, the King of France's fifteen-year-old sister. This annoyed the mainly Protestant Parliament which did not relish the prospect of a Catholic Queen bringing up her children in her own religion and, in any case, it would have been difficult to find a more unsuitable wife for Charles. Henrietta Maria was a pretty, featherheaded girl who grew into an obstinate woman, devoted to her husband but forever plaguing him with reckless advice to ignore Parliament and to rule as he pleased.

The war with Spain was disastrous. Buckingham shipped an army of hastily raised troops to Holland where the " raw and poor rascals " mostly perished of hunger and disease. A naval attack on Cadiz with rotten ships, some not refitted since the Armada, was a complete fiasco and then, as though in love with failure, Buckingham decided to make war on France! He had led an ill-equipped expedition to defeat at La Rochelle and was preparing further disasters, when an assassin killed him at Portsmouth.

By this time, Charles was on the worst possible terms with Parliament. Three times he sent them home when he found that the members, instead of granting him taxes, wanted to bring his friend Buckingham to trial. To obtain money for the war, he demanded " forced loans " from every county and imprisoned a number of the gentry who refused to pay. Parts of the country were placed under military law, men were seized for the army and soldiers were billeted upon householders without pay.

Charles was soon in such straits for money that he had to call Parliament and accept the Petition of Right, which declared the Englishman's right to be free from this kind of tyranny. But a King who believed in Divine Right did not feel obliged to keep promises and having brought the war to an end, he decided to rule without interference from a parliament.

For eleven years he managed to do so. The government muddled along on the money that could be raised by one means or another. Ship Money, a wartime tax paid in counties close to the sea, was demanded from all the counties and this aroused much indignation since it had not been passed by Parliament. John Hampden, a Buckinghamshire squire, refused to pay. The King's judges decided against him but he escaped arrest and was later to die fighting on Parliament's side. His example encouraged others to resist the royal tyranny.

Charles's chief ministers were now Sir Thomas Wentworth and William Laud, Archbishop of Canterbury. Wentworth believed in strong government and, as President of the Council in the north of England, he managed affairs with great efficiency, caring nothing for private persons but only for the good of the state. Made Earl of Strafford, he went to rule Ireland by the same stern system, which he called " Thorough ", and brought that turbulent country to a state of order it had not known for centuries. Wentworth's success made a deep impression on the King's opponents. They dreaded to think that " Black Tom Tyrant ", as they called him, might come to rule England in the same way.

If Strafford was feared, Archbishop Laud was hated. This sharp-tongued little man reformed the Church of England, inspected its parishes, punished the clergy for their errors and did his utmost to crush the Puritans by fines, imprisonment and penalties such as the cutting-off of ears.

Not content with wanting to make everyone in England worship in the same way, Charles and Laud rashly tried to do the same in Scotland. But most of the Lowland Scots were strong Presbyterians who believed in long sermons and plain services. Robes, ceremony and anything that reminded them of Catholic forms of worship filled them with horror. This did not please Laud and he ordered all Scottish churches to start using an English Prayer Book on a certain Sunday in 1637.

The cathedral of St Giles in Edinburgh was crowded when the Dean, wearing a white robe instead of the usual black, began to read the new prayers to his stern-faced congregation. He had not gone far when an old woman named Jenny Geddes, unable to bear what she believed to be the words of a Catholic service, started up, crying, "Thou false thief, wilt thou say Mass at my ear?" Snatching hold of her stool, she hurled it at the Dean's head, whereupon uproar broke out in the cathedral, with people shouting, "The Mass! The Mass! Down with Popery!" whilst others tore off the Dean's white surplice and well-nigh killed him. The Bishop himself was in danger until soldiers were called in to clear the church and restore order.

After this, all southern Scotland was up in arms. Thousands signed a document called the Covenant, binding themselves to fight for their form of religion, and Charles was forced to withdraw the hated Prayer Book. With his usual obstinacy, he would not leave the matter there. He decided to make the Scots obey by force of arms but, although he sent for Strafford to come over from Ireland, his unwilling conscripts, many of them Puritan lads, were no match for the determined Scots. In the Bishops' War, the Scots marched across the border, captured Newcastle and refused to go home until they were paid to do so. Having no money, Charles was forced to summon a parliament.

The Long Parliament, so called because it lasted for many years, assembled in 1640. Led by Hampden and John Pym, the members came to Westminster determined to make the King rule according to custom and law, and they were also set upon putting an end to Strafford.

" Black Tom " was about to train a royal army in the north, but he came to London at the King's request and advised him to arrest his opponents in Parliament. He himself went boldly to the House of Lords to hear an accusation of high treason which had been raised against him. " I will go and look my accusers in the face! " he said contemptuously.

When the Commons found that they could not prove treason, they passed a Bill of Attainder, an old way of getting rid of an opponent by simply declaring he was worthy of death. But the

Bill required the King's consent and Strafford, although lodged in the Tower, was certain that Charles would not allow him to be harmed. He had said so in a letter. Pym therefore took charge. His agents spread rumours of an attack on London, a mob was encouraged to surround the royal palace at Whitehall, where, rioting and howling for Strafford's death all day and night, they broke the King's nerve. With no soldiers for protection, terrified for his family's safety and upset by his tearful hysterical wife, he gave in and signed the death warrant.

At first Strafford could not believe that the King had betrayed him. Then he rose and said bitterly, " Put not your

trust in Princes." Three days later, Archbishop Laud, also in the Tower, thrust his hands through the grating of his cell door in order to bless Strafford as he passed by on his way to the scaffold. When the axe fell, the mob burst out in frenzied joy, " His head is off! Black Tom! His head is off! "

After this, the situation grew worse. The King agreed to all Parliament's demands but he was also looking round for support wherever he might find it. A Royalist party known as the Cavaliers began to arm ; street-mobs egged on by Puritan preachers, chanted, "No bishops!" and Pym drew up an insulting list of the King's faults.

Suddenly, Charles made up his mind to act. He would
arrest the leaders of the House of Commons, but instead of
doing so at once, he let the House of Lords know what he
intended and it was not until the following day that he went
to Westminster with 400 armed Cavaliers. Having seated himself in the Speaker's chair, he called out the names of five
members whom he regarded as his chief enemies. There was
no reply. Pym, Hampden and three others had already slipped
away to safety.

" Mr Speaker, where are those five members whose names
I have called? " demanded the King.

The Speaker fell upon his knees :

" Your Majesty," he replied, " I have neither eyes to see nor
tongue to speak in this place but as the House may direct me."

" 'Tis no matter," said Charles. " I think my eyes are as
good as another's. All my birds have flown."

Three days later, the royal family left London. While the
King moved to York to raise an army, the Queen went abroad

to pawn her jewels to buy arms and to try, with little success, to enlist support from foreign monarchs.

Parliament also made preparations for war. Pym engaged Philip Skippon, a professional soldier, to drill the citizen forces known as the Train Bands. Efforts were made to raise troops of cavalry, and in the country men like Hampden and Oliver Cromwell, a Huntingdonshire squire, began to train their tenants and the Puritan yeomen.

The first battle of the Civil War took place at Edgehill in the centre of England. Parliament's general, the Puritan Earl of Essex, advanced from London, but his cavalry was swept away by Prince Rupert, a tempestuous young giant who had fought in Germany and had come over to fight for his uncle, the King. While the Royalist horsemen gleefully pursued the enemy across country, a desperate struggle was waged on the field where Lord Lindsay, the King's commander, was killed and the Royal Standard was captured with Sir Edmund Verney's severed hand still clutching its pole. Just in time to save the day, Rupert returned with as many cavalry as he had been able to round up. Neither side had won but both claimed the victory and Essex sent urgent messages to Pym that London was in danger.

Rupert was all for dashing on to seize the capital before its defences had been put in order. With London taken, the war was as good as won. But Charles hesitated. He did not want any more bloodshed and his senior officers had already taken a strong dislike to Rupert's fiery contempt for their amateur soldiering. They advised caution and Charles moved away to Oxford where he set up his headquarters.

By the time the royal army advanced on London, Parliament's troops were barring the roads into the city. Entrenched in gardens and orchards where cavalry were useless, they put up so hot a resistance at Turnham Green that the Cavaliers retired to Oxford. However, for the next two years Charles seemed certain to win. Almost all the country districts, the west, all of

221

Wales and the north were on his side. Most (but not all) of the gentry came to serve him, bringing their sons and tenant-farmers, with good horses and all the money they could scrape together.

The Royalist cavalry outclassed all opposition and Rupert, hardly ever out of the saddle, was the despair of Parliament's leaders. They never knew where he would appear next, raising troops, setting up strong-points and winning cavalry engagements whenever he came across the enemy. When he and his brother Maurice captured Bristol, Parliament's defeat seemed only a matter of time. Its army was weak, especially in cavalry which Cromwell contemptuously described as " base and mean fellows . . . old decayed serving-men and tapsters "—and the Puritan squire went back to East Anglia to train a force of psalm-singing Puritans, men who feared God and would fight, not for plunder, but for religion and liberty.

Pym sent to the Scots for help ; Plymouth, Gloucester and Hull held firm and the tide of Royalist victories was checked. In truth, Parliament had the strength to win a long war, for London and most of the towns, with all their money and trade, were opposed to the King. So were the seaports and the navy, which made it difficult for Charles to obtain foreign help. As a result, he was always short of money, ammunition and reliable infantry.

Thus, after his early successes, the King's fortunes went downhill. Surrounded by scheming courtiers and quarrelsome generals, he never seemed able to take firm control or to find a strong man like Strafford to overawe the others. His friend Digby gave him nothing but bad advice and Rupert was too young and hot-headed to be supreme commander of the King's scattered forces.

In two great battles the war was lost. At Marston Moor, the Scots and Cromwell's new cavalry were too much for Rupert and, at Naseby, Fairfax and Cromwell destroyed the King's

infantry. After this defeat Charles could only wander aimlessly about with the remnant of an army. His last hope lay in Scotland. Here the valiant Marquis of Montrose had raised the Highlanders and in a most brilliant campaign had defeated the Covenanters and had taken Glasgow and Edinburgh. In response to the King's despairing pleas, he tried to persuade the Lowlanders to join him in a march into England but the clansmen were defeated, and when he learned that Charles had given

223

himself up to a Scottish army in Nottinghamshire, Montrose sorrowfully went to join the Queen in exile.

Rather than be captured by the Parliament men, Charles surrendered to the Scots. He thought they would treat him more kindly and he had hopes of winning them over altogether. But the Scots wanted their Presbyterian religion to be made the official religion of England, and when Charles would not agree they handed him over to Parliament.

Pym and Hampden were dead but it seemed clear that Parliament had won. The King was a prisoner at Holmby House and all that was needed was to make sure that he would rule properly after the army had been sent home. But the army would not go home. Their pay was much overdue and they were not sure that Parliament would favour the Puritan faith for which they had fought. So they appealed to Cromwell who cut through all the arguments by sending a troop of horse to bring the King to the army headquarters.

Charles went willingly and was soon lodged comfortably at Hampton Court. He was highly amused by the turn things had taken. With Parliament, the army and the Scots all at logger-heads, he felt sure that he would triumph : " When rogues fall out, honest men come into their own," he remarked. Thus he refused the army's generous terms on which he could have regained his throne. Instead, he haggled and argued and then astonished everyone by escaping to the Isle of Wight where he took refuge in Carisbrooke Castle.

As usual, he miscalculated. The governor was not a Royalist after all and kept his guest in close confinement. By this time, however, Charles was in touch with the Scots, promising to establish their religion if they would come to the rescue and overthrow the army. Cromwell was furious. In a short campaign his Ironsides defeated the Scots and he was then master of the situation.

He dealt with Parliament by sending Colonel Pride to

Charles I

surround the House with soldiers. As each member arrived, he was seized and turned away unless he supported Cromwell and the army leaders. After Pride's Purge, only about fifty members of the Long Parliament were left and it was now nicknamed the Rump Parliament since it was only the tail-end of one. But what was to be done with the King, " Charles Stuart, that man of blood ", as the Puritans called him? All faith in his word had gone. Only anger remained. The Rump Parliament did as it was told and voted to have the King put on trial for high treason.

Scarcely half of the one hundred judges who were called to Westminster Hall came to the trial. Charles refused to acknowledge the court or to answer any of the charges against him. He had ruled badly, not because he had meant to be a despot, but because he obstinately believed that as King he could do no wrong. Now, accused of terrible crimes and in peril of his life, he faced his enemies with the utmost dignity.

The court found him guilty of being a tyrant, traitor, murderer and public enemy and he was brought from St James's Palace through heavily guarded streets to Whitehall where a scaffold was erected outside the Banqueting Hall.

The people of London, and in the rest of the country, were horrified by the sentence but they had no leaders and the Royalists were weak and scattered. The army was in command and although Fairfax was opposed to execution, Cromwell was grimly determined.

On January 30th, 1649, Charles stepped on to the scaffold, looked towards the great crowd kept back by close ranks of soldiers and with calm deliberation knelt down at the block. When the executioner held up his severed head, a great groan burst from the crowd, " such a groan ", wrote an eye-witness, " as I never heard before and desire I may never hear again ".

Oliver Cromwell

After the execution, it was decreed that England should have no more kings. The House of Lords was done away with, all men were to be equal and the government was to be called a Commonwealth. But many people were outraged by the King's death. The Scots and Irish were particularly angry and in Ireland a rebellion broke out against the English government.

Cromwell therefore took the New Model Army to Dublin. He and his soldiers detested the Catholic religion and had not forgotten the massacre of Protestants during the previous Irish rebellion. With merciless severity Cromwell subdued the country, killing the priests, putting prisoners to the sword and transporting thousands more overseas. Catholics were deprived of their estates and the unhappy people were left to their poverty and despair. In Ireland, the name of Cromwell is still cursed.

Certain that he had only done his duty, Cromwell returned to deal with the Scots who had proclaimed the King's son Charles II. Montrose, who had come over from Holland, had already been captured and executed when Cromwell won a crushing victory at Dunbar, but young Charles still managed to slip away over the border, in the hope of raising the English Royalists. But they did not flock to join the Prince as he expected. They disliked the Scots and feared the Ironsides, so when Cromwell caught up with Charles at Worcester, his experienced army made short work of the Royalist troops.

With a handful of his officers, young Charles escaped from the battlefield and took refuge in the woods where an impoverished family of loyalists gave him shelter. With Cromwell's men scouring the countryside, it would have been folly to try to escape with a troop of horsemen, so the King's clothes were exchanged for a labourer's breeches and doublet, his face was daubed with soot and his long curls hacked off with a pair of shears. Thus disguised, he hid in thickets and barns, made an attempt by night to cross the Severn into Wales, and trudged on torn and bleeding feet to Boscobel House where, with a Royalist officer, he was obliged to perch for hours in a huge oak-tree from whose branches he could hear Cromwellian troopers discussing the reward for " Charles Stuart, a long dark man, above two yards high ".

After this, loyal friends moved him about from one house to another, often by night but presently by day when, dressed now as a serving-man to a colonel's sister, he rode to Bristol, failed to find a ship there and retraced his steps across southern England. By luck and his own cheerful presence of mind, he and his friends survived one narrow squeak after another. There were times when he had to pass close to a troop of Parliament's soldiers, to lie hid in the priest-hole of a Catholic home or in an upper room of a house where the servants were untrustworthy.

In one place his food had to be hoisted to him by rope and pulley in the chimney, and at another an old servant came to him, fell on his knees and confessed that he knew who he was. Indeed, the royal fugitive was recognised by dozens of persons but most were ready to risk their lives to help him, and the sharp-eyed ostler who reported his suspicions to the local military commander was just too late. Charles and his friends had left the inn and, taking a wrong turning, were soon lost in the darkness!

At last the skipper of a coal-brig was found who was willing to take two cavalier gentlemen across to France, and just six weeks after the Battle of Worcester the tattered figure of the King of England waded ashore on the coast of Normandy.

Meanwhile, " our chief of men ", as the Puritans called Cromwell, had become all-powerful. The plain-spoken country-man was a natural leader and it seemed to him that God had chosen him to take command. What he wanted was an England governed by justice and Godliness but the men of the Rump Parliament were interested only in keeping their own power. For the moment, he did not disturb them because there was much to do.

An efficient navy had to be got to sea to tackle the Royalist fleet with which Rupert was carrying on the war. In Robert Blake, a soldier with little experience of the sea, Cromwell found one of England's finest admirals, and after Blake had dispersed Rupert's ships, war broke out with Holland. The two countries were rivals in trade and there was ill-feeling because the Dutch would not recognise England's new government. Their admiral van Tromp hoisted a broom to his masthead to show that he had swept the English from the seas. But although Cromwell hated fighting against fellow-Protestants he had no intention of allow-ing his country to be defeated. A new fleet was fitted out and in a series of great battles, in which there were sometimes as many as 100 ships on either side, Blake and General Monk, another soldier-admiral, got the better of the Dutch and checked their sea power for the time being.

By now, Cromwell was thoroughly sick of the Rump Parlia-ment. It was governing badly and still refused to put an end to

229

its own existence, so, leaving a force of soldiers outside, he entered the House and sat for a while in his usual place, listening to the debate. Presently, he rose and began to speak of the wrong things Parliament had done. Pointing an accusing finger at one member after another, he reminded them of their sins and petty acts of meanness. His anger almost choked him. Suddenly clapping his hat upon his head to show that he held them in no respect, he burst out :

" It is not right that you should sit as a Parliament any longer. You have sat long enough! "

A member rose to protest. This was the last straw to Cromwell.

" I will put an end to your prating! " he shouted. " You are no Parliament. I say you are no Parliament."

Turning to a friend, he added, " Call them in! Call them in! " Thirty musketeers marched into the chamber and hustled the members out, as Cromwell continued to hurl reproaches at them for their evil ways. His eye fell upon the Mace, symbol of the Speaker's authority. " What are we to do with this bauble? " he asked one of the musketeers. " Take it away! "

The doors of the House of Commons were locked and there was no government in the land except the stern commander-in-chief of Britain's armies. He still wanted a good Parliament at Westminster but if he allowed free elections, the voters would undoubtedly choose a Royalist Parliament. So the Army Council of Officers did the choosing and put forward the names of 150 God-fearing persons, the first of whom was called Praise-God Barebone. But Barebone's Parliament had no notion of how to govern and its members soon agreed to abandon the task. At this, the army invited Cromwell to rule as Lord Protector.

For the first time in over half a century, England's name was respected on the continent. Peace was signed with the Dutch, alliances and trade agreements were made with the Protestant countries. Spain, still hostile, refused to allow free trade in the West Indies and persisted in capturing and persecuting English sailors whenever possible. When war broke out, Cromwell's power was plain to see, for the English fleet captured the rich sugar-island of Jamaica, intercepted the treasure-ships and sank sixteen galleons at Santa Cruz. On land, the New Model Army showed their fighting qualities in

Flanders where they beat a Spanish army and captured the frontier town of Dunkirk.

Great as they were, these triumphs did not make the Lord Protector happy. He tried his best to give the people good government with freedom of worship for all except the Catholics, but there was so much argument and discontent that he found himself becoming more of a tyrant than Charles I had ever tried to be. He dismissed judges who failed to support him, imposed heavy taxes to pay for the wars and when murmurings grew louder, he divided the country into districts under Military Law. His power depended not upon the laws of the land and the people's goodwill but solely upon the swords and muskets of his soldiers, and since the major-generals who ruled the local districts were strict Puritans, all kinds of harmless pleasures and sports were forbidden.

The people hated Cromwell's rule but they feared him too much to attempt to overthrow him. Power brought him no contentment but deep sorrow and the fear of assassination. Only in his family and his horses did he find happiness, and the death of his favourite daughter broke his heart. After ruling the country almost single-handed for nine years, he died at Whitehall, worn out by the difficulties of the task which he had taken upon himself.

His son Richard succeeded him but " Tumbledown Dick " had no wish to be a dictator and he sensibly resigned and went home to the country. By now even the army realised that the people wanted a king and a parliament as in the old days, and when General Monk marched down from Scotland to arrange matters, there was no opposition to the King's return. On May 28th, 1660, Charles II rode into London amid scenes of joy never known before or since that day.

Charles II

The gallant young man who so narrowly avoided capture after Worcester, had known hard times in exile. Penniless, surrounded by bickering cavaliers and idle companions, he had learnt to hide his own feelings and to trust no one. When he " came to his own " and recovered his kingdom, he still possessed charm and an easy smile but although he was clever and interested in sport, science and architecture, he was absolutely heartless and seemed to have no aim in life except to enjoy himself. Beneath this lazy good humour there was a hard determination to rule as he pleased and, at all costs, never to be forced to go on his " travels " again.

The new Cavalier Parliament was filled by the King's friends but although those who had condemned Charles I to death were made to suffer, there was a general pardon for the rest. Indeed, many a brave ruined Cavalier who had lost sons, money and land, complained of the King's ingratitude but, apart from remembering Rupert and some who had helped him to escape, Charles did little for his father's supporters. For the sake of peace and quiet, this may have been wise, but the Cavalier

233

Parliament insisted on passing harsh laws against those who did not conform to the Church of England and who were known as Nonconformists or Dissenters. Some of them, like John Bunyan who began to write *Pilgrim's Progress* in Bedford jail, endured years of imprisonment for their religious beliefs.

The Scots also suffered from these laws. Charles II had no intention of respecting the Covenant, and he not only brought back the bishops to Scotland but allowed them to turn 300 " Covenanter " ministers out of their churches. In south-west Scotland, faithful congregations defied the law by gathering together to listen to their banished minister in some secluded spot on the hillsides. The Earl of Lauderdale, in charge of Scottish affairs, retaliated by sending dragoons to break up the meetings and collect fines at the bayonet's point. Instead of being cowed, the Covenanters broke into open rebellion and some of their leaders were punished by hanging and torture. Hundreds were herded aboard ships and taken into exile in the West Indies.

Early in Charles II's reign, war broke out again with the Dutch. The King's brother, James, Duke of York, Prince Rupert and General Monk were capable admirals and the English seamen fought with their usual bravery, so that for a time, the enemy was held in check. But the navy was scandalously mismanaged. Dishonesty in the shipyards meant that the fleet was badly equipped and forever short of stores and victuals ; the sailors' pay was always in arrears and ships which ought to have been at sea were frequently laid up for economy. In 1667, the Dutch succeeded in sailing up the Thames and into the Medway to burn several warships and to carry off the *Royal Charles* as a prize. Furious at this humiliation, the nation laid the blame on Clarendon, the King's unpopular minister, and on Charles's extravagant gifts to his friends and lady-loves, but it was really Parliament's meanness that had brought the navy into such a dismal state.

Before the startling naval reverse at Chatham, the nation had already suffered two disasters in the capital. For many years, a disease known as the Plague was a regular visitor to towns during the summer months, but in 1665 London suffered an outbreak that was far more severe than usual. The sickness began unusually early in the year and, as the weather grew warmer, it increased at a tremendous rate in the city where filthy streets and rat-infested buildings were perfect breeding-places for disease. So many people became ill or panic-stricken that houses and shops were closed and business came to a stand-still. Deaths rose to close on seven thousand in one week and, with the churchyards full, bodies had to be carted away by night to be buried in great pits. The court and all who could fled to the country, and in the stricken capital hardly a soul dared venture out of doors : " Lord, how empty the streets are," wrote Samuel Pepys in his diary, for he and stout old Monk had stayed behind, " and they tell me that in Westminster, there is not a physician left, all being dead."

With winter's coming, the Plague slowly died away, but in the next year another disaster made the populace feel that the wrath of God had descended upon them. In September, 1666, after a long spell of dry weather, a fire broke out in a baker's shop in Pudding Lane, near London Bridge. Fanned by an easterly wind, the flames leapt from house to house and across the narrow streets until almost the entire city, from the Tower to the Temple, was blazing. Water-buckets, the primitive fire-engines and even the old method of pulling down houses were useless to check such a fire and it was not until gunpowder was used to blow up whole blocks of houses that the flames were brought under control.

In four days more than 13,000 houses, churches and public buildings had been destroyed, besides property valued at nearly ten million pounds. When at last the Great Fire was over, a wonderful opportunity presented itself to build a noble city with

235

wide streets and views of the river. Sir Christopher Wren made such a plan but the owners of houses and shops insisted on rebuilding their property in very much the same places as before. However, brick and stone largely took the place of timber, London became the most handsome capital in Europe and Wren devoted his genius to rebuilding the churches and St Paul's Cathedral.

The rest of the reign was an uneasy tale of plots, discontent and religious bitterness. Charles always admired France and the magnificence of his cousin Louis XIV who, from his sumptuous Palace at Versailles, was intent upon dazzling the world with his military conquests. Alarmed by the French King's ambition, Britain, Holland and Sweden formed an alliance to protect themselves, but Charles made a secret treaty with Louis, promising to help rather than to hinder his plans. In return for a large income, he would use the English fleet

against Holland and restore the Roman Catholic religion in England when the time was ripe.

By all the rules of war, little Holland should have been speedily crushed. But at sea the Dutch were a match for the English and on land William, Prince of Orange, fought with stubborn courage, even flooding great areas of his country to check the French armies. When Charles had come to the end of his money, he had to leave France to carry on the war alone but he still kept on good terms with Louis and was able to draw enough money from him to be able to do without Parliament for the latter part of his reign.

But he did not dare to introduce his own religion which he had kept secret for so many years. Riots and plots taught him how deeply, if unfairly, the people hated Roman Catholicism, and it was only on his death-bed that he finally admitted his faith.

James II

Because Charles II left no heir, his brother James, Duke of York, came to the throne. He started with great advantages, for Parliament voted him a good income for life and he could always count on Louis XIV for friendship. But James was a Roman Catholic and, unlike his brother, he did not keep his beliefs to himself. Almost at once, he made it clear that he meant to favour the Catholics.

A Protestant plan to overthrow James was launched from Holland. The leaders, a Scottish Covenanter called the Earl of Argyll and the handsome young Duke of Monmouth, decided to raise a two-fold rebellion. Argyll crossed from Holland and endeavoured to raise the Highlands by sending a fiery cross through the glens as a sign to the clansmen to prepare their weapons. Through jealousy and bad management, the rising collapsed and Argyll was taken and executed. Monmouth's rebellion in south-west England was a more serious threat to James.

The Duke landed at Lyme Regis and was proclaimed King

at Taunton. Thousands of Protestants came in from the surrounding countryside to join his standard but farm lads armed with scythes and old muskets were no match for the King's soldiers. At Sedgemoor, the royal army repulsed a brave attack by the rebels and then hunted them mercilessly across the countryside. " King Monmouth " was found hiding in a ditch and although he grovelled piteously before his uncle, he was speedily executed.

The King's vengeance did not end there. He sent Judge Jeffreys down to the west country where, at the Bloody Assizes, this ferocious man gleefully had over 300 persons put to death, including one poor woman whose only crime had been to feed a few exhausted fugitives. Hundreds of others were sent to slavery in the West Indies.

Two risings had been snuffed out so easily that James felt that he could now go ahead with his plans. An army, officered mostly by Catholics, was assembled just outside London, Catholics were appointed to high positions, judges who disagreed with the King were removed from their posts and Parliament itself was dismissed. James then announced what was called the Declaration of Indulgence. This abolished the laws against people who did not belong to the Church of England, and James thought he had made a master-stroke to win over the Dissenters. But the Dissenters saw through the trap. If they were to be free, so were the Catholics and they feared the Catholics far more than the Church of England. James ordered the Declaration to be read in every church but nearly all the clergymen refused to obey and seven bishops signed a paper telling the King that he was breaking the law. " This is rebellion," cried James, and ordered the bishops to the Tower.

As the prisoners were taken through the streets, people knelt down to ask for a blessing and by the time the Archbishop and his six companions were brought to trial, the whole country was seething with indignation. A jury found the bishops " Not Guilty " and that night the people lit bonfires, rang the bells and placed in their windows seven lighted candles, one taller than the rest. On that same night, some of the leading men of the kingdom sent a message to Holland asking William of Orange to come to England to save their liberties and the Protestant religion.

It was not only the trial of the bishops that brought about James II's overthrow. He had two grown-up daughters, Mary, wife of William of Orange, and Anne. Both were Protestants. But after his first wife died, James had married an Italian princess who was expecting a baby at about the time of the bishops' arrest. The child was a boy and although the story was put round that he was not the Queen's child at all but had been smuggled into the palace in a warming-pan, most people recognised the truth—that James now had a son and heir. This was serious news for the Protestants, because it meant that, unless they acted quickly, England would have a line of Roman Catholic monarchs.

Shortly after receiving the letter of invitation, William of Orange landed at Torbay in Devonshire with a small army and advanced cautiously inland.

James came out from London to oppose the invader but, apart from his Irish troops, he could not rely on his soldiers to fight. While he hesitated, he learned that Lord John Churchill, his best general, had gone over to William's camp and that his daughter Anne had deserted him. At this news, he fled, only to be captured by some fishermen and brought back. His presence was so embarrassing that he was allowed to escape a second time and his sole gesture of defiance was to drop the Great Seal into the Thames as he was rowed down river in a small boat. Without a blow being struck, the Glorious Revolution was over.

William and Mary

Although William of Orange's mother was an English princess and he had married James II's daughter, the Dutchman did not like England and had no wish to become its King. He agreed to come only because he wanted to save his beloved Holland from Louis XIV, and when he found that the English Parliament expected him to be lower than his wife, that is, to be Regent rather than King, he offered to go home again. At this, Parliament changed its tune and agreed to make William and Mary joint sovereigns. After his wife's death, he became William III.

Nor did the English people like " Dutch Billy " very much. He was a thin, misshapen little man, with a dry manner and no smiles or graces. However, he needed England's help and England wanted a Protestant on the throne. So they made the best of each other, and in time people came to respect William's courage and unflagging spirit.

241

In the more distant parts of Britain, support for James II was not dead and William had to deal with risings in Scotland and Ireland. He sent an army, under General Mackay, to attack Graham of Claverhouse, now Viscount Dundee, who had raised the Highlanders for King James. In the Pass of Killiecrankie, the half-naked clansmen routed the regular troops with one murderous charge, but their victory was useless, for a bullet killed Dundee and, without a leader, they soon drifted away to their glens.

Meanwhile, James II had arrived in Ireland with money and arms provided by Louis XIV. The Irish, ready to help James in order to get rid of their Protestant landlords, laid siege to Londonderry where the Protestant inhabitants, faced by certain death if they surrendered, held out desperately for 105 days. At this point, William himself landed and marched towards Dublin. James had drawn up his army along the bank of the river Boyne but, throwing caution aside, William ordered his troops to ford the river and attack. They did so with such spirit that James again lost his nerve and galloped away to take ship to France. Southern Ireland was subdued and peace was made on the understanding that the Irish Catholics should have decent liberty, but once they had laid down their arms they were treated as harshly as ever.

In Scotland, the government declared a pardon for all who had fought in the recent rising if they would take an oath of loyalty to King William. All the chiefs took the oath except MacIan, chief of the Macdonalds at Glencoe. He delayed for as long as possible and did not arrive at Fort William until the very last day, only to find that there was no one there to accept his oath. Hampered by snow, he made his way to the next town and took the oath six days late ; however, he had obeyed the law and he went home satisfied that all was well.

But Sir John Dalrymple, the Master of Stair, hated the Macdonalds, " that sect of thieves " he called them, and so did the Campbells. As the King's adviser, Dalrymple obtained permission to punish the chief for his delay and for this purpose he sent a force of 120 Campbells to Glencoe. With Highland courtesy, the old chief quartered his visitors as comfortably as possible in the cottages scattered up and down the glen. For more than a week, all was friendliness and good humour until the fatal morning when the Campbells rose early and slaughtered their hosts, killing them as they slept and shooting down those who tried to escape to the snowbound hills.

This crime was pinned upon William by his enemies. Certainly, he signed the order to punish the Macdonalds but it was doubtful if he understood what Dalrymple meant to do. What was certain was that the massacre of Glencoe kept alive the Highlanders' hatred of the English government.

William, however, was less concerned with the puzzling behaviour of his British subjects than with Louis XIV's designs. Helped by the English fleet, he beat him at sea and fought him on land in the Netherlands where, in a long drawn-out war of sieges and retreats, neither side gained much advantage. Louis' colossal extravagance was ruining France and he was glad to make peace for a time.

William was well satisfied to have saved Holland until, quite suddenly, all his life's work seemed to be ruined. The King of Spain was dying and Louis XIV's grandson appeared likely to gain the throne and all the Spanish possessions. France and Spain united would dominate Europe, and if this should happen Holland and England were doomed. William was preparing to fight again when his horse stumbled and threw him from the saddle. His injuries, trifling to a stronger man, proved too much for a frail body weakened by ceaseless work and campaigning. He died and was succeeded by his wife's sister, Anne.

Queen Anne

Queen Anne was an amiable woman whose dull-witted husband, George of Denmark, played no part in British affairs, so that she was entirely under the influence of Sarah Churchill, Duchess of Marlborough. The masterful Sarah saw to it that her husband was made commander of the army, and between them they practically ruled the country.

Fortunately, Marlborough was a great soldier, probably the greatest in Britain's history. Ambitious for fame and wealth, he was also charming and patient with his difficult Dutch allies and, rare in those days, he cared for his men, saw to their food and pay and lived with them so plainly on campaign that, in affection, they called him " Corporal John ". At first, his difficulties were immense. The British and Dutch armies were small, the Dutch rulers constantly interfered and his German and Austrian allies were proud and quarrelsome. However, having forced back the French in the Netherlands, Marlborough made a lightning move into Austria to save Vienna.

At Blenheim, he found the French and Bavarian army in a strong position, but declaring, " I rely on the bravery and

244

discipline of my troops," he won a victory so complete that it changed the course of the war.

A further series of victories reduced the spirit of the French soldiers until, at the mere mention of Marlborough's name, they felt that defeat was certain. France was beaten almost to her knees and old Louis XIV was appealing with pathetic dignity to his people to defend their own soil when Marlborough, the general who never lost a battle or failed to take a fortress, was dismissed from his command in disgrace.

He had always had enemies who resented his success and Sarah's influence but, although they put round stories that he enriched himself out of the money meant for the soldiers, they could do nothing as long as the Duchess controlled the Queen. But Anne had at last grown tired of Sarah's tantrums and she began to listen instead to the soothing voice of Mrs Masham, a lady whose Tory friends hated the great general. After a furious quarrel, the Queen plucked up courage to dismiss Sarah from the court. Marlborough's fall followed and the war with France was speedily brought to an end.

Britain gained Gibraltar, part of Canada and a good deal of respect and dislike abroad. Holland, weakened by the long

245

war, kept her freedom and France remained too exhausted to trouble the rest of Europe for the next quarter of a century.

The most important event of Queen Anne's reign at home was the Union with Scotland. Although the two countries had had the same King since the accession of James I and VI, Scotland had kept her separate Parliament, Church and trade. It was a trading disaster that actually hastened the Union, for the Scots put a great deal of money into the Darien Scheme, an ambitious plan to make the Isthmus of Darien (Panama) into the trading centre of the world. The scheme failed and the Scots, sore about their losses, were inclined to put the blame upon the greedy English who not only kept their own trade to themselves, but had done their best to ruin their neighbours' venture. However, when tempers had cooled, it was agreed that while Scotland kept her own Church and law courts, the two countries should have one Parliament, equal trading rights and the same coinage and weights and measures. The United Kingdom of Great Britain came into existence in 1707.

Queen Anne had a very large family but all her children died in infancy. As she grew older, she became ill and low-spirited. It seemed to her as if God had punished her for deserting her father and she hoped that her half-brother James Edward Stuart would come to the throne. Parliament and a majority of the people were totally opposed to a Catholic King, and when they found that James refused to change his religion, they began to look elsewhere for a Protestant monarch. They found one in Germany where George, the grandson of Elizabeth, "the Winter Queen", James I's daughter, was ruling the small kingdom or electorate of Hanover. George knew next to nothing about England but he *was* a Protestant. To keep the Stuarts out, Parliament invited him to accept the crown and although some of Anne's friends still hoped to bring in James Stuart, the Queen's sudden death upset their plans. At once, the Elector of Hanover was proclaimed King George I.

Hanover and Stuart

From the moment of George I's arrival, it was obvious that
Parliament would rule the country. A German king who spoke
no English could not have interfered if he had wanted to, and
George soon gave up attending meetings of the council. For his
part, the English were welcome to get on with their own affairs.
He much preferred Hanover where the docile people did as they
were told and he went back there as often as possible. George
was a stout, plain man with a good deal of common sense but no
charm or majesty. He was known to hate his eldest son and to
have shut his own wife up in a castle for life and there was little
about him or any of the Hanoverians to arouse the people's
affection. For the next hundred years, the royal family was
generally unpopular.

Almost at once the Jacobites, as the Stuart supporters were
called, tried to recover the throne. In 1715 the Earl of Mar

invited a number of Highland lords to a hunting-party which in reality was a gathering of the clans. The Standard of James VIII, " the Pretender ", was raised and from the north of England a smaller force of Jacobites, wearing the white cockade in their caps, moved towards the border.

If Mar had been anything of a general, he could have easily taken Edinburgh but " Bobbing John " had no notion of how to lead an army. He gave the government's troops, under Argyll, plenty of time to oppose him and when they met at Sheriffmuir, the battle was so half-hearted that neither side knew which had won. As a scornful jingle expressed it :

> " We ran and they ran, they ran and we ran,
> And we ran and they ran awa', man! "

James Edward Stuart arrived late from France bringing no help because Louis XIV had died, and in any case his mournful expression did nothing to fire his supporters' hearts. The " Fifteen " rising collapsed and the Pretender, taking Mar with him, slunk miserably back into exile. Lack of preparation and want of courage at the top had ruined the Stuart cause. When the next chance came, it was too late. By then Sir Robert Walpole had done his work.

Walpole was a wealthy landowner from Norfolk who became the country's chief minister during George I's reign. In fact, he was Britain's first Prime Minister, though that name was not yet in use. Stout, red-faced and jovial, Walpole believed that peace and quiet were better for the country than war. So he kept taxes low, encouraged manufacture and trade, and craftily smoothed away troubles whenever they arose. "Let sleeping dogs lie," was his answer to all problems and, under his rule, the country had twenty years of peace.

George II, who succeeded his father in 1727, heartily disliked Walpole, but Queen Caroline, far cleverer than her husband, persuaded him to keep the Norfolk squire in power. But as time

went by the old fox became unpopular. By cunning and bribery he kept control of everything in his own hands and some of the younger men felt that he cared nothing for their ability. Moreover, the nation was bored by peace and when a quarrel broke out with Spain, and a certain Captain Jenkins claimed to have had one of his ears cut off by a Spaniard, the people clamoured for war. At its outbreak they rang the church bells as though victory had already arrived. " They are ringing the bells now," remarked Walpole drily, " but they soon will be wringing their hands."

The war went badly, partly because Walpole himself had neglected to spend money on the navy and the army. Britain found herself fighting for Queen Maria Theresa of Austria against France and Spain and, on the continent, George II himself led an army to protect his cherished Hanover. At Dettingen, the last battle in which a British King took the field, a lively horse carried him towards the rear but, dismounting, he stoutly declared that he would fight on foot since his legs would never run away. Sword in hand and roaring, " Steady, my brave boys, steady! " he brought his troops to victory.

Shortly afterwards, however, his son, the Duke of Cumberland, was defeated by the French at Fontenoy. At this, the spirits of the Jacobites rose, especially as they now had an inspiring leader in Charles Edward, the handsome son of the Old Pretender.

Unfortunately for his hopes, a French invasion fleet was scattered by storms, and after this the French decided that the Scottish and English Jacobites were too weak to be worth helping. So when Charles Edward landed in Scotland to win back his father's kingdom, he was accompanied by only seven friends. Without large-scale French help, it was madness to attempt an uprising and the Prince received a cool reception from the Scottish chieftains.

But Charles Edward did not appeal to common sense. In

the name of honour and loyalty, he asked the clansmen to follow him and they could not refuse. When Cameron of Lochiel spoke of his doubts, Charles Edward retorted, " Lockiel may stay at home and learn his Prince's fate from the news-papers."

" Not so," cried Lochiel, " if you are resolved on that rash undertaking, I will go with you! "

Within days, over two thousand Highlanders had joined the Jacobite army which moved to Perth and on to Edinburgh where the Old Pretender was proclaimed King. A small force under General Cope was easily routed at Prestonpans and, for the next six weeks, Bonnie Prince Charlie held court at Holyrood winning the hearts of all who met him, but waiting in vain for news of a general uprising in his favour. Worse, the delay gave the government time to bring Cumberland and his army back from the continent.

At length, in November, 1745, the march on England began. Taking the westward route to avoid an English army at New-castle, Charles captured Carlisle and entered Lancashire with an army of about 5,000. The English Jacobites did not stir. Thirty years had passed since the last Stuart fiasco and under Walpole's comfortable rule, they had learned to put up with the Hanoverians. On December 4th, when Charles Edward reached Derby, only 130 miles from London, his discouraged chieftains refused to march another step. Their men were already begin-ning to slip away and two English armies lay between them and home. It was madness to go on. But at this stage it was probably folly to go back. They did not know that London was in a panic and King George was making ready to leave. Anything could have happened if they had gone on, but on " Black Friday " they turned about and began the long march back. Charles, who had formerly marched gaily with the troops, now rode in dejected silence.

Cumberland was presently at their heels but Lord George

251

Murray beat him off and the Prince and his army reached Glasgow after marching six hundred miles in less than two months. They defeated a royal army at Falkirk but instead of capturing Stirling Castle, Charles was persuaded to retire into the Highlands. Cumberland came on remorselessly. At Culloden Moor, near Inverness, he at last caught up with the Jacobite army and although the Highlanders fought with all their desperate valour, they were utterly defeated. Two officers seized Charles's bridle and forced him from the field and Cumberland was left to crush resistance with such blood-thirsty cruelty that he earned the name of " Butcher ".

With a price of £30,000 upon his head, Charles wandered about the Highlands and the Western Isles for five months, hunted by the government troops but protected by the loyalty of people to whom thirty guineas would have been a fortune. Not one betrayed him. In caves and huts, they fed and clothed him and led him by secret paths to fresh hiding-places.

Once, when capture seemed certain, a lady named Flora MacDonald brought him a dress in order to disguise him as " Betty Burke ", her Irish maid, and, although the tall " maid " took overlong strides and managed her skirts clumsily, Flora succeeded in taking the Prince past the soldiers to another island.

At last a boat was found to carry the gallant youth away to France. He never returned to Scotland. Many years later, when an unhappy old drunkard named Charles Edward Stuart died in Rome, his name was forgotten and unmourned except in Scotland. There they still cherished the pattern of " Betty Burke's " dress and sang of that brave lad " born to be King ". But the Jacobite cause was dead.

Rise of an Empire

For more than a century, despite all the troubles at home, Britain—and England in particular—had been getting richer. Trade produced bigger and quicker profits than farming or manufactures, and more English ships put out to sea for lawful trade than for the old-style piracy. There were still expeditions to the Spanish Main but men like William Dampier who lived for years among the buccaneers and ended by becoming a celebrated navigator, tended to become merchant captains rather than sea-robbers. They could find employment with various enterprises such as the African Company, the Levant Company in the Mediterranean, the Hudson Bay Company and the rich East India Company. There were sugar plantations in Barbados which produced more wealth than all the North American colonies, fisheries off Newfoundland and the Baltic trade in rope, timber and tallow. As the profits came home to the rich merchants and were spread out to lesser business-men and tradesmen, England took on a more gracious, prosperous air.

Trade had to be fought for and protected. The Forty-five

253

Rise of an Empire

Rebellion was only a part of the wider struggle into which Britain was drawn. The wars on the continent between Frederick the Great of Prussia and most of the rest of Europe did not interest the British government very much, apart from the King's nervousness for Hanover.

But across the oceans were matters of great importance. The Spaniards were still trying to keep all the South American trade to themselves, and the French plan to link their colony in Canada to Louisiana in the south was a threat to the English colonies along the coast of North America. Since Captain John Smith's time, more than a million settlers had made their homes there and as they pushed inland, building villages and clearing the woods for farms, they found that the French, often in alliance with the Red Indians, were their enemies.

In India there was much fiercer rivalry. For over a century the East India Company had been sending home cargoes of luxuries, and there were French merchants engaged in the same profitable business. The country itself had fallen into disorder. There was no strong government but a number of Indian princes constantly at war with each other. The Europeans therefore built forts and enlisted local troops to protect their warehouses and an English or a French governor, with a few disciplined troops under European officers, could become extremely powerful by aiding one prince against another. It was clear that if one side ousted the other, the victor would possess the richest trade in the world.

For a time the French made much better progress. With a clever governor named Dupleix, they gained control of most of southern India and were on the point of putting an end to English influence when a harum-scarum clerk, who had recently taken to soldiering, changed the situation.

Robert Clive was taken prisoner when the French captured Madras, but having escaped by disguising himself as an Indian, he joined the East India Company's force and volunteered to
254

attack Arcot, capital of the French-controlled province. He expected that this would draw off a huge army which was besieging Trichinopoly, the last town in which the British had some interest. His daring plan succeeded. With only 200 European troops and about 300 Indian sepoys, he took Arcot and held its crumbling walls for fifty days against an army of 10,000. British prestige was saved. The prince whom they supported ousted the French candidate and Dupleix was sent home in disgrace. Clive, no longer the black sheep of his family, returned to England with a fortune.

When the Seven Years War broke out in 1756, Britain was seen to be hard-pressed everywhere—in Europe, in North America and in India. Admiral Byng was executed on his own quarter-deck for failing to recapture the island of Minorca, the Duke of Cumberland surrendered an army on the continent; Frederick the Great, now Britain's ally, was severely defeated several times and the French general, Montcalm, appeared

255

certain to secure the whole of Canada. These disasters brought to power William Pitt, a country gentleman who had long been prominent in Parliament as a sarcastic critic of the government and the King. George II detested Pitt but he had to accept him as his chief minister, for Pitt, " that terrible cornet of horse ", was very popular in the country and had enormous confidence in himself. " I know I can save this country," he declared, " and no one else can! "

With energy and boldness, he attacked France so that she never knew where the next blow would fall, supplied Frederick the Great with gold to keep his armies in the field, strengthened the British forces on the continent and used the navy to support operations all over the world. Above all, he had the gift of choosing good commanders and of inspiring men with his own determination. " No man ", it was said, " ever entered his room who did not feel himself braver at his return than when he went in."

Clive had already returned to India when Sarajah Dowlah, a young prince who favoured the French, captured the English trading-post at Calcutta. One hundred and forty-six prisoners were crammed into a tiny room where all but twenty-three died from thirst and suffocation during a single night. News of this incident, the Black Hole of Calcutta, brought Clive up from Madras to recapture the trading-post. The " heaven-born general ", as Pitt called him, then decided to depose Sarajah Dowlah in order to prevent the French taking control of Bengal, a province larger than Great Britain itself. With a tiny force, he completely routed Dowlah's vast army at the battle of Plassey and in the next three years, aided by Colonel Eyre Coote's fighting regiments and an efficient naval squadron working off the coasts, he destroyed all traces of French influence in India.

The Taking of Quebec

One of several officers brought to Pitt's notice at this time was James Wolfe, a thin red-haired youngster with a sloping chin and little of the soldier's military bearing. However, Wolfe had fought at Dettingen and Culloden and had distinguished himself in raids upon the French coast, besides offending some of his senior officers by his unmannerly remarks about the feeble way in which the army was run. When Pitt had him promoted to general and sent to attack the great French port of Louisbourg in America, they complained to George II that Wolfe was mad. The fellow read books and poetry, they said, and he had no respect for his seniors :

" Mad, is he ? " growled the old King. " Then I hope he will bite some others of my generals ! "

Wolfe captured Louisbourg, and was ordered to take Quebec, the fortress-town which the French had built on the St Lawrence

River. Situated high above the river and strongly defended by more than a hundred guns and by Montcalm's army, the town appeared to be untakable. From their lofty position, the French disdainfully watched the British landing troops on the bank of the river. No army would ever scale their cliffs and, in any case, the Canadian winter would force the enemy to retire. With first-class service from Admiral Saunders, Wolfe got guns and men up the river ; he bombarded Quebec and made an unsuccessful attack upon Montcalm's outlying camp but there seemed to be no prospect of getting near to the town, let alone of capturing it.

As summer wore on, Wolfe fell ill and by the time he had hit upon a plan, he was so weak that he had to beg the army doctor to merely " patch " him up and kill his pain for a few days. He broke camp, moved troops up and down the river to make the French doubtful of his intentions and had the warships open an all-night bombardment of the town. In the darkness, he landed with 1,700 picked men at a tiny cove at the foot of the cliffs where he had seen women of Quebec washing their clothes in the river. With a spy-glass, he had picked out the zig-zag path which they used and it was on this path that he based his hopes.

A party of volunteers hauled themselves up the cliff, over-powered the guard at the top and signalled to their companions to follow. More boats drifted down river and by dawn Wolfe had an army of 4,500 men with two field-guns drawn up on the Plains of Abraham, a mile or so from Quebec. Deciding to act before the British could bring up reinforcements, Montcalm hastily formed his men into columns of attack and led them against the enemy. On Wolfe's order, the British held their fire until the French were within forty paces of their ranks. The volley burst out and under cover of the smoke, the British re-loaded, advanced twenty paces and fired again. Then they charged. Within moments, the battle had become a rout and the French army had fled, save here and there, where their white-coated regulars fought to the end. By then, Wolfe was dead and Montcalm was dying of his wounds.

The sharp-shooters had marked Wolfe's bright new uniform and he was hit early on but he somehow gave the order to charge : " Hold me up! " he muttered to an officer. " They must not see me fall! " The soldiers advanced and he heard shouts and cheers. Someone told him the French were on the run. He raised himself and gave orders to cut off their retreat. He knew that his gamble had succeeded ; Quebec and Canada, too, would be taken by the British. " I die content," he whispered. As Pitt said later, he died in the moment when his fame began.

In that same year, 1759, when Quebec was captured and the news of Plassey arrived, English regiments helped to win a victory at Minden which saved Frederick the Great : Admiral Boscawen beat one French fleet at sea and Admiral Hawke destroyed another in Quiberon Bay to put an end to the threat of invasion. This was the Year of Victories when people said that the church bells were wearing out from so much joyous pealing.

It was also the high-water mark of Pitt's success for, in the following year, George II died and his son, George III, was soon able to bring the war to an end. He wanted to be rid of Pitt and to have his own friends in power. It was clear that Britain had made enormous gains from the war and was now supreme in trade and upon the seas. But Frederick the Great felt left in the lurch by his ally and he never forgave George III's treachery. As for Pitt, he took the title of Earl of Chatham and retired to his country house, growling angrily about the terms of the peace.

The Navy and Captain Cook

The Royal Navy, on which Britain's power rested for the next 150 years, had known many ups and downs since Henry VIII's reign. It fell into ruins and was rebuilt by Sir John Hawkins for Queen Elizabeth, who could also call upon large numbers of armed merchantmen and privateers when danger was at hand. Peace with Spain and Charles I's money difficulties again reduced the fleet to a sorry state and although there was a revival in Cromwell's time, the Dutch War in Charles II's reign revealed the helplessness of an island that neglected its navy.

The weakness was not solely due to dishonesty and neglect. Officers were part-timers, posted to a ship, as a rule, when war broke out and likely to return to private life after the danger had passed. Some were court favourites who, finding it fashionable to " serve a commission " against the Dutch, obtained command of a ship without much experience of the sea or any intention of making the navy their career. Needless to say, these " fair-weather officers " were not liked by the " tarpaulin " captains, men of little polish or education who had served in

260

ships since their boyhood days. In Charles II's reign, Samuel Pepys, Secretary of the Admiralty, devoted his life to correcting this state of affairs and it was due to his efforts that the navy came to have trained officers who had passed examinations in seamanship.

Thus, by the time of the Georges, the navy had become a regular, instead of a part-time, career. The seamen were little changed ; they were still merchant sailors and fishermen who joined or were forced to serve in the royal ships. The admirals were still mostly from noble families but those in the next grade, the captains, had come up from the bottom, starting as a rule as midshipmen, and earning their promotion the hard way. Most of them were sons of lesser gentry and because the favour of a high-placed relative was useful, they usually rose more easily than the few who came up from the lower deck or from the merchant service. However, they were all trained, professional sailors.

A notable episode in the navy's development was Anson's voyage round the world. In 1740 Captain George Anson was despatched with six ships to " vex " the Spaniards in the Pacific. He carried out his orders perfectly, capturing a port and a huge treasure galleon and playing havoc with Spanish trade. Then, like Drake, he crossed the Pacific and came home via the Cape, having survived countless dangers and the loss of 626 of his 961 men in the first year of the four-year voyage. His superb leadership produced results far greater than the treasure on board the *Centurion*. Anson was promoted to admiral and in time at least eight of the junior officers who served under him also reached admiral's rank, so that the experience and inspiration of that great voyage provided a lasting tradition in the navy.

Admiral Saunders, who carried General Wolfe and his army to Quebec, had been one of Anson's officers and when the fleet reached the St Lawrence, Saunders chose a quiet Yorkshireman named Cook to sail ahead in the *Mercury* to make charts of the river's shoals and sandbanks. Cook carried out his task so well that, to the astonishment of the French, the British fleet was able to drop anchor below Quebec without losing a single vessel.

James Cook had earned his first pennies scaring crows but, at fifteen, he was at sea in a Whitby collier engaged in carrying coal down the coast to London. His master taught the serious-minded apprentice all he knew of navigation and Cook had become mate of the collier, when he decided to enlist in the navy as an able seaman. He rose slowly, for he had no advantages of birth or education, but his outstanding abilities had already been noticed when he was chosen to chart the St Lawrence.

Nine years later, when the Admiralty proposed to send a ship to the Pacific to study the path of the planet Venus and to make reports upon the geography, people and botany of that vast area, Lieutenant Cook was given command of the *Endeavour*. With a crew of eighty-five, some scientists and artists, he rounded Cape Horn and reached the island of Tahiti where the scientists pursued their observations, and the sailors made friends with the easy-going natives.

Cook then sailed into almost unknown seas. A continent called Terra Australis was supposed to lie to the south ; a Dutchman named Tasman had brought home some vague reports and William Dampier had reached Western Australia. Lack of water had forced Dampier to depart and no one knew the size or extent of this southern land nor anything about the thousands of islands scattered in the ocean. The *Endeavour* reached New Zealand which was found to consist of two islands, inhabited by the fierce Maoris. Having made careful charts, Cook sailed on to Australia where he explored the east coast for 2,000 miles and almost lost his ship on the Barrier Reef before returning to England.

The voyage had taken three years and thirty out of the crew of eighty-five had died, mostly from scurvy, so when Cook, promoted to the rank of captain, sailed again, he made sure that his men ate less salt meat than usual but far more fruit and vegetables than they liked. A sailor who disobeyed him was given a dozen lashes, but at the end of the second voyage which also lasted three years and took the *Resolution* far into the icy

waters of the Antarctic, only one man out of 118 had died of sickness.

For his third voyage as a commander, Cook again chose the sturdy *Resolution* and he was accompanied by a second vessel, the *Discovery*. This was to be an even more extensive voyage of exploration, not only of the South Pacific but of the Arctic Ocean in search of the North-West Passage. When no trace of a way to the Atlantic could be found, the ships headed south again to cruise among the islands where Cook and his sailors were by now well-known to the natives.

At Hawaii, where Cook was regarded as a god-like person, the natives were as friendly as ever but their habit of stealing anything they fancied caused a good deal of annoyance. One day, Cook went ashore with a small party of marines to talk to a friendly old chief about the theft of one of the ship's boats. He invited him to accompany him back on board, probably hoping to detain him there until the missing boat was returned. The chief cheerfully agreed but on the way to the beach, his wives and relatives became alarmed and set up a loud wailing. This brought an excited crowd to the scene and by the time Cook and his companions had reached the water's edge, they were so closely pressed that the marines could not have used their weapons. Seeing this, a boat-party, just off-shore, fired some warning shots, upon which Cook, who had kept perfectly calm, turned and called out to the boats to cease firing. As he turned, he was stabbed in the back and quickly clubbed to death in the shallow water.

Thus, on his third great voyage, Cook was killed in a petty squabble by the people whom he had always treated with kindness and understanding. He was one of the world's most notable discoverers, a leader and a man of noble character.

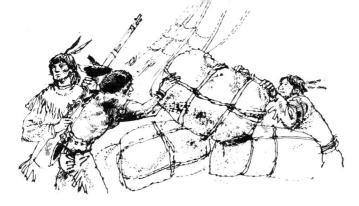

The American Colonies

While Cook was voyaging in the South Seas there occurred in North America a dispute so ill-tempered that it led to a war and to the rise of a new nation.

By this time, the American settlers numbered more than two million and nearly all of them or their fathers had crossed the ocean because they had been unhappy or oppressed at home. By hard toil they had built homes and businesses and it was not surprising that many of them, especially in the Puritan colonies of New England, felt no love for Britain. They grumbled about the law which forbade them to trade with any other country and they disliked the haughty officials who came out to manage their affairs and to accuse them of smuggling when they did undercover business with the French and the Dutch. Nor did they feel any gratitude for the armed protection they had been given in the recent wars and they saw no reason to pay for the soldiers who were defending their frontiers against the Red Indians.

George III, a pleasant, stupid young man, was determined to play a bigger part in his country's affairs than George I or George II had done. Remembering his mother's advice to " be a king ", he managed to build up a party of " King's Friends " in Parliament so that he could rule through ministers of his own choosing. Unfortunately, he chose men not for their cleverness but for their willingness to please him and Pitt was now too old and ill to oppose him.

Thus, when George and his ministers decided that the colonies should pay part of the cost of their own defence, the

265

matter was handled badly.

The government put taxes on a few articles such as glass, paper and tea, and the colonists refused to pay. They raised the cry of " No taxation without representation ", meaning that it was not fair for them to have to pay taxes ordered by Parliament at Westminster where they had no members. Pitt came out of retirement to support them and all the taxes were taken off except the one on tea.

By a special arrangement, tea was actually cheaper than before but a party of indignant colonists, dressed as Red Indians, boarded three ships in Boston harbour and threw their cargoes of tea into the water.

It was the King's turn to get angry, and after the Boston Tea Party his minister, Lord North, punished the colony by closing the port. At this, the colonists drew up a petition to the King, setting out their grievances but also stating their loyalty to the crown. George III ignored the petition.

Fighting broke out in New England when a force of British soldiers was sent to seize a store of arms at Lexington. As they marched inland, the redcoats were sniped at from the woods by " Minute men ", so-called because they were ready to turn out at a minute's notice. Then came the battle of Bunker's Hill. This piece of high land overlooking Boston harbour had been occupied by the local citizen-soldiers who were only driven off after the regular troops had suffered heavy casualties. The War of American Independence had begun.

Having blundered into war, George III and his ministers appeared to have no idea how to win it. Their red-coated soldiers, many of them hired from Germany, were commanded by officers who were baffled by an enemy who refused to fight European-style battles but preferred to use their knowledge of a vast wooded country in order to ambush and harrass the regulars. In any case, the British commanders felt that they had merely to sit still and wait for the opposition to collapse.

The colonists lacked artillery and warships ; they were ill-equipped, quarrelsome and at times even treacherous, so that a commander like Wolfe or Clive would have speedily brought the war to an end. However, there was no plan of action but only confusing orders from London, and the colonists were held together by their commander-in-chief, George Washington, a man of superb tenacity and courage. At length, after three years spent " in teaching the Americans how to fight ", the British suffered a major reverse when General Burgoyne's army of 8,000 men was surrounded and captured at Saratoga.

In a European campaign the surrender of one small army would not have mattered very much but in America it lost the war. Britain's enemies could see that the colonists had a chance of victory and France and Spain entered the war. Holland joined them and most of the other countries of Europe agreed to defy the British navy's practice of searching neutral ships for cargoes intended for America. When foreign warships arrived in American waters, the Royal Navy was outnumbered and this temporary loss of sea-power was decisive. Lord Cornwallis, commanding a British army at Yorktown, was in no particular danger from George Washington's forces until a French fleet appeared off the coast. This completely changed the situation and Cornwallis was compelled to surrender.

" O God! It is all over! " cried Lord North when he heard the news. This was true, for although Admiral Rodney regained command of the sea by defeating the French and Spanish fleets near some islands called the Saints, his victory came too late. Britain had to recognise the independence of the American colonies in order to deal with her other enemies. Despite having been bested by a few thousand armed settlers, Britain fended off France and Spain without great difficulty and when peace was made, the only important losses were the thirteen American colonies and Minorca. Canada, India and Gibraltar, all threatened during the war, remained in the empire.

Inventors and Engineers

George III's failure in America put an end to his ambition to " be a king " and his opponents, the Whigs, took over the government. However, when they proved to be as selfish and greedy as the ministers whom they had attacked, George III took a daring step to get rid of them. As First Lord of the Treasury or prime minister, he appointed William Pitt, son of Pitt the elder. Pitt was only twenty-four. He was an earnest unsmiling young man who had studied hard to follow in his father's steps, but he had few supporters in the House of Commons and the Whigs declared it was ridiculous to put the country's government into the hands of anyone so young. It was, they said :

> " A sight to make surrounding nations stare,
> A kingdom trusted to a schoolboy's care."

But the " schoolboy " had the people's support. They remembered how old Pitt had saved the country and they gave his son the chance to prove himself. For the next twenty years, Pitt the Younger remained prime minister. Scorning to enrich himself as many other politicians had done, he insisted that officials should be more honest and hardworking than in the past and he did much to encourage trade and manufacture.

Until the eighteenth century the country's prosperity rested mainly on farming and sea-trade. Manufacturing, even of cloth, was mostly carried on at home and in small workshops ; coal was little used except in household grates and two-thirds of all the iron came from abroad. Then there arose a group of

269

inventors whose ideas made Britain into the chief manufacturing country in the world.

A Lancashire man named James Kay invented a shuttle which, by means of springs, returned to the weaver's right hand, leaving his left hand free to operate a bar or batten. The Flying Shuttle speeded up weaving so much that faster spinning was required and James Hargreaves, a poor cottager, realised how this could be done when he saw his wife's spinning wheel fall over and continue to spin on its side. His *Spinning Jenny* with its upright spindles was further improved by Richard Arkwright, a barber whose journeys to buy human hair for wig-making took him into the cottages of Lancashire cloth-workers. His inventive mind was fascinated by the problem of how to produce thread still faster for the weavers, and with the help of a clockmaker he began to experiment. The work had to be carried out in secret because the workers feared that machines would put an end to their own jobs but, after many setbacks, the partners succeeded in producing an efficient spinning-frame.

Arkwright's machines were driven by water-power, which meant that workers had to work together in mills or factories built near streams. When Samuel Crompton used the ideas of earlier inventors to produce an improved machine called a *Mule*, spinning became so quick that it was the turn of the weavers to cry out for better looms. Power, more reliable than water, was needed. For many years, steam-engines invented by Thomas Newcomen, had been used to pump water out of shallow mines, but they were clumsy machines requiring a great deal of fuel to produce a small amount of power. One day, early in the reign of George III, a model of Newcomen's engine was sent for repair to an instrument-maker at Glasgow University named James Watt. This brilliant Scot discovered how the engine's faults might be overcome but he could not have produced a successful steam-engine without the patient help of Matthew Boulton, owner of a Birmingham engineering works, who became his

270

partner. Together, they turned out hundreds of steam-engines to pump water and to drive machines of every kind, including the power-looms invented by the Reverend Cartwright.

Steam-power created a new world of machines and factories, of skilled engineers, mechanics and ill-paid workers. Difficulties of all kinds had to be overcome. The engineers were hampered by a shortage of iron but as charcoal gave way to coal for smelting, the iron industry moved north where ironmasters, like John " Iron Mad " Wilkinson, produced the enormous quantities of metal which the surging industries demanded.

Another difficulty was the state of the roads. To move heavy loads of materials by wagon was a slow and costly business but when James Brindley, an uneducated genius, built the Worsley Canal for the Duke of Bridgewater, the price of coal in Manchester fell by half. This led to the building of canals to link the navigable rivers to the factory and mining areas.

In barely fifty years, large parts of Britain were transformed. The bleak moors and quiet valleys of Yorkshire, Lancashire, South Wales and Lanarkshire became crowded with manufacturing and mining villages where the workers, drawn in from the countryside, came to live in buildings flung up as cheaply and quickly as possible, usually without sanitation, comfort or any of the decencies of life. It was a harsh and brutal age, but it was also an age of elegance and opportunity. While the rich, many of whom had recently won their wealth in India or in the new industries, could enjoy luxury in its most gracious forms, the poorest classes lived in brutish squalor. But, bad as the contrast was between England's rich and poor, it was mild compared with conditions in France.

Trafalgar

In France, apparently so powerful and rich, the peasants suffered monstrous oppression in order to support the most splendid and most idle aristocracy in the world. Despite its magnificence, the country was almost bankrupt and the workers were near to starvation. A food riot in Paris grew into a revolution and Louis XVI, a harmless simpleton, and his unpopular wife, Marie Antoinette, were executed, along with hundreds of aristocrats who had failed to flee abroad.

Those who believed in liberty and justice were thrust aside by the leaders of the blood-thirsty Paris mob. Appalling crimes took place and government, snatched by one or another group of petty villains, fell into ruin while the ragged armies of France repelled its enemies along the frontiers. The European powers, notably Austria, Prussia and Great Britain, had little sympathy for Louis XVI or for the French aristocrats in exile but the revolution alarmed them, especially when the French declared that they would help any people who rose against their rulers.

War broke out and it was during a British naval attack on Toulon that the port was saved by a young artillery officer named Napoleon Bonaparte. He was a Corsican of Italian descent who had attended a French military college shortly before the revolution. War and the disappearance of most of the aristocratic officers gave him the chance to rise, and at twenty-six, Bonaparte was a general. By a series of brilliant victories in Italy, he defeated Austria and then, fired by a dream of conquering an empire in the East, he took an army to Egypt. His plans were dashed when Admiral Nelson sailed into Aboukir Bay and destroyed his fleet as it lay at anchor at the mouth of the Nile. At this reverse, Napoleon abandoned his army and returned to Paris where, with the people's acclaim, he overthrew the government and made himself absolute master of France.

As First Consul and presently as Emperor, he magically restored the fortunes of France. The swarthy little Corsican was a genius whose superhuman energy enabled him to govern the country, to win campaigns and to dominate everyone from officials and generals to kings and queens. Victory followed victory until half of Europe had been defeated in the field or cowed into submission by a dictator whose matchless armies were filled by officers chosen for their ability in battle and by soldiers who worshipped their invincible commander.

Pitt conducted the war against France in much the same style as his father had done forty years earlier, though with less energy and fire. The navy held the seas and English gold supported the armies of allies on the continent, but when these allies were beaten, all that stood between Napoleon and complete victory was the English Channel. Once across that narrow strait, the Grand Army would make short work of Britain's meagre forces.

One hundred and fifty thousand of the finest troops in the world were assembled on the cliffs of Boulogne ; the barges and stores lay ready for the invasion and all that was needed for complete success was a few days' control of the Channel. To a general of Napoleon's capacity, it would have been easy to solve such a problem on land but the French navy was shut up in harbour and Napoleon could only rage at his admirals' failure to move their ships as quickly and precisely as cavalry or guns. At last, however, Admiral Villeneuve managed to get his ships out of Toulon harbour while the watching British squadron had been withdrawn for a refit. Nelson, furious at having been given the slip, chased Villeneuve to the West Indies and back across the Atlantic towards the approaches to the Channel where the French ran into an English squadron.

Trafalgar

Villeneuve turned away and took refuge in Cadiz harbour. Napoleon's invasion plan was ruined and, in disgust, he broke camp at Boulogne and marched away to destroy the armies of Austria and Russia at Ulm and Austerlitz. The news killed Pitt. All his hopes had been pinned on his latest alliance and men said the "Austerlitz look" never left his face until his death a few weeks later. He was only forty-six and he died in despair, murmuring, "My country! How I leave my country!"

The outlook was indeed dark. The combined armies of Europe seemed unable to withstand Napoleon whose latest triumph, a crushing victory over the Prussians and a treaty with the Tsar of Russia, gave him control of the entire continent. Moreover, he intended to use this power to kill Britain's trade by closing all the ports and markets of Europe to her goods. This, he felt certain, would bring that "nation of shopkeepers" to their knees.

One victory relieved the gloom. While Napoleon was beating the Austrians, his navy was destroyed at Trafalgar by Lord Nelson, the best-loved of all sea-commanders. This slight, spare man who had gone to sea from his father's Norfolk vicarage at the age of thirteen and had suffered scurvy, fever and the loss of

an arm and an eye in his country's service, possessed the same
kind of passionate heroism that fired James Wolfe. In him was
the same contempt for senior authority, the same dedication to
his profession and his men and the same resolve for a victory so
complete that it would bring immortality.

After Villeneuve had escaped into Cadiz, Nelson rejoined
the fleet off the coast of Spain, where he lay at a distance,
concealing his strength and moving ships away in hope of
enticing the enemy out. At length, one of the frigates, poised
to carry news of a move, brought word that the French and
Spanish ships had left harbour and were standing out to sea.

At once, Nelson ordered his fleet to carry out the pre-
arranged plan. His captains knew what was needed and the
Admiral had only to signal " General Chase South-East " for
them to take up their stations in two columns which moved
slowly towards the enemy on the lightest of breezes. As they
closed in, Nelson's flag-ship showed another signal, " England
Expects That Every Man This Day Will Do His Duty ".

" What is Nelson signalling about? " cried one captain.
" We all know what we have to do! " But the seamen greeted
the message with cheers which rolled across the water from one

ship to the next and a band played " Britons Strike Home " as the black-and-yellow-painted three-deckers moved into a storm of fire from the strung-out French fleet. With Nelson in the *Victory* leading one column and Collingwood in the *Royal Sovereign* leading the other, they pierced the enemy line at right angles in two places, and, having done so, every ship in the British fleet, except for one or two in the rear, found an opponent for the " pell-mell " battle which followed. At close quarters, when the great ships came alongside each other, riggings became hopelessly entangled aloft, broadsides raked the decks and boarding-parties slashed away as volleys were presented at point-blank range.

In this kind of fighting, the French were no match for their enemy's experience. In Nelson's ships, 450 men were killed but Villeneuve lost nearly 5,000; the rear and centre of his fleet were destroyed and Napoleon's navy ceased to exist.

Trafalgar was the greatest British victory of all time. It brought command of the seas for a century and made certain that Britain could not be defeated by the French Emperor. But at home the news was received with sorrow and tears. Nelson was dead. At the height of the battle, he was walking the twenty-foot length of his quarter-deck wearing a uniform coat bright with the four embroidered stars of his Orders of Knighthood, when a French sharp-shooter up on the mizzen-mast of the *Redoubtable* leaned forward and shot him at a range of only fifteen yards.

The loss of one maimed little admiral stunned the nation, for the people loved him and had already made him their national hero. His sailors, those hard-drinking ruffians, wept for him. A young sailor wrote of him to his parents, " all the men in our ship who have seen him are such soft toads, they have done nothing but blast their eyes and cry ever since he was killed . . . Chaps that fought like the Devil sit down and cry like a wench."

276

Waterloo

In order to make all Europe obey his order to do no trade
with Britain, Napoleon drove out the royal family of Portugal
and put his own brother upon the Spanish throne. This was to
close the last way in for English goods, but the Portuguese and
the Spaniards broke into revolt and called to Britain for help.
Thanks to the navy, a small British army was landed in Portugal
which became the base for the prolonged struggle known as the
Peninsular War.

In command of the British force was a beak-nosed martinet
whose experience of fighting on the dusty plains of India stood
him in good stead in Spain's parched and mountainous countryside. He was Arthur Wellesley, later Duke of Wellington. This
unbending aristocrat who regarded Nelson as a showman, his

277

officers as dandified boobies and his men as the scum of the earth, came to Spain with one ambition—to beat the French. He knew how to do it and he had the patience to carry out his plan in the face of every difficulty. To Wellington, war was a matter of preparation and hard sense. He understood the problems. The French, led by Napoleon's best marshals, had vastly superior numbers and the confidence that victory belonged always to them. The country could barely support its poverty-stricken peasants, let alone an army on campaign. As allies, the Portuguese were brave but undisciplined and the Spaniards were useless in formal battles against the French. Defeat would result in the recall of the British troops and victory must take a long, long time to secure. In fact it took four years.

During that time Wellington crossed and recrossed Spain, beating the French in battle, drawing them after him to exhaust their supplies, falling back to the fortified lines he had constructed outside Lisbon and advancing warily back into Spain when the enemy retreated. In this drawn-out contest, he transformed his ill-conditioned troops into the finest little army in Europe. He had called them " a rabble " and he made them into his " fine fellows ". " With that army, I could have done anything," he declared. They did not love " Old Nosey " in the way that men loved Marlborough and Nelson but they trusted him. The sight of his long nose was worth ten thousand men any day, they said.

At Vimiero, Talavera, Busaco, Albuera and Salamanca, Wellington beat the French, as he said he would. After Vitoria, he drove them out of Spain, and at Toulouse he beat them on French soil. It was after that battle that he heard the astounding news of Napoleon's abdication.

While he was abusing his marshals for their failures in Spain, Napoleon had been preparing the defeat of Russia. By 1812 he was ready, and at the head of the finest army that ever marched

278

in column, he advanced to Moscow. The Russians fought and retreated, burning the countryside as they went. Moscow was empty. Amid the ruins, Napoleon waited for the Tsar's peace proposals but none came ; there was no one to deal with, no visible army to fight and, worse still, no supplies in the capital to support his own army through the winter. As snow began to fall he gave the order to retreat from Moscow, but he was already far too late. Cold and hunger destroyed the Grand Army. Out of that magnificent host, half a million strong, barely 40,000 men survived the march back. By then they were no longer recognisable as soldiers, and Napoleon had long since deserted them. He had raced ahead to raise fresh armies for, scenting his downfall, Europe was up in arms against him. He fought brilliantly but his enemies were too numerous. Paris fell and the French turned against the man who had heaped so much glory and disaster upon his adopted country. Napoleon abdicated and was sent into exile on the island of Elba.

In less than a year he escaped and returned to France. The people, already sick of defeat, welcomed him with joy and his old soldiers flocked back into the ranks. The allies who had disbanded their forces, hastily scraped together an army and asked Wellington to proceed to Belgium to take command. It was a mixed collection of troops and he regretted that most of his Peninsular veterans were missing. Still, he had the Guards and some reliable infantry and there were the Prussians some way off, under Blücher, a tough old general whom he trusted.

Napoleon moved north out of France and defeated Blücher. Believing that the Prussians were done for, he then came on to deal with Wellington, who was waiting for him behind a ridge near the village of Waterloo. There was a long slope up to the ridge and Wellington garrisoned three forward positions as strong-points to hold up the enemy.

The attack started at noon when the French made furious assaults on the outposts and surged in columns against the army

279

behind the ridge. Wellington met them as he had met them in Spain, with volleys, with British squares and, when the opportunity arose, with the bayonet. It was desperate work, " hard pounding ", Wellington called it, " we must see who can pound the hardest ". He was everywhere, encouraging his tired troops, praising the Guards, calling for one more brave effort. Constantly, he looked for the Prussians. Blücher, old " Marshal Forwards ", would not fail him but he wanted him badly. In the late afternoon, a movement was sighted away to the left. It was the Prussians.

Napoleon increased his effort to overwhelm the British. In four massed charges the French cavalry was hurled against the infantry squares which held firm " as though rooted to earth "; the Prussians were checked and as dusk began to fall the Imperial Guard was ordered up the slope. With majestic calm, 6000 picked soldiers, the very aristocrats of Napoleon's army, advanced in parade order to the tap of the drum, their officers out in front with drawn swords. The British waited behind their ridge. At fifty paces, they stood up and fired one terrible volley. The enemy line wavered. A deep voice called out, " Now's the time, my boys! " and the British sprang forward with the bayonet. The Imperial Guard broke and fled down the slope as the Prussians burst through on the left and the battle became a rout.

White-faced and still blaming his defeat on Marshal Ney's cavalry tactics, Napoleon got into his carriage and made for Paris. Unable to raise yet another army, he surrendered to the British from whom he expected better treatment than from the vengeful Prussians. This time there was to be no escape. Exiled to St Helena in the South Atlantic, the Corsican Emperor of France died there after six years of captivity.

The Railways

Twenty-five years of revolution and war on the continent had made little difference to the lives of the people in Britain. They had seen nothing of the enemy or of the violent overthrow of governments and ruling classes. Their old King, George III, now blind and mad, still occupied the throne ; his fat son, the vain, talented Prince Regent, was unpopular and so was the government, but the aristocracy continued to rule the country. The rich were richer than ever and the poor still toiled long hours in field and factory.

During the years following Waterloo, Britain learned something of the turmoil that had affected the nations of Europe. Unemployment, dear bread and taxes on food and drink led to discontent and riots. Angry crowds attacked factories to smash the machines which seemed to have taken away their jobs and eleven persons were killed at " Peterloo " when soldiers tried to disperse a meeting in St Peter's Field, Manchester. Rumours of armed gatherings and talk of revolution alarmed the government. But Britain was not as desperate as Louis XVI's France. Poverty and injustice existed on every side but the workers had not reached such depths of misery that they were ready to kill their masters. In any case, they lacked leaders and were forbidden to form unions or even to hold meetings. The situation grew quieter as trade picked up and jobs became more plentiful.

Coal and iron had turned Britain into an industrial nation. These were the materials that made it possible to produce the goods that the world wanted—clothes, hardware, machinery, pottery, guns and glass. As industry gathered pace, a speedier method was needed to carry goods about the country and down

281

to the ports. Canal-barges were slow and horse-drawn wagons were slower still. Great efforts were made to improve the roads and John Macadam and Thomas Telford were busily engaged on laying their new highways when a young man named Stephenson went to the mining village of Wylam, near New-castle, to look at a moving steam-engine named *Puffing Billy*.

George Stephenson came from a family so poor that he was out to work at eight years of age, and at fourteen he was earning a man's wage of a shilling a day for looking after a pumping-engine. Unable to read and write until he was grown up, the lad had the born engineer's gift to take engines to pieces and to make them work better. This was why he went to watch *Puffing Billy* pull coal trucks along an iron track.

There had been various attempts to build steam locomotives long before Stephenson ever saw one, but most people regarded them as extravagant oddities. Horses were cheaper and much more reliable. Stephenson, however, became convinced that he could build an efficient locomotive and with help from his employers he constructed one named *Blücher*. It was far from perfect but good enough to encourage the idea of a railway that

282

would carry goods and passengers. Given the post of chief engineer, Stephenson laid the track from Stockton to Darlington in Durham and, just ten years after Waterloo, he himself drove the first train along it at the astounding speed of 12 mph. When his locomotive, *The Rocket*, beat all its rivals for service on the new Manchester to Liverpool line, the Railway Age had begun.

People tumbled over each other in their eagerness to subscribe money to buy land and to hire the gangs of labourers who laid the tracks along which Stephenson's engines were to run. Within twenty years Britain had the world's first railway network, with over 5,000 miles of track, signalling and electric telegraph systems and a high standard of service and speed. This remarkable achievement which changed life in Britain more rapidly than any other happening in history, owed almost everything to one man. Hardly anywhere, at home or abroad, was the building of a railway contemplated without " Geordie " Stephenson's advice. His *Rocket* was the father of every other steam-locomotive that ever ran, for its design provided the basic principle of steam locomotion during the 120 years when steam ruled the world's railways.

Help for the Poor

Such rapid changes in transport and industry brought fortunes to a few and a better standard of life to a great many others. The changes also brought suffering. In the enthusiasm for " progress ", there was no time to bother about those who were too weak or too young to defend themselves. Thus, men worked for wages that barely kept them alive, women and girls dragged coal-trucks in the mines and children were sent to the factories almost as soon as they could walk, since even the smallest could earn a few pence for crawling under machines to clean the parts.

In return for their labour, the poor lived worse than animals. It seemed to be nobody's concern that the children grew up bent and diseased, that a great part of the nation was under-nourished, ignorant and dirty. Indeed, most people believed that it would be wrong to interfere with the laws of nature. The poor must stay poor because if wages went up, profits would fall, business would dry up and everyone would be ruined.

Here and there a few people refused to accept this comfortable notion. Robert Owen, himself a poor boy who went to work at seven and supported himself entirely from the age of ten, became part-owner and manager of a huge spinning-mill at New Lanark in Scotland. His pity was roused by the condition of the child-workers, most of them orphans and foundlings sent from the workhouses to toil for thirteen or fourteen hours a day for six and a half days a week in the hot, damp atmosphere of a cotton-mill. Owen shocked public opinion by providing better houses and cheaper food for his workers ; he encouraged them to be clean and honest, he paid them higher wages and opened
284

a school for the children. People declared him mad. His soft-headed ideas would bring ruin to his partners, and although Owen proved that better wages and conditions could still produce good profits, he was regarded as a crank for the rest of his life. Certainly most of his later plans failed and he lost his fortune, but his ideas lived on and the workers never forgot him.

There were others, besides Owen, who cared about the poor. John Wesley travelled the country for fifty years, preaching to outdoor congregations of miners, weavers, spinners, foundry-men, fishermen and labourers. He suffered persecution and his life was often in danger. Besides bringing religion and a new sense of self-respect and decency to hundreds of thousands of workers who had never entered a church, he also helped to found schools and orphanages.

A man from an entirely different background from Owen was Anthony Ashley Cooper, the seventh Earl of Shaftesbury. Born into a rich aristocratic family, he grew up with the same passionate determination to put right some of the evils of his time. He believed that the best way to do this was to change some of the laws and to bring in new ones, and after years of ridicule and abuse, he persuaded Parliament to reduce factory hours of work to ten hours a day for most workers and less for young children, to stop women and children working under-ground in the mines and to forbid the employment of little boys as chimney-sweeps. Outside Parliament, " our Earl ", as the workers called Shaftesbury, did much to help the men and women who had started the " Ragged Schools " for the home-less waifs who lived in the streets. Like Elizabeth Fry, who forced people to feel ashamed of the inhuman treatment of lunatics and prisoners, and like countless other Victorians who refused to accept injustice as a normal part of life, Shaftesbury was upheld by a deep religious faith.

During the 1840's, the " Hungry Forties ", there occurred the Irish Famine, when a then unknown disease destroyed the

potatoes on which the vast majority of the Irish lived. More than a million died of starvation and almost as many again emigrated to the United States and Canada. This tragedy convinced Sir Robert Peel, the prime minister, that he must abolish the Corn Laws so that foreign corn could come readily into the country. In this way, he hoped to help the poor by bringing down the price of bread.

Abolishing the Corn Laws ruined Peel's career and did nothing to help the Irish or the poor. The price of wheat remained much the same and Ireland's plight was as desperate as ever. In the rest of Britain, however, conditions began to improve when a trade boom and a number of good harvests made life easier for the workers.

Queen Victoria

As the old Duke of Wellington remarked, the country was
" getting on to its legs again ". Business picked up, the railways
were still expanding and the ports were crammed with British
goods on their way to customers overseas, for by now Britain was
selling more than all the other nations put together. The
288

empire was growing bigger and richer, as small wars and annexations brought fresh territories in India, Africa and the Pacific under British rule.

Wealth flowed into Britain. It failed to reach the poorest class but increasing numbers of the people came to have a share in the country's progress. They were proud of their success and felt that old " Pam ", Lord Palmerston, was quite right when he bullied foreign governments and made them understand Britain's power. More thoughtful people considered that the British had a special mission to bring justice and good government to those unfortunate countries which had never known these blessings. This sense of belonging to a gifted, superior nation was increased by a changed attitude towards the crown.

When William IV died, he was succeeded by his niece, Princess Victoria. She was only eighteen but although in childhood she had been over-sheltered by a domineering mother, she at once behaved with remarkable dignity and charm. In place of the Hanoverians whom no one could admire, the people now had a vivacious girl on the throne who was painstakingly anxious to be a good and dutiful Queen. It was not long before Victoria married Prince Albert, a German cousin, and although her serious-minded husband was never popular, their marriage was blissfully successful. Family happiness and an earnest interest in the country's affairs took the place of the old scandals and quarrels. The court became respectable and dull, for Albert shared none of the Queen's natural gaiety. Unfortunately, his early death reduced her to such a state of gloom that it seemed as if she had retired into perpetual mourning. However, when she was older, she fell under the spell of the witty and amusing prime minister, Benjamin Disraeli, who coaxed her into reappearing in public ; and by the latter part of her immensely long reign, this obstinate, astute little woman had earned for the royal family an affectionate respect so deep that it has never since been seriously weakened.

289

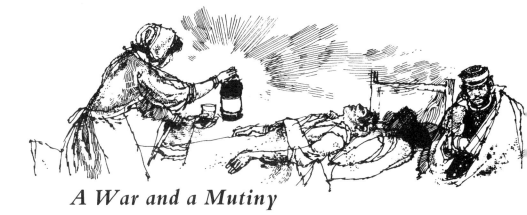

A War and a Mutiny

During Queen Victoria's reign, there were one or two set-backs to the British people's self-confidence. Having become accustomed to the idea that they managed all things better than anyone else, they were shocked to discover that when it came to war, their army was wretchedly equipped and badly led.

The Crimean War was fought to prevent Russia overthrowing the Turkish Empire, and all the fighting took place in the Crimea, a part of southern Russia where the British and their French allies attempted to capture the Black Sea port of Sebastopol. Troops, many of them sent from India, were landed in summer kit, without the supplies, tents, greatcoats and boots that were needed to sustain them through the Russian winter. Bad as the arrangements were for the fighting-men, they were even worse for the sick and wounded. The base hospital was miles away across the Black Sea where, in a filthy ruinous barracks, men died like flies from fever, frostbite and sheer neglect. In the entire place, there was not a bandage, a bowl, a bottle of medicine or even a spoon. All had been forgotten or had never arrived.

For the first time in history, thanks to the recently invented electric telegraph, the public were able to read up-to-date reports of the war in their newspapers. They read how the soldiers fought with matchless courage at Alma and Inkerman, and how the Light Brigade charged so gloriously and uselessly at Balaclava. With mounting anger, they also read of the shocking conditions in which these brave fellows were forced to live and die. The public indignation brought results. Stores and equipment were despatched to the front and money was collected to send out a team of nurses under the leadership of the only woman in England with expert knowledge of hospitals and nursing.

In the eyes of her parents and of most Victorians, Miss Florence Nightingale was an extremely odd person. Brought up to the leisured life of a rich young lady, she had insisted upon having a career, and against her family's wishes she had gone abroad to study nursing, an occupation which was normally followed only by the lowest and most ignorant of women. By the time of the Crimean War, she had become lady-super-intendent of a London hospital for sick gentlewomen, and it was therefore to Miss Nightingale that the government turned when it decided to send out a party of nurses to look after the wounded.

Knowing a great deal about how to overcome stupidity and prejudice, she arrived at the hospital base of Scutari in Turkey. The hostility of the army authorities did not dismay her any more than the filth and stench of that vast barracks where the sick and the dead lay side by side on floors oozing with damp. She pursed her mouth and waited for the army to seek her assistance. The arrival of fresh shiploads of wounded turned a difficult situation into chaos and in desperation the army officers turned to the fierce little woman in a black dress with white collar and cuffs. At least she had thirty-eight nurses and large sums of money to buy all the stores that were needed.

Miss Nightingale took command. Her first action was to produce not medicine but two hundred scrubbing-brushes. Floors and walls were scoured, barrow-loads of filth were wheeled away, a kitchen was opened to cook decent food for the men, a laundry was organised to wash their bedding and lice-ridden shirts, and fresh air was let into the entire place. Then she began to nurse the sick. As one of the wounded soldiers said, " We felt we were in Heaven . . . What a comfort it was to see her pass even . . . We lay there in hundreds but we could kiss her shadow as it fell." Those in authority found her a hard and efficient organiser with a sharp tongue and a ruthless knack of getting her own way, but all the tenderness and compassion in her nature went out to those broken men who lay waiting for her to come to them. " I became ", she said, " mother to 50,000 soldiers." She not only nursed them but wrote their letters, saved their pay, sent it home to their wives and made them regard themselves as decent human beings.

Florence Nightingale wrought a miracle, not only because she saved the lives of hundreds of men for whom she almost died from camp fever, but because, by her example and ceaseless work for the next fifty years, she transformed hospitals and the nursing profession. She was also one of the little band of enthusiasts who, like Elizabeth Garrett Anderson, the first woman doctor, made it possible for women to have education and careers.

Hardly had the Crimean War ended than the nation was shocked to learn of a violent uprising in the empire. The Indian Mutiny affected only a small part of the huge continent where British rule was accepted by millions of the inhabitants. To the vast majority, the British brought peaceful, orderly government and their rule was opposed chiefly by the warlike tribesmen who lived by pillaging their neighbours, and by religious leaders who did not wish the people's ancient customs and beliefs to be interfered with. The mutiny was sparked off by what seemed to be an insult to religion.

The army, which contained a great many Indian soldiers, known as sepoys, was issued with a new rifle cartridge coated with grease. Rumour had it that the grease was made from the fat of cows, animals sacred to the Hindus, or from the fat of pigs, animals considered unclean by the followers of Mohammed, or from a mixture of both. Aided by an old prophecy that the British were due to be ousted from India that very year, the rumour provoked a regiment to mutiny. At Meerut the sepoys killed their officers and were joined by more soldiers, freed

292

prisoners and some of the populace. They laid siege to Delhi, Cawnpore and Lucknow. At Cawnpore a massacre took place, but Delhi and Lucknow held out until fresh troops arrived to relieve the hard-pressed defenders and presently to subdue the entire province. As a result of the mutiny, the powers of the old East India Company were taken over by the British government and the Queen appointed a Viceroy to rule in her absence. The huge country settled down again to ninety years of fairly peaceful government.

The handful of British officials and soldiers who ruled India and the rest of the empire made mistakes and were sometimes guilty of arrogance and tactlessness, but most of them were filled with an honourable desire to do their duty. They believed that it was their mission to bring civilised justice to backward peoples and it was with ideals of service and adventure that so many hundreds of young men set off to distant parts of the world.

Livingstone in Africa

Australia, New Zealand, the Pacific Islands, Burma and the coastal fringe of China attracted adventurers and settlers in search of land, gold and trade. Some wanted none of these things. They were the explorers and missionaries, and Africa, more than anywhere else, drew them like a magnet.

North Africa and the coastal regions of East and West Africa had been known for centuries, and in the south the Dutch had founded a colony which was by now under British rule, but the heart of Africa was a vast continent unknown to Europeans.

The first probings into the interior were made during the Napoleonic wars by a group of wealthy Englishmen interested in geography. They sent out Mungo Park to explore the River Niger and presently the government provided money to further exploration which fired the enthusiasm of Victorian gentlemen for " Christianity and commerce ". Missionary societies were founded and early in Queen Victoria's reign there arrived at Cape Town a young man named David Livingstone.

Born in poverty near Glasgow, Livingstone had taught himself Latin at ten years of age as he stood at work in a cotton mill. By intense efforts, he passed his examinations to become a doctor of medicine and his first intention was to serve as a missionary in China. By chance, however, he turned one evening into a meeting-hall where a returned missionary was speaking of his work in South Africa. When Livingstone heard him say, " On a clear morning, I can see from the hills of Kuruman, the smoke of a thousand villages where no missionary has ever been," he

294

made up his mind that he would carry the Gospel and his medical knowledge to the Africans.

After working for a time at a mission station 100 miles up-country, Livingstone travelled farther north to start a new missionary settlement in country which had never before seen a white man. Here, with the aid of his wife Mary, he won the friendship of the native people who willingly acted as guides on his journeys to distant kraals where he preached and tended the sick. The urge to go farther and farther on took him across the dreaded Kalahari Desert and then, having made a nightmare journey with his wife and babies in an ox-wagon, he left them in the care of a friendly chief and pushed on alone to the great Zambesi River. Reluctantly, he decided that the climate was too unhealthy for his family and that he must see them safely off to England before he could explore further. After accompanying them to Cape Town, he made the immense journey back to Linyanti, in the heart of Africa.

With a few stores crammed into a tin box and some of his black friends as escorts, Livingstone set out westwards towards " the white man's sea ". For months they travelled along rivers, through forests and across great grasslands and by the time they reached the ocean, fever and hunger had reduced Livingstone almost to a skeleton. After a period for rest, he set out again to keep his promise to return his faithful tribesmen to their chief. The journey took a year but having reached Linyanti, he continued eastwards down the Zambesi towards the Indian Ocean, discovering the Victoria Falls on the way and passing through a country terrorised by the Arab slave-dealers. In four years he had explored and mapped a huge area of Africa, and on his return to England his book about his travels not only made him a public hero but led to a wave of enthusiasm for African exploration. The Royal Geographical Society sent out Burton and Speke to find the source of the Nile and paid the expenses of Livingstone's next expedition which was to last for five years.

Livingstone in Africa

After this, he could have retired to enjoy the fortune which his books had earned but Africa drew him back. His wife had died of fever and the gaunt missionary spent another six years exploring the upper reaches of the Congo in Central Africa. His last journey was made in order to map the huge tract of land between Zanzibar and Lake Tanganyika. When he set out with Susi, his black servant, and several others, the doctor was far from well, for the strain of his journeys and innumerable bouts of fever had weakened even his tough frame. The going was exceptionally difficult and the loss of his medicine chest meant that he could no longer control the fever. Too weak to walk during the last part of the journey, he was carried on a litter made from boughs until they reached Ujiji on the shore of Lake Tanganyika, Here, at the centre of the Arab slave-trade,

he recovered sufficiently to begin exploring the surrounding country and to encourage the inhabitants to resist the slavers.

For four years no news of Livingstone reached the outside world and public alarm reached such a pitch that an American newspaper sent out an expedition led by an adventurous reporter named H. M. Stanley. Following every clue that he could pick up in East Africa, Stanley eventually tracked the missing hero to Ujiji. News of the approaching party of strangers had been carried ahead and Stanley had to push his way through a crowd of excited Africans to enter the village. He saw a tall, bearded white man standing outside a hut. He looked ill and confused by the commotion. Stanley advanced towards him, took off his hat and said: " Dr Livingstone, I presume? "

The two men liked each other and Stanley, who had himself

known great hardship in his early life and was presently to become a celebrated explorer, did everything possible to nurse the sick doctor back to health and to persuade him to go home. It was no use. " I must finish my task," said Livingstone.

With the new stores, he set out on another journey of exploration but his strength had gone, and one morning Susi found that his master had died in the night kneeling in prayer by his bed. In loving sorrow, his black servants buried his heart beside Lake Bangweolo and then they wrapped his body in bark and carried it a thousand miles to the coast so that his own countrymen could bury him in Westminster Abbey.

Not all the white men who ventured into Africa's interior came with the ideals of Livingstone. Besides the traders and the diamond- and gold-prospectors, there were the riff-raff of a dozen nations, all on the look-out for a living by any means whatsoever. In the south, the Dutch settlers, known as Boers, were dour, Old Testament-reading farmers who believed that the black people were an inferior race ordained by providence to work for the white men. Resentful at British rule and at the arrival of missionaries, many of the Boers decided to leave Cape Colony and to trek north into the vast grasslands of the interior where they could raise cattle and live without interference.

Thus the Boer republics of the Transvaal and the Orange Free State came into existence, but it was not long before the Boers, in their widely scattered farms, found themselves unable to control the warlike Zulus. Reluctantly, they had to accept Britain's annexation of the Transvaal. The Zulus proved to be formidable warriors and it was only after some setbacks and hard fighting that the British troops managed to defeat their chief, Cetewayo. At once, the Boers clamoured for the return of their independence and this was granted by Mr Gladstone, leader of the Liberals.

Gladstone and Disraeli

William Ewart Gladstone had recently become prime minister after waging a thunderous election campaign against his rival, Disraeli. At a time when there were no sporting heroes or popular stars, people took a tremendous interest in parliamentary affairs and they followed the contest between these two politicians with as much excitement as if it had been a heavyweight boxing championship.

Speeches in the House of Commons were reported in full in the daily newspapers, were discussed, read aloud and argued over in homes and public-houses. Year in and year out, the battle between Gladstone and Disraeli seemed, to their separate supporters, to be no less than a fight between good and evil.

Disraeli, leader of the Conservatives, was a Jew who had started his career without money or aristocratic connections. Yet he had arrived at the head of the party which represented wealth and the traditional right of the English gentry to rule the country. When he first entered Parliament, his appearance and manner aroused such ridicule that he was forced to bring his first speech to an end with these words : " I will sit down now

299

but the time will come when you will hear me! " Everything about him seemed to offend the Conservatives—his foreign name and appearance, his dandified clothes (he often wore green trousers, fancy waistcoats and an assortment of rings and watch-chains), his black hair arranged into a curl on his forehead and, above all, his cool and venomously witty manner of speaking. But the brilliant outsider triumphed. After Peel fell from office, Disraeli rebuilt the Conservative party and gave it a new policy —growth of British power abroad and improvement in the people's lives at home. When, as he said, he " climbed to the top of the greasy pole " to become prime minister, he won Queen Victoria's confidence to an extraordinary degree. Flattering her, making her laugh with his amusing anecdotes, he drew her back into public life, so that she came to dote upon the dazzling charmer who brought her the title of Empress of India and secured the Suez Canal for Britain.

Her affection for " Dizzy " was matched by her dislike for Gladstone. The great Liberal, to whom politics were part of his religion, was never at ease in the Queen's presence. As solemn and awe-inspiring as one of the ancient prophets, he spoke as if he were addressing a vast audience, fixing them with his piercing gaze as the tremendous sentences rolled over them like a flood. Queen Victoria did not like being lectured and she made no attempt to conceal her exasperation with Gladstone's manner and opinions.

" The Grand Old Man ", as his supporters called him, bore the sovereign's dislike with patience, for nothing could change his views of what was right. He believed in reform and pro-gress, with peace abroad and justice for the weaker nations. Thus, he wanted the Irish to be allowed to rule themselves and he was opposed to the use of force and the expansion of the empire.

War in South Africa

In keeping with his principles, Gladstone had restored independence to the Boers when an event took place which changed the situation in South Africa. Gold was discovered in Transvaal and a horde of adventurers poured into the farming province in search of fortunes. The gold-rush town of Johannesburg sprang up overnight and the newcomers, mostly British, soon outnumbered the Boers. In fear of losing control of the country, the Boer president, Paul Kruger, refused to give the newcomers—the " Uitlanders "—the right to vote, though they were made to pay heavy taxes.

By this time the most commanding figure in South Africa was Cecil Rhodes. He had come out from England after leaving school and by luck and ability had made a fortune in the diamond-fields before he was twenty. Immensely rich and

eager for power, Rhodes was also an idealist who loved Africa
and genuinely believed that its black peoples would be happiest
under British rule. With all the zest of his masterful character,
he set to work to make his dream come true of an English-
speaking land that would stretch from Cape Town to Cairo.
The Boers, whom he despised, presented a stumbling-block to
his plans. Having used his influence as prime minister of Cape
Colony to extend British territory to the south and west of the
Boer republics, Rhodes formed a company to develop a huge
expanse of almost uninhabited territory lying north of Transvaal.
A railway line was built to provide a link with Cape Town and
settlers began to move into the new country which was presently
named Rhodesia.

The Boers naturally regarded these activities with alarm.
Knowing that Rhodes owned a large share of the gold mines in
Transvaal, they rightly suspected that his next move would be
an attempt to gain control of their country. With his friend,
Dr Jameson, Rhodes concocted a plan to bring about an uprising
of the Uitlanders in Johannesburg. At the head of a small force
of mounted police, Jameson was to make an armed dash into
Transvaal but the plans went wrong and Jameson's Raid was a
sensational failure. A few of the mounted raiders were killed
and the rest surrendered, so that the only results were to put an
end to Rhodes' career and to inflame the bad feeling between
the Boers and the British. Emboldened by this success and by
offers of German weapons, the Boers made preparations to drive
the British clean out of South Africa. They could put 60,000
resolute, well-mounted marksmen into the field against fewer
than 15,000 British regulars and when Kruger learned that
reinforcements had been ordered to the Cape, he sent a truculent
demand for their recall and followed this up by ordering an
attack on British territory.

The war began with a series of disasters for Britain which
reached their peak in " Black Week " when an astonished world

learned that the forces of the most powerful empire in history had been defeated three times by the Boer farmers of two tiny republics. What was more surprising, however, was the Boer failure to follow up their early successes. They had superior numbers, far better artillery, and hosts of supporters and Dutch relatives in the British territories. Instead of sweeping through to the Cape, they wasted time and effort on besieging the little towns of Kimberley, Mafeking and Ladysmith.

This mistake gave the British time to bring in reinforcements. The garrisons of the three towns held out until the new commanders, Lord Roberts and Lord Kitchener, were able to counter-attack. Kimberley and Ladysmith were relieved and as the Boers retreated, a British column advanced towards Mafeking, the most northerly outpost. This small town had been completely surrounded for months but its small garrison was commanded by Colonel Baden-Powell with such courage and bluff that it was able to withstand enemy attacks and all the privations of a siege for 217 days.

The relief of Mafeking caused a tremendous outburst of joy in London but it did not end the war. With Pretoria, their capital, taken and Kruger a fugitive, the Boers still refused to surrender. Guerilla " commandos " under Botha, De Wet and Smuts defied Kitchener for nearly two years, roaming the vast country, attacking British posts and drawing supplies and information from the scattered farms. It was impossible to surround or catch them and in the end Kitchener found there was no answer except to destroy their farms and put their families into camps.

At last peace was made on terms which brave men could accept. Though nothing could bring back the children who had died in the camps, a gift of three million pounds was made by Britain to restore the farms and the two Boer republics were promised self-government at an early date.

Edwardian Days

The war was still dragging towards its end when Queen Victoria died. During her reign of more than sixty-three years, Britain had advanced to the summit of power and influence in the world and people rightly supposed that the old Queen's death had brought an age to its close.

Some of them feared that the reputation of the crown would decline, for the new monarch, " a jolly old sport " to his more vulgar subjects, was chiefly known for his love of racehorses and pretty women. However, Edward VII at once showed that his mother had been wrong to distrust his ability for so many years. Besides taking up his duties with regal dignity, he helped to bring about a friendly understanding with France and took an astute interest in the country's affairs. The outlook seemed better than ever. There was a lively, more cheerful spirit in the country, an air of prosperous content and a new government full of plans to improve the lives of working people.

All kinds of inventions and devices appeared to point to an increase in progress and happiness. Motor-cars, developed at first in Germany and France, were now being made in England, for the law which required a man to walk ahead of a motor-car carrying a red flag had been repealed and the King himself was an enthusiastic motorist. Two brothers named Wright built a flying-machine in America that actually flew and this exciting news was soon followed by the appearance in the sky of aeroplanes and gliders. For less adventurous people, there were bicycles with rubber tyres, cheap railway trips to the seaside, electric tramcars and underground trains, moving pictures in the first cinemas and the voices of celebrated singers issuing

305

from gramophone horns. There was scientific progress, too, with marvellous discoveries such as wireless, radium and X-rays which added to the sense of adventure aroused by the almost superhuman qualities of endurance displayed by the Antarctic heroes, Shackleton and Scott. At a less exciting level, new schools and public libraries were being built and workers began to have a weekly half-holiday.

Further improvements in the people's everyday lives were introduced by the new Liberal government which was probably the most talented and civilised government this country has ever had. Led by Mr Asquith, a clever, aloof lawyer, the Liberals brought in old-age pensions, unemployment pay, sick benefits, labour exchanges and a host of lesser reforms to help those who were poor and unfortunate. To carry out the main part of this programme, Asquith appointed two ministers who were to prove themselves the outstanding politicians of the century. They came from utterly different backgrounds but they resembled each other in the force of their personalities, in their ambition and driving determination to get things done. Their names were David Lloyd George and Winston Churchill.

David Lloyd George was brought up in a Welsh village in the house of his uncle, a cobbler who was a local preacher and a man of strong character. The boy went to the village school and showed such brilliance that his uncle decided that he should become a lawyer. Since there was no one to teach him Latin and French, uncle and nephew slogged painfully through grammar-books and dictionaries until David had learned sufficient to be able to pass his first Law examination and to enter a firm of solicitors. He lived in lodgings, working in an office by day and studying by candlelight at night until, after six years, he was ready to take his final examination in London. Whilst there, he visited the House of Commons and saw his idol, Mr Gladstone, rise to make a speech. One day, he vowed, he too would speak in Parliament.

There followed several years of building up a solicitor's practice, mostly for people as poor as he had been, and when he was elected to Parliament by 18 votes, he had to give up most of his income, for in those days M.P.s were not paid. The short, good-looking Welshman with a great mane of hair quickly made an impression upon the House. On Welsh affairs, temperance and religious matters, he spoke with passionate eloquence, but he was still a back-bencher, without influence or powerful friends, and the Liberals had small hopes of taking office. Then came the Boer War and young Lloyd George appeared to have ruined his career. In the face of the nation's aggressive patriotism, he sided with the Boers and became so unpopular that on one occasion he narrowly escaped death at the hands of an enraged crowd.

The war and the public's anger passed away and when a Liberal government was elected, Lloyd George had risen to become one of its leading members. His chance had come and he seized it eagerly. At the Board of Trade and presently as Chancellor of the Exchequer, he worked like a dynamo to bring in reforms which would help the poor, the old and the unemployed. In this work, which infuriated his political enemies,

307

he was supported by his admiring colleague, Winston Churchill.

Churchill had known nothing of the older man's poverty and struggle. Born into an aristocratic family, son of the brilliant Lord Randolph Churchill and educated at a famous school, Winston was a dunce. He would not or could not learn sufficient Latin to make any advance and his sole achievements were in reciting poetry and in fencing. In despair, his father sent him into the army where, to everyone's surprise, he did rather well and was posted as a cavalry officer to India. Here, he distinguished himself in several ways. He not only became a crack polo player but he actually began to educate himself, reading with an appetite he had never showed at school and beginning to write articles for newspapers at home. This occupation put him into hot water with his superiors for, after taking part in a campaign against the tribesmen of the North West Frontier, he had the nerve to write a book criticising the commanders. A desire to be present wherever things were happening took him next to Egypt where he got himself attached to Kitchener's army in the campaign to conquer the Sudan and he charged with the cavalry at Omdurman.

Having quitted the army, Churchill went to South Africa as a war-correspondent and was captured by the Boers after displaying much courage during an attack on an armoured train. His thrilling escape from a prisoner-of-war camp made worldwide news and, as a public hero, he came home to stand for Parliament. It was not long before this high-spirited fellow was in the Liberal government, working heart and soul alongside Lloyd George and subduing for the time being his military interests in favour of workmen's hours and insurance.

In their efforts to deal with poverty and injustice at home, the Liberals tended to overlook affairs outside Britain and it was suddenly and, it seemed, by accident that they found themselves at war.

The Great War

In a dusty little town named Sarajevo, a Serbian student shot and killed the Archduke Ferdinand of Austria. Violence was common enough in Balkan politics and the crime aroused interest but no alarm in London. Austria, however, saw in the assassination the opportunity to destroy Serbia, a Balkan country which had long been an irritating obstacle to her aims in that part of Europe. The Austrian threats to Serbia were supported by Germany. But Russia regarded herself as the Serbs' champion and would go to the rescue if an attack were made. This would bring in France, because she was Russia's ally and had not Britain made a friendly agreement with France?

In this complicated situation, there were a few who realised that the murder at Sarajevo could lead to a world war. But in Britain most people dismissed the danger. Why should they go to war because of a quarrel in the Balkans? Talks were starting and the trouble would soon blow over.

But the real cause of the trouble lay much deeper. For forty years, Germany had been growing stronger and more truculent. Her people were told that, whereas other nations had empires and world-wide trade they, the cleverest and most hardworking people in Europe, had been left out in the cold. The chief culprits were Britain and France who greedily refused to share the good things of the earth and so, while the German Kaiser, Queen Victoria's grandson, swaggered and boasted, his generals prepared for war. Their plan was simple. The German armies would sweep through Belgium into France with a great scything blow that would crush France so swiftly that the campaign would

309

be over before her ally Russia could move. The British, strong only at sea, would be powerless to interfere. By 1914 the German generals were ready and the murder at Sarajevo provided the excuse that was needed.

At the mention of Belgium, however, the mood of the British people changed. Britain, like Germany and all the great powers, had agreed that Belgium should be neutral and no armies should ever invade her territory. Yet the Germans were proposing to ignore the rights of a small country which had not given the slightest offence. For the British, this was enough. They cared nothing for the Serbs or the Russians ; the agreement with France had been hidden from them but the attack on " brave little Belgium " affronted their sense of fair play. Almost to a man, they agreed that they must fight to teach the bully a lesson. The navy, thanks to Churchill, was at action stations and with the confidence of a nation which had always triumphed, they believed it would " all be over by Christmas ".

The most deadly war in the world's history lasted for more than four years and cost the lives of ten million soldiers and of countless civilians. Yet it was indeed almost over in the first few weeks. The German armies swept into France and came close to Paris before the French and, on their left, the small but superb British army held firm, checked the onslaught and drove the enemy back to the River Aisne.

Then there developed a war which not even the generals had foreseen. The destructive force of heavy artillery and the murderous power of machine-gun fire made it impossible for the armies to stand up and fight, so they dug themselves into the earth in trenches that stretched across France from the Alps to the sea. To get at their enemy, soldiers had to clamber into the open, cross " no-man's land " towards a forest of barbed wire protecting the opposite trenches. The defenders invariably mowed down the attackers and those who did manage to reach

the enemy line found that there were other lines behind, with strongpoints and communication-trenches making an impassable network of defence. The old ways of fighting with cavalry and outflanking movements were useless and so the soldiers dug themselves in and endured the mud and the shelling, the big attacks which the generals felt obliged to launch, the appalling loss of life and the tragic farce of trying to break an unbreakable deadlock.

All kinds of efforts were made for victory. The Germans used poison gas, the Allies developed the first tanks and failed to employ them properly ; both sides relied on gigantic artillery bombardments and on trying to starve the other's civilian population. Aeroplanes which began as scouts turned to bombing, submarines became deadlier than surface warships, fresh allies were dragged in until half the world was engaged in the struggle and entire nations gave up everything in order to produce guns, shells and yet more armies for the slaughter.

In eastern Europe, the war was less like a siege but equally bloody. The huge, ill-armed, badly commanded Russian armies blundered to and fro, suffering terrible defeats from the Germans but almost crushing the Austrians and their allies. The need to help Russia, whose soldiers went into action sometimes without even a rifle apiece, led to an attempt to break into south-east Europe. Lloyd George and Churchill both favoured the idea of an attack through the Balkans but it was Churchill's plan to capture Constantinople that won grudging approval. The naval attack on the Dardanelles failed narrowly and by the time troops were landed on Gallipoli shore, the plan was doomed. Surprise had gone, the Turks fought stubbornly and the generals in France had never released sufficient men to give the landings a chance. The bold stroke became a heartbreaking failure and Churchill left the government to return to soldiering in France.

As Churchill fell and Asquith's authority faded, Lloyd George came to power. The war was going badly, for Gallipoli was followed by gigantic losses on the Western Front, where the French were badly weakened and the British were short of shells and ammunition. At sea, the German fleet was brought to battle at Jutland, only to escape into the darkness after inflicting some unexpected damage to the British ships and, shortly afterwards, Lord Kitchener, the veteran hero, was drowned at sea.

The one man who seemed as full of confidence as ever was Lloyd George. By forceful methods, he made the factories produce an ever-increasing flow of war-supplies and it seemed to many people that here was the leader the country needed. Asquith was ousted and Lloyd George took his place as Prime Minister. To many Liberals this was treachery and they never forgave him. King George V disliked the " Welsh Wizard ", Haig, the commander-in-chief, and most of the generals detested him and there were good reasons for many others to distrust him.

He was tricky and vain, dangerous to his enemies and faithless to his friends but he was also a great man, with a genius for getting impossible things done, for overcoming difficulties and for driving on in the face of every setback. He was called " the man who won the war " and he deserved the name.

Mass warfare threw up very few heroes at the top. In the long bitter struggle, there were hardly any successes but countless losses and disappointments ; Haig was too silent to be popular, Churchill and Admiral Beatty both possessed courage and flair but no luck, and one of the very few who caught the public's imagination was an eccentric archaeologist named T. E. Lawrence who aided the Arab revolt against the Turks, though the real victor was General Allenby. In truth, the heroes of the war were the soldiers in the trenches and the seamen who braved the submarines to keep Britain from starvation.

After three years, the collapse of Russia, near-mutiny in the French army, the defeat of the Italians and disastrous losses of merchant-ships brought the allies almost to their knees. The Germans, strengthened by their armies from the Eastern Front, then launched a series of tremendous attacks mainly upon the British, drove them back and actually broke right through into open country. Once again, they came within striking distance of Paris, but, once again, the allies, now under a supreme commander, Marshal Foch, held out as fresh American troops began to arrive in ever-increasing numbers. When exhaustion brought the German advance to a halt, Foch and Haig took their chance to hit back at the most vulnerable parts of the enemy front. The Germans retired fighting but the allies, scenting victory, kept up the pressure so remorselessly that they swept on until suddenly it was clear that the enemy was in full retreat towards his own frontier. Like magic, Austria, Turkey and Bulgaria collapsed, the German fleet mutinied, civilians rioted in Germany, the Kaiser fled to Holland and the war was over.

Between the Wars

Victory had come at last but, as in the years after Waterloo, it was followed by hard times and suffering. Trade failed to pick up and soon there were a million or more men without jobs.

A tragic struggle now took place in Ireland. Before the war Asquith had been ready to give the Irish the right to rule themselves, and this induced the Protestants of Ulster to declare that they would fight rather than be ruled by a Roman Catholic majority. The war postponed the struggle, but Irish feelings were inflamed by the execution of the leaders of a rising in Dublin. Soon there was no room for moderation, as Irish republicans attacked the police and the British government recruited a force known as the Black and Tans who met terror with terror. At last Lloyd George seemed to have made a settlement when a treaty was signed giving Home Rule to Southern Ireland, but " the troubles " were not yet over, for civil war broke out between those who accepted the treaty and those who denounced it.

By this time, Lloyd George's great reputation was on the wane. His popularity was slipping away and there was no loyal party at his back. The Conservatives were tired of a man they had never liked, the Liberals would not rally to him and although Lloyd George remained the ablest politician in the country, he never held office again.

The story of the next seventeen years is a melancholy one of

314

a nation bewildered by its troubles and lack of leadership. Unemployment became a kind of malign bogey which no-one seemed able to banish, and the very industries on which Britain's prosperity had been founded—coal, iron, cotton and shipbuilding—were the hardest hit. Some parts of the country, South Wales, Lancashire, the North-east and Scotland, became known as Distressed Areas where as many as twenty or thirty men out of every 100 had no work to do. There were strikes, including a General Strike that fizzled out after nine days, hunger-marches and pay-cuts ; but unemployment never dropped below a million until the next war made every man's labour necessary.

The country's leaders during this period were Stanley Baldwin, Ramsay MacDonald and Neville Chamberlain, men of more ability and honesty than their critics have allowed but none was great enough to solve the problems at home or to deal with the dangers abroad. Hardly anyone listened to Lloyd George who had positive plans to tackle unemployment, or to Churchill who growled out warnings about Germany's rising strength. Distrusted and frequently derided, they stood on the sidelines watching the lesser men take charge.

The picture was not entirely gloomy during the twenties and thirties, for parts of the country, mainly the Midlands and the south, regained their prosperity thanks to light industries, motor-cars and a great increase in building. Britain still led the world in aircraft manufacture, civil aviation, car-racing and most kinds of sport, so that the popular heroes included Major Seagrave, the racing-driver, Jack Hobbs, Lord Nuffield and Amy Johnson, the girl-pilot from Hull who thrilled everyone by flying alone to Australia. In science and medicine, Sir Ernest Rutherford was the pioneer of nuclear physics, Robert Watson Watt discovered radar, Frank Whittle invented the jet-engine and Alexander Fleming, a Scot working at a London hospital, discovered penicillin, the drug which saved innumerable lives during the Second World War.

Victory at all Costs

For more than a dozen years, people lived in hope that a major war would never happen again. They put their faith in the League of Nations which had been set up at Geneva to settle the nations' quarrels by peaceful discussion and it was not until the thirties when Japan attacked China and the Italian dictator, Mussolini, invaded Abyssinia that they began to realise that the League was powerless to stop the big aggressor. This unhappy truth had already been recognised by Adolf Hitler.

There was nothing in Hitler's early life to suggest that he possessed even average ability, let alone the power to dominate a nation and to commit the most monstrous crimes in the world's history. His schooldays and youth were a story of failure to pass examinations or to secure a regular job and during his service in the 1914–18 War, he rose no higher than the rank of corporal. After the war, this morose day-dreamer joined an obscure political party in Munich where it was discovered at meetings that he did possess one gift. He was an orator who could pour out a torrent of words which had an almost mesmeric effect upon his audience. The message of his speeches was hatred— hatred of Germany's defeat, of the peace settlement, of socialists, communists and, above all, Jews.

Hitler would probably have continued to be no more than an unpleasant nuisance in Munich had it not been for the Great Depression in world trade. Germany's recovery crashed into ruins ; more than six million men became unemployed

316

and, in this situation, people were prepared to listen to a fanatic who claimed to be able to restore the country's greatness. His political party, known as the Nazis, took control of Parliament, and with the aid of a gang of henchmen as wicked and ruthless as their leader, the laws were overthrown, all other parties abolished and all opposition crushed. Hitler became president and commander-in-chief of the German army. He was now a complete dictator, and with terrifying swiftness he put his programme into gear.

Unemployment was overcome by the manufacture of arms, the German army and air force increased at a tremendous rate and, piece by piece, all the losses of the war were recovered. Part of the Rhineland opposite to France was re-occupied by troops, Austria, whose union with Germany was forbidden by the Treaty of Versailles, was taken over, enthusiastic support was given to Mussolini and Franco, the dictators of Italy and Spain, and demands were made on Czechoslovakia to hand over a large part of Czech territory inhabited by German-speaking citizens.

The League of Nations and France and Britain, in particular, watched Hitler's behaviour with nervous dismay. They protested but did little more, partly because their peoples wanted to have nothing to do with war and partly because Hitler outwitted them by constantly promising that each move was his last step towards uniting his country. Many people felt that if Germany's grievances were removed, she would behave sensibly and would see, as they did, that peace was better than war.

This attitude was called " appeasement " and Neville Chamberlain, the British prime minister, believed in it wholeheartedly. He was sure that if he could meet the dictators face to face, he would talk them into a reasonable frame of mind. So, when Germany's threats to Czechoslovakia seemed about to cause a European war, Chamberlain flew to Munich to meet Hitler. The French prime minister was there, too, and

between them they agreed that Czechoslovakia should give Hitler what he wanted. There would be no war and the people of Britain went mad with joyous relief.

But not quite everybody. Churchill pointed out that the unfortunate Czechs had been betrayed and were now defence-less : it was, he said, not a victory but complete and utter defeat.

His words were true. Within six months, Hitler had seized the rest of Czechoslovakia and had begun to threaten Poland. This alarmed even Chamberlain and in a belated effort to stop the aggressor, he promised to support Poland. At this stage the offer was ludicrous and Hitler, who had already made a secret agreement with Russia, knew that no help from Britain and France could reach the Poles. On September 1st, 1939, he invaded Poland and it is said that he was astonished when Britain and France declared themselves at war with Germany.

As in 1914, it was only at the last moment that the British realised that they must fight to prevent one country from dominating Europe. With frantic speed they tried to arm themselves, but neither they nor the French could do anything to prevent the destruction of Poland and, for the first winter, so little happened that this was called the " phoney war ".

By spring 1940, however, Hitler was ready for his next leap. Norway was invaded and conquered in a few days and, at this,

318

the British people lost all patience with Chamberlain and in reality it was they, and not the politicians, who called in Churchill to take his place. They remembered that he had warned them over and over again of the dangers of appeasement and they knew that although they had derided him as an old war-monger, had questioned his judgement and seen him out of office for many years, he possessed above all else the quality they now needed so badly in a leader—courage. Meanwhile, the Germans had crushed Holland with horrifying speed and their matchless armoured divisions, their powerful air arm and a huge confident army stood poised to spring at France. The real war had come and Churchill spoke to the nation :

" I have nothing to offer but blood, toil, tears and sweat," he said. " You ask, ' What is our policy? ' I will say : it is to wage war, by sea, land and air, with all our might and with all the strength that God can give us . . . You ask, ' What is our aim? ' I can answer in one word : Victory—victory at all costs, victory in spite of all terror ; victory, however long and hard the road may be."

There followed the complete collapse of France, the loss of

the army's equipment at Dunkirk, the RAF's narrow but decisive victory in the Battle of Britain, the night-bombing, defeat in Greece, Crete and North Africa. By now Britain was alone, still clinging to the hope that Churchill had given them that somehow victory would come. Europe belonged to Hitler and there were more catastrophes to come in the Far East where Singapore, Hong Kong and Burma fell to the Japanese.

Then the tide turned and there were allies fighting the same enemy, not because they came to Britain's rescue but because Hitler attacked Russia and the Japanese destroyed an American fleet at Pearl Harbor. Instead of defeats, there was news of victories—Alamein, Stalingrad and Midway Island. Italy was invaded and at long last the allied armies were back in France, forcing a way in at Normandy and steadily, painfully boring on towards Germany as the Russians closed in from the east. In the end Germany was pounded to defeat and Hitler died in the ruins of Berlin. In 1945 the dropping of two atomic bombs brought the surrender of Japan.

Churchill fulfilled his promise and went out of office immediately he had done so. No single man can win a war. There were other great leaders and generals in the struggle—Roosevelt, Eisenhower, Zhukov, MacArthur and Montgomery —but Churchill saw it through from start to finish and by his will for victory made it possible for other leaders to arise, for the conquered peoples to go on hoping and for the British people to survive. As it happened, it *was* victory at all costs, and costs which are still being paid—economic difficulty, supremacy of the United States, Russian domination of eastern Europe. But Churchill expressed the will of the British people that they should not give in and he showed them, that given courage and leadership, they could achieve miracles, not merely in battle but in the fairer realms of unity, decency and justice. They still can.

INDEX

Index

Index

Index

Index